THE RIVER WAR

THE RIVER WAR

*An account of the re-conquest
of the Soudan*

WINSTON S. CHURCHILL

PRION

This edition first published in 1997 in Great Britain by
PRION
32-34 Gordon House Road,
London NW5 1LP

ISBN 1-85375-264-9

Cover design by Bob Eames
Cover image courtesy of the E.T. Archive
Printed and bound in Great Britain
by Creative Print and Design, Wales

CONTENTS

THIS BOOK IS INSCRIBED

TO

THE MARQUESS OF SALISBURY, K.G.

UNDER WHOSE WISE DIRECTION

THE CONSERVATIVE PARTY HAVE LONG ENJOYED POWER

AND THE NATION PROSPERITY

DURING WHOSE ADMINISTRATIONS THE

REORGANISATION OF EGYPT HAS BEEN MAINLY ACCOMPLISHED

AND UPON WHOSE ADVICE HER MAJESTY DETERMINED

TO ORDER THE RECONQUEST OF THE SOUDAN

MAPS AND PLANS

FOREWORD
by Winston S. Churchill (The Younger)

Close on a century has passed since my Grandfather, a 23-year-old cavalry officer and sometime correspondent for the *Morning Post*, wrote *The River War*. I am delighted – as I know he himself would be – that, thanks to this abridged edition, a whole new generation of readers can become acquainted with one of Churchill's finest, and perhaps most exciting, works.

The significance of this book does not rest in the importance of Britain's efforts shortly before the turn of the century to subjugate the Sudan, nor even in its deciding moment, the Battle of Omdurman, all of which in the perspective of history and, most especially, of the scale of the world wars that have ensued, have been lost in the mists of time. Its true significance rests above all in the fact that it is the first major historical work of the man who 40 years on, more than any other single individual, was to save the world from Hitler.

Nor is this the work of an academic historian writing from the safety and seclusion of an ivory tower amid the spires of Oxford or Cambridge. On the contrary, it is the testimony of a brilliant, courageous and resourceful young officer in the field, a soldier of fortune determined to be where the action was, desperate to prove himself in battle in the hope – impecunious as he was – of launching himself upon a career in politics.

The "Young Winston" deployed all his resources of influence and persuasion – most notably his beautiful, American-born mother, Jennie Jerome, or Lady Randolph Churchill as she then was – to get himself attached to the British Expeditionary Force under Field Marshal Lord Kitchener, that was embarking upon the dangerous task of reconquering the Sudan. Pulling every string he could, and in the teeth of Kitchener's fierce opposition, indeed specific refusal to have him on his staff, Churchill succeeded in getting himself attached to the 21st Lancers. As a result, he found himself taking part in one of the last great cavalry charges in the history of the British Army.

His account captures the excitement and drama, both of the skirmishes and the Battle, in a way that only a participant could. Writing for an audience before the days of television, or even the cinema, he uses all his skill as a future artist (who would have nearly 500 canvasses to his credit by his death) to conjure up for his reader a picture of the sights, sounds and colours of the Sudan, its peoples and, above all, the dramatic actions in which so many thousands were to perish.

The outcome of the struggle between the disciplined and well equipped British-led force and the Dervish masses, armed with ageing rifles and swords, may not have been in doubt for, in the famous rhyme of Hilaire Belloc: "Whatever happens we have got, the Maxim gun - and they have not!", but for a cavalry officer, armed only with a lance and a pistol, the odds were much more equal.

Bearing in mind that the British Empire was then at its height and that jingoism was in fashion, what perhaps the reader will find most remarkable of all is the fairness and detachment with which Churchill writes of their Dervish opponents, together with the sympathy and understanding that he expresses for their religious leader, the Mahdi. This was a characteristic that he was to display soon afterwards in the Boer War where he was taken prisoner. Referring to the Boers in the House of Commons he incurred much wrath and criticism when he declared: "If I were a Boer in the field - and if I were a Boer I should *hope* I would be in the field...".

Furthermore, before the Sudan campaign was ended, this

junior lieutenant of horse would not hold back from criticising in forthright terms his Commander-in-Chief for what he regarded as the inhuman treatment meted out to the enemy wounded. This work, even in its abbreviated form, shows the remarkable moral fibre of a young officer preparing himself for a later destiny and, through it all, his formidable developing power as a writer.

W. S. C., London, 1997

INTRODUCTION [1]

Nearly thirty-five years have passed since this book was written and I am very glad that it is now to take a renewed lease of life.

In those distant days the world was tranquil and our country relatively rich and powerful. The Royal Navy was more than equal to the next two or three navies put together. England was largely the world's manufacturer, and London was its unchallenged financial centre. With these great advantages we pursued a steady and modest policy of avoiding foreign entanglements, and only reluctantly accepted new possessions or responsibilities.

In spite, however, of the wishes of many of the statesmen of both political parties, England was drawn into Egypt. After the bombardment of Alexandria in 1881, when the French fleet sailed away before the action, we became to all intents and purposes the paramount power. The marvellous work of creating good government and prosperity for the Egyptians, which will for ever be linked with the name of Lord Cromer, was soon in full progress. A small band of first-class Englishmen, keeping themselves in the background, directed the whole process of reform and reconstruction with virtually sovereign power.

It was at this moment that the Rebellion of the Mahdi plunged the vast, remote provinces of the Soudan into bloodshed and confusion. Mr Gladstone's Government had no other wish than to escape from Egypt at the earliest possible moment. They viewed with horror being involved in the Soudan. The disturbances and disasters which befell the Egyptian armies and administration

[1] *Specially written for the Third Edition.*

xiii

further stimulated their eagerness to quit the Nile valley. They unhesitatingly resolved to relinquish the Soudan to barbarism. General Gordon was sent to Khartoum to wind up affairs and bring away the surviving officials, soldiers and Egyptian colonists and traders.

Easier said than done! Once arrived at Khartoum, he made it a point of honour not to leave until he had safely evacuated all those committed to his charge. He was soon 'hemmed in' – the expression is Mr Gladstone's, who resented the word 'surrounded' – and the long blockade began. If General Gordon considered his honour involved in rescuing the Egyptians in the Soudan, Great Britain soon found an even stronger obligation to rescue *him*. Lord Hartington, the Liberal Secretary of State for War, moved very slowly; but when he considered his honour was involved, nothing could turn him from his path. Gordon must be rescued at all costs. Expeditions both by the winding Nile and by short-cuts across the desert were launched. After fierce fighting the Desert column reached Metemma, where Gordon's gunboats awaited them. The relievers arrived before Khartoum two days too late. The city was already in the hands of the Dervish mob. Gordon and nearly all the people he would not desert had been massacred. The evacuation of the Soudan was thus complete.

However, the story had sunk deeply into British hearts. The overthrow of Mr Gladstone on Home Rule in 1886 inaugurated what was practically twenty years of Conservative rule. Very slowly, patiently, cautiously and frugally the British Government set about the recovery of the ruined territory. The results achieved in Egypt were now so remarkable as to be the source of general pride. At the head of the Egyptian Army stood Kitchener, a British officer of exceptional capacity and growing repute. More than ten years after the sack of Khartoum, the first advance into the Dongola Province began, and two years later, in 1898, the armies of the savage Dervish empire were shattered and largely destroyed in the Battle of Omdurman. Thirteen years from General Gordon's death his countrymen resumed undisputed control over the city he had defended to the death.

The pacification, restoration and orderly development of the Soudan is a story in itself. It repeated in another form far to the southward the successes which our administrators had achieved along the lower Nile. The Soudan became an unbreakable link between Great Britain and Egypt. Neither can ever relinquish respective rights and interests there.

In these later times and in the moral exhaustion which followed victory in the Great War, successive British governments have adopted weak and unworthy policies in Egypt. Proposals have even been entertained to remove the British garrison from Cairo. Thus far their baseness and folly have fortunately been averted. It has therefore not been necessary to come to an issue with the Egyptian Government about the title-deeds of the Soudan.

I have always been in favour of preserving both the British relation with Egypt and the Egyptian relation with the Soudan. I trust both British and Egyptian statesmen and administrators will work together with goodwill and for the common advantage for centuries to come. These views are, however, highly controversial. A generation has grown up which knows little of why we are in Egypt and the Soudan, and what our work there has been. Uninstructed and ignorant impressions colour the decisions not only of parliaments but of cabinets. It is my hope that the story which these pages contain may be some help and encouragement to those young men and women who have still confidence in the destiny of Britain in the Orient. They may learn from it how much harder it is to build up and acquire, than to squander and cast away.

W. S.C. 1933

THE RECONQUEST OF THE SOUDAN

BY

WINSTON SPENCER CHURCHILL

AUTHOR OF 'THE STORY OF THE MALAKAND FIELD FORCE, 1897'

EDITED BY COL. F. RHODES, D.S.O.

Illustrated by Angus McNeill, Seaforth Highlanders

IN TWO VOLUMES

VOLUME I.

LONGMANS, GREEN, AND CO.
39 PATERNOSTER ROW, LONDON
NEW YORK AND BOMBAY
1899

CHAPTER 1

THE REBELLION OF THE MAHDI

The north-eastern quarter of the continent of Africa is drained and watered by the Nile. Among and about the headstreams and tributaries of this mighty river lie the wide and fertile provinces of the Egyptian Soudan. Situated in the very centre of the land, these remote regions are on every side divided from the seas by five hundred miles of mountain, swamp, or desert. The great river is their only means of growth, their only channel of progress. It is by the Nile alone that their commerce can reach the outer markets, or European civilisation can penetrate the inner darkness. The Soudan is joined to Egypt by the Nile, as a diver is connected with the surface by his air-pipe. Without it there is only suffocation.

The town of Khartoum,[1] at the confluence of the Blue and White Niles, is the great spout through which the merchandise collected from a wide area streams northwards to the Mediterranean shore. It marks the extreme northern limit of the fertile Soudan. Between Khartoum and Assuan the river flows for twelve hundred miles through deserts of surpassing desolation. At last the wilderness recedes and the living world broadens out again into Egypt and the Delta.

The real Soudan, known to the statesman and the explorer, lies far to the south – moist, undulating, and exuberant. But there is another Soudan, which some mistake for the true, whose solitudes oppress the Nile from the Egyptian frontier to Omdurman. This great tract, which may conveniently be called 'The Military

[1] *Map, 'The Soudan', p. 54*

1

Soudan', stretches with apparent indefiniteness over the face of the continent. Level plains of smooth sand are interrupted only by occasional peaks of rock – black, stark, and shapeless. Rainless storms dance tirelessly over the hot, crisp surface of the ground. The fine sand, driven by the wind, gathers into deep drifts, and silts among the dark rocks of the hills, exactly as snow hangs about an Alpine summit; only it is a fiery snow, such as might fall in hell.

Through the desert flows the river – a thread of blue silk drawn across an enormous brown drugget; and even this thread is brown for half the year. Where the water laps the sand and soaks into the banks there grows an avenue of vegetation which seems very beautiful and luxuriant by contrast with what lies beyond. Yet the character of the vegetation is inhospitable. Thorn-bushes, bristling like hedgehogs, everywhere predominate and with their prickly tangles obstruct the path. Only the palms by the brink are kindly, and men journeying along the Nile must look often towards their bushy tops, where among the spreading foliage the red and yellow glint of date clusters proclaims the ripening of a generous crop.

There is life only by the Nile. If a man were to leave the river, he might journey westward and find no human habitation, nor the smoke of a cooking fire, except the lonely tent of a Kabbabish Arab or the encampment of a trader's caravan, till he reached the coast-line of America. Or he might go east and find nothing but sand and sea and sun until Bombay rose above the horizon. The thread of fresh water is itself solitary in regions where all living things lack company.

Through all the centuries the great river has performed the annual miracle of its flood. Every year when the rains fall and the mountain snows of Central Africa begin to melt, the headstreams become torrents and the great lakes are filled to the brim. A vast expanse of low, swampy lands, crossed by secondary channels and flooded for many miles, regulates the flow, and by a sponge-like action prevents the excess of one year from causing the deficiency of the next. Gradually the flood begins. The Bahr-el-Ghazal from a channel of stagnant pools and marshes becomes a broad and navigable stream. The Sobat and the Atbara from dry watercourses with occasional pools, in which the fish and crocodiles are crowded, turn to rushing rivers. After its confluence with the Atbara no drop of water reaches the Nile, and it flows for seven hundred miles through the sands or rushes in cataracts among the rocks of the Nubian Desert. Nevertheless, in spite of the tremendous diminution in volume caused by the dryness of the earth and air and the heat of the sun – all of which drink greedily – the river below Assuan is sufficiently great to supply nine millions of people with as much water as their utmost science and energies can draw, and yet to pour into the Mediterranean a low-water surplus current of 61,500 cubic feet per second. Nor is its water its only gift. As the Nile rises its complexion is changed. The clear blue river becomes thick and red, laden with the magic mud that can raise cities from the desert sand and make the wilderness a garden.

South of Khartoum and of 'The Military Soudan' the land becomes more fruitful. The tributaries of the Nile multiply the areas of riparian fertility. A considerable rainfall, increasing as the Equator is approached, enables the intervening spaces to support vegetation and consequently human life. The greater part of the country is feverish and unhealthy, nor can Europeans long sustain the attacks of its climate. Nevertheless it is by no means valueless. On the east the province of Sennar used to produce abundant grain, and might easily produce no less abundant cotton. Westward the vast territories of Kordofan and Darfur afford grazing-grounds to a multitude of cattle, and give means of livelihood to great numbers of Baggara or cow-herd Arabs, who may also pursue with activity and stratagem the fleet giraffe and the still fleeter ostrich. To the south-east lies Bahr-el-Ghazal, a great tract of country occupied by dense woods and plentifully watered. Further south and nearer the Equator the forests and marshes become exuberant with tropical growths, and the whole face of the land is moist and green. Amid groves of gigantic trees and through plains of high waving grass the stately elephant roams in herds which occasionally number four hundred, hardly ever disturbed by a well-armed hunter. The ivory of their tusks constitutes the wealth of the Equatorial Province. All other kinds of large beasts known to man inhabit these obscure retreats. The fierce rhinoceros crashes through the undergrowth. Among the reeds of melancholy swamps huge hippopotami, crocodiles, and buffaloes prosper and increase. Antelope of every known and many unclassified species; serpents of peculiar venom; countless millions of birds, butterflies, and beetles are among the offspring of prolific Nature.

The human inhabitants of the Soudan would not, but for their vices and misfortunes, be disproportioned in numbers to the *fauna* or less happy. War, slavery, and oppression have, however, afflicted them until the total population of the whole country does not exceed at the most liberal estimate three million souls. The Soudanese are of many tribes, but two main races can be clearly distinguished: the aboriginal natives, and the Arab settlers. The indigenous inhabitants of the country were negroes as black as coal. They displayed the virtues of barbarism. They were brave and honest. The smallness of their intelligence excused the degradation of their habits. Yet their eulogy must be short, for though their customs, language, and appearance vary, the history of all is a confused legend of strife and misery, and their condition is one of equal squalor and want.

Although the negroes are the more numerous, the Arabs exceed in power. During the second century of the Mohammedan era, when the inhabitants of Arabia went forth to conquer the world, one adventurous army struck south. The first pioneers were followed at intervals by continual immigrations of Arabs not only from Arabia but also across the deserts from Egypt and Morocco. The element thus introduced has spread and is spreading throughout the Soudan, as water soaks into a dry sponge. The aboriginals absorbed the invaders they could not repel. The stronger race imposed its customs and language on the negroes. The vigour of their blood sensibly altered the facial appearance of the Soudanese. For more than a thousand years the influence of Mohammedanism, which appears to possess a strange fascination for negroid races, has been permeating the Soudan, and the whole of the black race is gradually adopting the new religion and developing Arab characteristics. In the districts of the north, the evolution is complete, and the Arabs of the Soudan are a race formed by the interbreeding of negro and Arab, and yet distinct from both. In the more remote and inaccessible regions which lie to the south and west the negro race remains as yet unchanged by the Arab influence. And between these extremes every degree of mixture is to be found. In some tribes pure Arabic is spoken, and prior to the rise of the Mahdi the orthodox Moslem faith was practised. In others Arabic has merely modified the ancient dialects, and the Mohammedan religion has been adapted to the older superstitions.

The stronger race soon began to prey upon the simple aboriginals; some of the Arab tribes were camel-breeders; some were goat-herds; some were Baggaras or cow-herds. But all, without exception, were hunters of men. To the great slave-market at Jedda a continual stream of negro captives has flowed for hundreds of years. The invention of gunpowder and the adoption by the Arabs of firearms facilitated the traffic by placing the ignorant negroes at a further disadvantage. Thus the situation in the Soudan for several centuries may be summed up as follows: The dominant race of Arab invaders was unceasingly spreading its blood, religion, customs, and language among the black aboriginal population, and at the same time it harried and enslaved them.

All this was unheeded by the outer world, from which the Soudan is separated by the deserts. The impulse of conquest which hurried the French and English to Canada and the Indies, which sent the Dutch to the Cape and the Spaniards to Peru, spread to

Africa and led the Egyptians to the Soudan. In the year 1819 Mohammed Ali, availing himself of the disorders alike as an excuse and an opportunity, sent his son Ismail up the Nile with a great army. The Arab tribes, torn by dissension, exhausted by thirty years of general war, and no longer inspired by their neglected religion, offered a weak resistance. Their slaves, having known the worst of life, were apathetic. The whole vast territory was conquered with very little fighting, and the victorious army, leaving garrisons, returned in triumph to the Delta.

From 1819 to 1883 Egypt ruled the Soudan. Her rule was not kindly, wise, or profitable. Its aim was to exploit, not to improve the local population. For the rough injustice of the sword there were substituted the intricacies of corruption and bribery. The land was undeveloped and poor. It barely sustained its inhabitants. The additional burden of a considerable foreign garrison and a crowd of rapacious officials increased the severity of the economic conditions. Famines were periodical. Corrupt and incapable Governors-General succeeded each other at Khartoum with bewildering rapidity. The success of their administration was measured by the Ministries in Egypt by the amount of money they could extort from the natives; among the officials in the Soudan, by the number of useless offices they could create. There were a few bright examples of honest men, but these, by providing a contrast, only increased the discontents.

The rule of Egypt was iniquitous: yet it preserved the magnificent appearance of Imperial dominion. The Egyptian Pro-consul lived in state at the confluence of the Niles. The representatives of foreign Powers established themselves in the city. The trade of the south converged upon Khartoum. Thither were sent the ivory of Equatoria, the ostrich feathers of Kordofan, gum from Darfur, grain from Sennar, and taxes collected from all the regions. Complex and imposing reports of revenue and expenditure were annually compiled. An elaborate and dignified correspondence was maintained between Egypt and its great dependency. Yet all

was a hateful sham.[1] The arbitrary and exce
lected only at the point of the bayonet. If
arrears, his neighbours were raised against hi...
were recalcitrant, a military expedition was despatch
the ability of the Arabs to pay depended on their success a.
hunters. When there had been a good catch, the revenue profite.
The Egyptian Government had joined the International League
against the slave trade. They continued, however, indirectly but
deliberately, to make money out of it.[2]

The authority of a tyrannical Government was supported by
the presence of a worthless army. Nearly 40,000 men were distributed among eight main and numerous minor garrisons.
Isolated in a roadless country by enormous distances and natural
obstacles, and living in the midst of large savage populations of
fanatical character and warlike habits, the Viceregal forces might
depend for their safety only on the skill of their officers, the
excellence of their discipline, and the superiority of their
weapons. But the Egyptian officers were at that time distinguished
for nothing but their public incapacity and private misbehaviour.
The evil reputation of the Soudan and its climate deterred the
more educated or more wealthy from serving in such distant
regions, and none went south who could avoid it. The officers
remained for long periods, many all their lives, in the obscurity of
the remote provinces. Some had been sent there in disgrace, others
in disfavour. Many were hopeless and habitual drunkards. Nearly all
were dishonest. All were indolent and incapable.

Under such leadership the finest soldiery would have soon
degenerated. The Egyptians in the Soudan were not fine soldiers.
Like their officers, they were the worst part of the Khedivial
Army. Their training was imperfect; their discipline was lax; their

---

[1] 'The government of the Egyptians in these far-off countries is nothing else but
one of brigandage of the very worst description.' *Colonel Gordon in Central Africa,
11th April 1879.*
[2] *Egypt, No. 11, 1883.*

7

urage was low. Nor was even this all the weakness and peril of
.heir position; for while the regular troops were thus demoralised,
there existed a powerful local irregular force of Bazingers
(Soudanese riflemen), as well armed as the soldiers, more numerous,
more courageous, and who regarded the alien garrisons with fear
that continually diminished and hate that continually grew. And
behind regulars and irregulars alike the wild Arab tribes of the
desert and the hardy blacks of the forests, goaded by suffering and
injustice, thought the foreigners the cause of all their woes, and
were delayed only by their inability to combine from sweeping
them off the face of the earth. Never was there such a house of
cards as the Egyptian dominion in the Soudan.

The names of two men of character and fame are for ever
connected with the actual outburst. One was an English general,
the other an Arab priest; yet, in spite of the great gulf and vivid
contrast between their conditions, they resembled each other in
many respects. Both were earnest and enthusiastic men of keen
sympathies and passionate emotions. Both were powerfully
swayed by religious fervour. Both exerted great personal influence
on all who came in contact with them. Both were reformers. In
the end they fought to the death, but for an important part of
their lives their influence on the fortunes of the Soudan was
exerted in the same direction. Mohammed Ahmed, 'The Mahdi',
will be discussed in his own place. Charles Gordon needs little
introduction.

It is impossible to study any part of Charles Gordon's career
without being drawn to all the rest. As his wild and varied fortunes
lead him from Sebastopol to Pekin, from Gravesend to South Africa,
from Mauritius to the Soudan, the reader follows fascinated. Every
scene is strange, terrible, or dramatic. Yet, remarkable as are the
scenes, the actor is the more extraordinary. Potentates of many
lands and different degree – the Emperor of China, the King of
the Belgians, the Premier of Cape Colony, the Khedive of Egypt
– competed to secure his services. The importance of his offices

varied no less than their nature. One day he was a subaltern of sappers; on another he commanded the Chinese Army; the next he directed an orphanage; or was Governor-General of the Soudan, with supreme powers of life and death and peace and war. But in whatever capacity he laboured he was true to his reputation. Whether he is portrayed bitterly criticising to Graham the tactics of the assault on the Redan; or pulling the head of Lar Wang from under his bedstead and waving it in paroxysms of indignation before the astonished eyes of Sir Halliday Macartney; or riding alone into the camp of the rebel Suliman and receiving the respectful salutes of those who had meant to kill him; or telling the Khedive Ismail that he 'must have the whole Soudan to govern'; or reducing his salary to half the regulation amount because 'he thought it was too much'; we perceive a man careless alike of the frowns of men or the smiles of women, of life or comfort, wealth or fame.

It was a pity that one, thus gloriously free from the ordinary restraining influences of human society, should have found in his own character so little mental ballast. His moods were capricious and uncertain, his passions violent, his impulses sudden and inconsistent. The mortal enemy of the morning had become a trusted ally before the night. The friend he loved today he loathed tomorrow. Scheme after scheme formed in his fertile brain, and jostled confusingly together. All in succession were pressed with enthusiasm. All at times were rejected with disdain. His virtues are famous among men; his daring and resource might turn the tide of war; his energy would have animated a whole people; but it must also be set down that few more uncertain and impracticable forces than Gordon have ever been introduced into administration and diplomacy.

Although the Egyptian Government might loudly proclaim their detestation of slavery, their behaviour in the Soudan was viewed with suspicion by the European Powers, and particularly by Great Britain. To vindicate his sincerity the Khedive Ismail in

1874 appointed Gordon to be Governor of the Equatorial Province in succession to Sir Samuel Baker. The mission, which may have been originally instituted as a pretence, soon became in Gordon's energetic hands very real. The slave dealers had committed every variety of atrocity for which the most odious traffic in the world afforded occasion; but when, under the leadership of Zubehr Rahamna, they refused to pay their annual tribute, it was felt in Cairo that their crimes had cried aloud for chastisement.

Zubehr is sufficiently described when it has been said that he was the most notorious slave dealer Africa has ever produced. His infamy had spread beyond the limits of the continent which was the scene of his exploits to the distant nations of the north and west. In reality, his rule was a distinct advance on the anarchy which had preceded it, and certainly he was no worse than others of his vile trade. His scale of business was, however, more extended.

As early as 1869 he was practically the independent ruler of the Bahr-el-Ghazal. The Khedive resolved to assert his rights. A small Egyptian force was sent to subdue the rebel slaver who not only disgraced humanity but refused to pay tribute. Like most of the Khedivial expeditions they came, they saw, they ran away. Zubehr *apologised* for defeating the Viceregal soldiers and remained supreme in the Bahr-el-Ghazal. Thence he planned the conquest of Darfur, at that time an independent kingdom. The Egyptian Government were glad to join with him in the enterprise. The man they had been unable to conquer, they found it expedient to assist. The operations were successful. The King of Darfur, who was distinguished no less for his valour than for his folly, was killed. The whole country was subdued. The whole population available after the battles became slaves. Zubehr thus wielded a formidable power. The Khedivial Government, thinking to ensure his loyalty, created him a Pasha – a rank which he could scarcely disgrace; and the authority of the rebel was thus unwillingly recognised by the ruler. Such was the situation when Gordon first came to the Soudan.

It was beyond the power of the new Governor of the Equatorial Province at once to destroy the slave-hunting confederacy. Zubehr was enticed to Cairo, and, once there, the Government refused to allow their faithful ally and distinguished guest to go back to his happy-hunting grounds. Although the slave dealers were thus robbed of their great leader, they were still strong, and Zubehr's son, the brave Suliman, found a considerable following. Furious at his father's captivity, and alarmed lest his own should follow, he meditated revolt. But the Governor-General, mounted on a swift camel and attired in full uniform, rode alone into the rebel camp and compelled the submission of its chiefs before they could recover from their amazement. The confederacy was severely shaken, and when, in the following year, Suliman again revolted, the Egyptian troops under Gessi Pasha were able to disperse his forces and induce him to surrender on terms.

Towards the end of 1879 Gordon left the Soudan. With short intervals he had spent five busy years in its provinces. His energy had stirred the country. He had struck at the root of the slave trade, he had attacked the system of slavery, and, as slavery was the greatest institution in the land, he had undermined the whole social system. He was, as he knew himself, the herald of the storm. Oppressed yet ferocious races had learned that they had rights; the misery of the Soudanese was lessened, but their knowledge had increased. The whole population was unsettled, and the wheels of change began slowly to revolve; nor did they stop until they had accomplished an enormous revolution.

Down to the year 1881 there was no fanatical movement in the Soudan. In their utter misery the hopeless inhabitants had neglected even the practices of religion. They were nevertheless prepared for any enterprise, however desperate, which might free them from the Egyptian yoke. All that delayed them was the want of some leader who could combine the tribes and restore their broken spirits, and in the summer of 1881 the leader appeared.

The man who was the proximate cause of the River War was born by the banks of the Nile, not very far from Dongola. His family were poor and of no account in the province. But as the Prophet had claimed a royal descent, and as a Sacred Example was sprung from David's line, Mohammed Ahmed asserted that he was of the 'Ashraf',[1] and the assertion, since it cannot be disproved, may be accepted. His father was a humble priest; yet he contrived to give his son some education in the practices of religion, the principles of the Koran, and the art of writing. Then he died while on a journey to Khartoum, and left the future Mahdi, still a child, to the mercies of the world. A boy deprived of a father's care often develops an independence and vigour of thought which may restore in after life the heavy loss of early days. It was so with Mohammed Ahmed. He looked around for an occupation and subsistence. A large proportion of the population of religious countries pass their lives at leisure, supported by the patient labour of the devout. The young man determined to follow the profession for which he felt his talents suited. He became a priest. He journeyed to Khartoum as soon as his religious education was completed, and became a disciple of the renowned and holy Sheikh, Mohammed Sherif.

His devotion to his superior, to his studies and to the practice of austerities, and a strange personal influence he was already beginning to show, won him by degrees a few disciples of his own: and with them he retired to the island of Abba. Here by the waters of the White Nile Mohammed Ahmed lived for several years. His two brothers, who were boat-builders in the neighbourhood, supported him by their industry. We read that he 'hollowed out for himself a cave in the mud bank, and lived in almost entire seclusion, fasting often for days'.[2]

---

[1] *Descendants of the Prophet.*

[2] *I take this passage from* Fire and Sword in the Soudan, *by Slatin. His is the most graphic and trustworthy of all known records of the Mahdi. He had terrible opportunities of collecting information. I have followed his version* (chapter iv) *very closely on this subject.*

This virtuous and frugal existence was disturbed and terminated by an untoward event. The renowned and holy Sheikh made a feast to celebrate the circumcision of his sons. Sherif, according to the lax practice of the time, granted a dispensation from any sins committed during the festivities, and proclaimed in God's name the suspension of the rules against singing and dancing by which the religious orders were bound. The ascetic of Abba island, with the recklessness of the reformer, protested against the demoralisation of the age, and loudly affirmed the doctrine that God alone could forgive sins. These things were speedily brought to the ears of the renowned Sheikh, and in all the righteous indignation that accompanies detected wrong-doing, he summoned Mohammed Ahmed before him. The latter obeyed. He respected his superior. He submissively entreated forgiveness; but in vain. Sherif felt that some sort of discipline must be maintained among his flock. Rising in anger, he drove the presumptuous disciple from his presence with bitter words, and expunged his name from the order of the elect.

Mohammed went home. He was greatly distressed. Placing a heavy wooden collar on his neck, clad in sackcloth and sprinkled with ashes, he again returned to his spiritual leader, and in this penitential guise implored pardon. He was ignominiously ejected. Nor did he venture to revisit the unforgiving Sheikh. But it happened that in a few weeks Sherif had occasion to journey to the island of Abba. His former disciple appeared suddenly before him, still clad in sackcloth and defiled by ashes. Careless of his plain misery, and unmoved by his loyalty, which was the more remarkable since it was disinterested, the implacable Sheikh poured forth a stream of invective. Among the insults, one went home: 'Be off, you wretched Dongolawi.'

Abuse by class is a dangerous though effective practice. A man will perhaps tolerate an offensive word applied to himself, but will be infuriated if his nation, his rank, or his profession is insulted. Mohammed Ahmed rose. All that man could do to make amends

13

he had done. Now he had been publicly called 'a wretched Dongolawi'. Reaching his house, he informed his disciples – for they had not abandoned him in all his trouble – that the Sheikh had finally cast him off, and that he would now take his discarded allegiance elsewhere. The rival, the Sheikh el Koreishi, lived near Mesalamia. He was jealous of Sherif and was therefore delighted to receive a letter from Mohammed Ahmed announcing his breach with his former superior and offering his most devoted services. He returned a cordial invitation, and the priest of Abba island made all preparation for the journey.

This new development seems to have startled the unforgiving Sherif. It was no part of his policy to alienate his followers, still less to add to those of his rival. After all, the quality of mercy was high and noble. He would at last graciously forgive the impulsive but repentant disciple. He wrote him a letter to this effect. But it was now too late. Mohammed replied with grave dignity that he had committed no crime, that he sought no forgiveness, and that 'a wretched Dongolawi' would not offend by his presence the renowned Sheikh el Sherif. After this indulgence he departed to Mesalamia.

But the fame of his doings spread far and wide throughout the land. Mohammed did not hesitate to declare that he had done what he had done as a protest against the decay of religious fervour and the torpor of the times. Rumour, loud-tongued, carried it about the land that a great Reformer was come to purify the faith and break the stony apathy which paralysed the hearts of Islam.

Throughout Nubia the Shukri belief prevails: some day, in a time of shame and trouble, a second great Prophet will arise – a *Mahdi* who shall lead the faithful nearer God and sustain the religion. The people of the Soudan always look inquiringly to any ascetic who rises to fame, and the question is often repeated, 'Art thou he that should come, or do we look for another?' Of this powerful element of disturbance Mohammed Ahmed resolved to avail himself. He requested and obtained the permission of the Sheikh Koreishi to return to Abba, where he was well known, and with which island village his name was connected, and so came back in triumph to the scene of his disgrace. Thither many pilgrims began to resort. He journeyed preaching through Kordofan, and while he spoke of the purification of the religion, they thought that the burning words might be applied to the freedom of the soil. He supported his sermons by writings, which were widely read. When a few months later the Sheikh Koreishi died, the priest of Abba proceeded forthwith to erect a tomb to his memory, directing and controlling the voluntary labours of the reverent Arabs who carried the stones.

While Mohammed was thus occupied he received the support of a man, less virtuous than but nearly as famous as himself. Abdullah was one of four brothers, the sons of an obscure priest; but he inherited no great love of religion or devotion to its observances. He was a man of determination and capacity. He set before himself two distinct ambitions, both of which he accomplished: to free the Soudan of foreigners, and to rule it himself. So soon as he saw Mohammed Ahmed rising to fame and displaying qualities of courage and energy, he hastened to throw himself at his feet and assure him of his devotion.

Mohammed Ahmed received his new adherent kindly, but without enthusiasm. For some months Abdullah carried stones to build the tomb of the Sheikh el Koreishi. Gradually they got to know each other. 'But long before he entrusted me with his secret,' said Abdullah to Slatin,[1] 'I knew that he was "the expected Guide".' And though the world might think that the 'Messenger of God' was sent to lead men to happiness in heaven, Abdullah attached to the phrase a significance of his own, and knew that he should lead him to power on earth. The two formed a strong combination. The Mahdi – for such Mohammed Ahmed had already in secret announced himself – brought the wild enthusiasm

[1] *Slatin*, Fire and Sword, *p. 131.*

15

of religion, the glamour of a stainless life, and the influence of superstition into the movement. But if he were the soul of the plot, Abdullah was the brain. He was the man of the world, the practical politician, the general.

There now commenced a great conspiracy against the Egyptian Government. The Mahdi began to collect adherents and to extend his influence in all parts of the country. He made a second journey through Kordofan, and received everywhere promises of support from all classes. As the ramifications of the plot spread they were perceived by the renowned Sheikh Sherif, who warned the Egyptian Government. They, knowing his envy and hatred of his former disciple, discounted his evidence and for some time paid no attention to the gathering of the storm. But presently more trustworthy witnesses confirmed his statements, and Raouf Pasha, then Governor-General, finding himself confronted with a growing agitation, sent a messenger to the island of Abba, to summon Mohammed Ahmed to Khartoum to justify his behaviour and explain his intentions. The news of the despatch of the messenger was swiftly carried to the Mahdi. He consulted with his trusty lieutenant. They decided without further delay to defy the Government. When it is remembered how easily an organised army, even though it be in a bad condition, can stamp out the beginnings of revolt among a population, the courage of their resolve must be admired.

The messenger arrived. He was received with courtesy by Abdullah, and forthwith conducted before the Mahdi. He delivered his message, and urged Mohammed Ahmed to comply with the orders of the Governor-General. The Mahdi listened for some time in silence, but with increasing emotion; and when the messenger advised him, as he valued his own safety, to journey to Khartoum, if only to justify himself, his passion overcame him. 'What!' he shouted, rising suddenly and striking his breast with his hand. 'By the grace of God and his Prophet I am master of this country, and never shall I go to Khartoum to justify myself.'[1] The terrified messenger withdrew. The rebellion of the Mahdi had begun.

Both the priest and the Governor-General prepared for military enterprise. The Mahdi proclaimed a holy war against the foreigners, alike the enemies of God and the scourge of men. He roused the local tribes. He wrote letters to all parts of the Soudan, calling upon the people to fight for a purified religion, the freedom of the soil, and God's holy prophet 'the expected Mahdi'. He promised the honour of men to those who lived, the favour of God to those who fell, and lastly that the land should be cleared of the miserable 'Turk'. 'Better', he said, and it became the watchword of the revolt, 'thousands of graves than a dollar tax.'[2]

Nor was Raouf Pasha idle. He sent two companies of infantry each commanded by a Captain, with one gun by steamer to Abba to arrest the fanatic who disturbed the public peace. At sunset on an August evening in 1881 the steamer arrived at Abba. Both landed with their companies and proceeded by different routes under the cover of darkness to the village where the Mahdi dwelt. Arriving simultaneously from opposite directions, they fired into each other, and, in the midst of this mistaken combat, the Mahdi rushed upon them with his scanty following and destroyed them impartially. A few soldiers succeeded in reaching the bank of the river. But the captain of the steamer would run no risks, and those who could not swim out to the vessel were left to their fate. With such tidings the expedition returned to Khartoum.

The effect of the success was electrical. The news spread throughout the Soudan. Men with sticks had slain men with rifles. A priest had destroyed the soldiers of the Government. Surely this was the Expected One. Abdullah, however, had no illusions. More troops would be sent. They were too near to Khartoum. Prudence counselled flight to regions more remote. But before this new *Hegira* the Mahdi appointed his four Khalifas, in accordance with

[1] *Slatin*, Fire and Sword, *p. 135.*
[2] *Ohrwalder*, Ten Years' Captivity in the Mahdi's Camp.

prophecy and precedent. The first was Abdullah. Of the others it is only necessary at this moment to notice Ali-Wad-Helu, the chief of one of the local tribes, and among the first to rally to the standard of revolt.

Then the retreat began; but it was more like a triumphal progress. Attended by a considerable following, and preceded by tales of the most wonderful miracles and prodigies, the Mahdi retired to a mountain in Kordofan to which he gave the name of Jebel Masa, that being the mountain whence 'the expected Guide' is declared in the Koran sooner or later to appear. He was now out of reach of Khartoum, but within reach of Fashoda. The Egyptian Governor of that town, Rishid Bey, a man of more enterprise and even less military knowledge than is usual in his race, determined to make an attempt to seize the rebel and disperse his following. Taking no precautions, he fell on the 9th of December into an ambush, was attacked unprepared, and was himself with 1,400 men, slaughtered by the ill-armed but valiant Arabs.

The Government, thoroughly alarmed by the serious aspect the revolt had assumed, organised a great expedition. Four thousand troops under Yusef, a Pasha of distinguished reputation, were sent against the rebels. Meanwhile the Mahdi and his followers suffered the extremes of want. Their cause was as yet too perilous for the rich to join. Only the poor flocked to the holy standard. All that Mohammed possessed he gave away, keeping nothing for himself, excepting only a horse to lead his followers in battle. Abdullah walked. Nevertheless the rebels were half-famished, and armed with scarcely any more deadly weapons than sticks and stones. The army of the Government anticipated an easy victory. Their contempt for the enemy was supreme. They did not even trouble themselves to post sentries by night, but slept calmly inside a slender thorn fence, unwatched save by their tireless foes. And so it came to pass that in the half-light of the early morning of the 7th of June the Mahdi, his ragged Khalifas, and his almost naked army rushed upon them, and slew them to a man.

The victory was decisive. Southern Kordofan was at the feet of the priest of Abba. Stores of arms and ammunition had fallen into his hands. Thousands of every class hastened to join his standard. No one doubted that he was the divine messenger sent to free them from their oppressors. The whole of the Arab tribes all over the Soudan rose at once. The smaller Egyptian posts, the tax-gatherers and local administrators, were massacred in every district. Only the larger garrisons maintained themselves in the principal towns. They were at once blockaded. All communications were interrupted. All legal authority was defied. Only the Mahdi was obeyed.

It is now necessary to look for a moment to Egypt. The misgovernment which in the Soudan had caused the rebellion of the Mahdi, in Egypt produced the revolt of Arabi Pasha. As the people of the Soudan longed to be rid of the foreign oppressors – the so-called 'Turks' – so those of the Delta were eager to free themselves from the foreign regulators and the real Turkish influence. While men who lived by the sources of the Nile asserted that tribes did not exist for officials to harry, others who dwelt at its mouth protested that nations were not made to be exploited by creditors or aliens. Mohammed Ahmed broke the Egyptian yoke; Arabi gave expression to the hatred of the Egyptians for the Turks. But although the hardy Arabs might scatter the effete Egyptians, the effete Egyptians were not likely to disturb the solid battalions of Europe. After much hesitation and many attempts at compromise, the Liberal Administration of Mr Gladstone sent a fleet which reduced the forts of Alexandria to silence and the city to anarchy. The bombardment of the fleet was followed by the invasion of a powerful army. Twenty-five thousand men were landed in Egypt. The Egyptian armies were slaughtered or captured. Their patriotic but commonplace leader was sentenced to death and condemned to exile, and Great Britain assumed the direction of Egyptian affairs.

The British soon restored law and order in Egypt, and the

question of the revolt in the Soudan came before the English advisers of the Khedive. Notwithstanding the poverty and military misfortunes which depressed the people of the Delta, the desire to hold their southern provinces was evident. The British Government, which at that time was determined to pursue a policy of non-interference in the Soudan, gave a tacit consent, and another great expedition was prepared to suppress the False Prophet, as the English and Egyptians deemed him.

During the summer of 1883 the Egyptian troops gradually concentrated at Khartoum until a considerable army was formed. It was perhaps the worst army that has ever marched to war. One extract from General Hicks's letters will suffice. Writing on the 8th of June, 1883, to Sir E. Wood, he says incidentally: 'Fifty-one men of the Krupp battery deserted on the way here, although in chains.' The officers and men who had been defeated fighting for their own liberties at Tel-el-Kebir were sent to be destroyed, fighting to take away the liberties of others in the Soudan. They had no spirit, no discipline, hardly any training, and in a force of over eight thousand men there were scarcely a dozen capable officers. The two who were the most notable of these few – General Hicks, who commanded, and Colonel Farquhar, the Chief of the Staff – must be remarked.

El Obeid, the chief town of Kordofan, had fallen to the Mahdi before the ill-fated expedition left Khartoum; but the fact that Slatin Bey, an Austrian officer in the Egyptian service, was still maintaining himself in Darfur provided it with an object. On the 9th of September Hicks and his army (the actual strength of which was 7,000 infantry, 400 mounted Bashi Bazuks, 500 cavalry, 100 Circassians, 10 mounted guns, 4 Krupps, and 6 Nordenfeldt machine guns) left Omdurman and marched to Duem. Although the actual command of the expedition was vested in the English officer, Ala-ed-Din Pasha, the Governor-General who had succeeded Raouf Pasha, exercised an uncertain authority. Differences of opinion were frequent, though all the officers were agreed in taking the darkest views of their chances. The miserable host toiled slowly onward towards its destruction, marching in a south-westerly direction through Shat and Rahad.

On the approach of the Government troops the Mahdi had marched out of El Obeid and established himself in the open country. More than forty thousand men collected round his standard, and the Arabs were now armed with several thousand rifles and a few cannon, as well as a great number of swords and spears. To these proportions had the little band of followers who fought at Abba grown! The disparity of the forces was apparent before the battle. The Mahdi thereupon wrote to Hicks, calling on him to surrender and offering terms. His proposals were treated with disdain, although the probable result of an engagement was clear.

The collision took place on the 3rd of November. All through that day the Egyptians struggled slowly forward, in great want of water, losing continually from the fire of the Soudanese riflemen, and leaving several guns behind them. On the next morning they were confronted by the main body of the Arab Army, and their attempts to advance further were defeated with heavy loss. Scarcely five hundred Egyptians escaped death; hardly as many of the Arabs fell. The European officers perished fighting to the end; and the general met his fate sword in hand, his personal valour and physical strength exciting the admiration even of the fearless enemy, so that in chivalrous respect they buried his body with barbaric honours. Mohammed Ahmed celebrated his victory with a salute of one hundred guns; and well he might, for the Soudan was now his.

It is customary to lay to the charge of Mohammed Ahmed all the blood that was spilled. To my mind it seems that he may divide the responsibility with the unjust rulers who oppressed the land, with the incapable commanders who muddled away the lives of their men, with the vacillating Ministers who aggravated the misfortunes. But, whatever is set to the Mahdi's account, it should not be forgotten that he put life and soul into the hearts of his countrymen, and freed his native land of foreigners. The poor miserable natives, eating only a handful of grain, toiling half-naked and without hope, found a new, if terrible magnificence added to life. Within their humble breasts the spirit of the Mahdi roused the fires of patriotism and religion. There are many Christians who reverence the faith of Islam and yet regard the Mahdi merely as a commonplace religious impostor whom force of circumstances elevated to notoriety. In a certain sense, this may be true. But I know not how a genuine may be distinguished from a spurious Prophet, except by the measure of his success. The triumphs of the Mahdi were in his lifetime far greater than those of the founder of the Mohammedan faith; and the chief difference between orthodox Mohammedanism and Mahdism was that the original impulse was opposed only by decaying systems of government and society and the recent movement came in contact with civilisation and the machinery of science. Recognising this, I do not share the popular opinion, and I believe that if in future years prosperity should come to the peoples of the Upper Nile, and learning and happiness follow in its train, then the first Arab historian who shall investigate the early annals of that new nation will not forget, foremost among the heroes of his race, to write the name of Mohammed Ahmed.

CHAPTER 2

THE FATE OF THE ENVOY

The triumph no less than the plunder which had rewarded the Mahdi's victories had called into existence a military spirit distinct from the warlike passions of the tribesmen – the spirit of the professional soldier.

The siege of Khartoum was carried on while this new influence was taking the place of the original forces of revolt. There was a period when a neutral point was obtained and the Mahdist power languished. But the invasion of the Eastern Soudan by the British troops in the spring and the necessary advance of the relieving columns in the winter of 1884 revived the patriotic element. The tribes who had made a great effort to free themselves from foreign domination saw in the operations of Sir Gerald Graham and Lord Wolseley an attempt to bring them again under the yoke. The impulse which was given to the Mahdi's cause was sufficient to raise a fierce opposition to the invading forces. The delay in the despatch of the relief expedition had sealed the fate of Khartoum, and the fall of the town established the supremacy of the military spirit on which the Dervish Empire was afterwards founded.

In order to describe conveniently the changing character of the revolt, I have anticipated the story and must revert to a period when the social and racial influences were already weakening and the military spirit was not yet grown strong. If the defeat of Yusef Pasha decided the whole people of the Soudan to rise in arms and strike for their liberties, the defeat of Hicks satisfied the British

Government that those liberties were won. Had Egypt been left to herself, other desperate efforts would have been made. But the British Government had finally abandoned the policy of non-interference with Egyptian action in the Soudan. They 'advised' its abandonment. The Khedive bowed to superior authority. The Minister resigned. The policy of evacuation was firmly adopted. 'Let us', said the Ministers, 'collect the garrisons and come away.' It was simple to decide on the course to be pursued, but almost impossible to follow it. Several of the Egyptian garrisons, as in Darfur and El Obeid, had already fallen. The others were either besieged, like Sennar, Tokar, and Sinkat, or cut off from the north, as in the case of the Equatorial Province, by the area of rebellion. The capital of the Soudan was, however, as yet unmolested; and as its Egyptian population exceeded the aggregate of the provincial towns, the first task of the Egyptian Government was obvious.

Mr Gladstone's Administration had repressed the revolt of Arabi Pasha. Through their policy the British were in armed occupation of Egypt. British officers were reorganising the army. A British official supervised the finances. A British plenipotentiary 'advised' the re-established Tewfik. A British fleet lay attentive before the ruins of Alexandria, and it was evident that Great Britain could annex the country in name as well as in fact. But Imperialism was not the object of the Radical Cabinet. As they were now determined that the Egyptians should evacuate the Soudan, so they had always been resolved that the British should evacuate Egypt.

The British Government watched with anxious solicitude the efforts of Egypt to evacuate the Soudan and bring the garrisons safely home. They utterly declined to assist with military force, but they were generous with their advice. Everybody at that time distrusted the capacities of the Egyptians, and it was thought the evacuation might be accomplished if it were entrusted to stronger and more honest men than were bred by the banks of the Nile. The Ministers looked about them, wondering how they could assist the Egyptian Government without risk or expense to themselves, and in an evil hour for their fame and fortunes someone whispered the word 'Gordon'. Forthwith they proceeded to telegraph to Cairo: 'Would General Charles Gordon be of any use to you or to the Egyptian Government; and, if so, in what capacity?' The Egyptian Government replied through Sir Evelyn Baring that as the movement in the Soudan was partly religious they were 'very much averse' from the appointment of a Christian in high command. The eyes of all those who possessed local knowledge were turned to a different person. There was one man who might stem the tide of Mahdism, who might perhaps restore the falling dominion of Egypt, who might at least save the garrisons of the Soudan. In their necessity and distress the Khedivial advisers and the British plenipotentiary looked as a desperate remedy to the man whose liberty they had curtailed, whose property they had confiscated, and whose son they had executed – Zubehr Pasha.

This was the agent for whom the Government of Egypt hankered. The idea was supported by all who were acquainted with the local conditions. A week after Sir Evelyn Baring had declined General Gordon's services he wrote: 'Whatever may be Zubehr's faults, he is said to be a man of great energy and resolution. The Egyptian Government considers that his services may be very useful....Baker Pasha is anxious to avail himself of Zubehr Pasha's services.'[1] It is certain that had the Egyptian Government been a free agent, Zubehr would have been sent to the Soudan as its Sultan, and assisted by arms, money, and perhaps by men, to make head against the Mahdi. It is probable that at this particular period the Mahdi would have collapsed before a man whose fame was nearly equal to, and whose resources would have been much greater than, his own. But the British Ministry would countenance no dealings with such a man. They scouted the idea of Zubehr, and by so doing increased their obligation to suggest an alternative. Zubehr being rejected, Gordon remained.

[1] *Sir Evelyn Baring, letter of 9th December 1883.*

It is known that from the very first Sir Evelyn Baring was bitterly opposed to General Gordon's appointment. No personal friendship existed between them, and the Administrator dreaded the return to the feverish complications of Egyptian politics of the man who had always been identified with unrest, improvisation, and disturbance. The pressure was, however, too strong for him to withstand. Nubar Pasha, the Foreign Office, the British public, everyone clamoured for the appointment. At length Baring yielded, and, as soon as his consent had been obtained, the Government turned with delight to Gordon. On the 17th of January Lord Wolseley requested him to come to England. On the 18th he met the Cabinet. That same night he started on the long journey from which he was never to return.

Gordon embarked on his mission in high spirits, sustained by that belief in personality which too often misleads great men and beautiful women. It was, he said, the greatest honour ever conferred upon him.

The Ministers were intensely relieved. The most unbounded confidence was reposed in the envoy. His interview with the Khedive was 'very satisfactory'. His complete authority was proclaimed to all the notables and natives of the Soudan.[1] He was assured of the support of the Egyptian Government.[2] One hundred thousand pounds was placed to his credit, and he was informed that further sums would be supplied when this was exhausted. He was assured that no effort would be wanting on the part of the Cairene authorities, whether English or Egyptian, to afford him all the support and co-operation in their power.[3] Under these propitious auguries the dismal and disastrous enterprise began.

His task was clearly defined. 'You will bear in mind', wrote Sir Evelyn Baring, 'that the main end to be pursued is the evacuation of the Soudan.' 'The object ... of your mission to the Soudan',

[1] *Proclamation of the Khedive, 26th January 1884.*
[2] *Sir Evelyn Baring to Major-General Gordon, 25th January 1884.*
[3] *Sir Evelyn Baring to Major-General Gordon, 25th January 1884.*

declared the Khedive, 'is to carry into execution the evacuation of those territories and to withdraw our troops, civil officials, and such of the inhabitants ... as may wish to leave for Egypt ... and after the evacuation to take the necessary steps for establishing an organised Government in the different provinces.' Nor was he himself under any misconception. He drew up a memorandum when on board the *Tanjore* in which he fully acquiesced in the evacuation of the Soudan. In a sentence which breathes the same spirit as Mr Gladstone's famous expression, 'a people rightly struggling to be free', he wrote: 'I must say that it would be an iniquity to conquer these peoples and then hand them back to the Egyptians without guarantees of future good government.' Finally, he unhesitatingly asserted: 'No one who has ever lived in the Soudan can escape the reflection "What a useless possession is this land!"' And Colonel Stewart, who accompanied him and endorsed the memorandum, added: 'And what a huge encumbrance to Egypt!' Thus far there was complete agreement between the British envoy and the Liberal Cabinet.

On the 22nd of February he arrived at Khartoum. He was received with rejoicing by the whole population. Those who had been about to fly for the north took fresh heart. They believed that behind the figure of the envoy stood the resources of an Empire. The Mahdi and the gathering Dervishes were perplexed and alarmed. Gordon had come. The armies would follow.

Whatever confidence the General had felt in the power of his personal influence had been dispelled on the journey to Khartoum. He saw himself confronted with a tremendous racial movement. The people of the Soudan had risen against foreigners. His only troops were Soudanese. He was himself a foreigner. Foremost among the leaders of the revolt were the Arab slave dealers, furious at the attempted suppression of their trade. No one, not even Sir Samuel Baker, had tried harder to suppress it than Gordon. Lastly, the whole movement had assumed a fanatical character. Islam marched against the infidel. Gordon was a

Christian. His own soldiers were under the spell they were to try to destroy. Every influence was hostile, and in particular hostile to his person. On the very day of his arrival at Khartoum, while the townsfolk were cheering his name in the streets and the batteries were firing joyful salutes, while the people of England thought his mission already accomplished, General Gordon sat himself down and telegraphed a formal request to Cairo for Zubehr Pasha.

The whole story of his relations with Zubehr is extremely characteristic. Zubehr's son, Suliman, had been executed, if not by Gordon's orders, at least during his administration of the Soudan and with his complete approval. He had hardly started from London on his new mission, when he telegraphed to Sir Evelyn Baring, telling him that Zubehr was a most dangerous man and requesting that he might be at once deported to Cyprus. The General arrived in Cairo like a whirlwind close behind his telegram, and was very angry to hear that Zubehr was still in Egypt. Before starting up the river he went to see Sherif Pasha. In the ex-Minister's ante-room he met the very man he had determined to avoid – Zubehr. He greeted him with effusion. They had a long talk about the Soudan, after which Gordon hurried to the Agency and informed Sir Evelyn Baring that Zubehr must accompany him to Khartoum at once. Baring did not himself disapprove of the plan. But he thought the change in Gordon's attitude too sudden to be relied on. Tomorrow he might change again. He begged the General to think more seriously of the matter. Gordon with his usual frankness admitted that his change of mind had been very sudden. He had been conscious, he said, of a 'mystic feeling' that Zubehr was necessary to save the situation in the Soudan.

Her Majesty's Government refused absolutely to have anything to do with Zubehr. They declined to allow the Egyptian Government to employ him. The historians of the future may occupy their leisure and exercise their wits in deciding whether the Ministers and the people were right or wrong.

But if the justice of the decision is doubtful, its consequences were obvious. Either the British Government were concerned with the Soudan, or they were not. If they were not, then they had no reason or right to prohibit the appointment of Zubehr. If they were, they were bound to see that the garrisons were rescued. England had not misgoverned the Soudan, had not raised the revolt or planted the garrisons. All that Egypt had a right to expect was commiseration. But the moment Zubehr was prohibited the situation was changed. The refusal to permit his employment was tantamount to an admission that affairs in the Soudan involved the honour of England as well as the honour of Egypt. When the British people – for this was not merely the act of the Government – adopted a high moral attitude with regard to Zubehr, they bound themselves to rescue the garrisons, peaceably if possible, forcibly if necessary.

Gordon considered that he was personally pledged to effect the evacuation of Khartoum by the garrison and civil servants. He had appointed some of the inhabitants to positions of trust, thus compromising them with the Mahdi. Others had undoubtedly been encouraged to delay their departure by his arrival. He therefore considered that his honour was involved in their safety. Henceforward he was inflexible. Neither rewards nor threats could move him. Nothing that men could offer would induce him to leave Khartoum till its inhabitants were rescued. The Government on their side were equally stubborn. Nothing, however sacred, should induce them to send troops to Khartoum.

The deadlock was complete. To some men the Foreign Office might have suggested lines of retreat, covered by the highest official praise. Others would have welcomed an order to leave so perilous a post. But the man they had sent was the one man of all others who was beyond their control, who cared nothing for what they could give or take away. So events dragged on their wretched course. Gordon's proposals became more and more impracticable as the best courses he could devise were successively vetoed by the

Government. He had asked for Zubebr. Zubehr was refused. He had requested Turkish troops. Turkish troops were refused. He had asked for Mohammedan regiments from India. The Government regretted their inability to comply. He asked for a *Firman* from the Sultan to strengthen his position. It was 'peremptorily refused'. He proposed to go south in his steamers to Equatoria. The Government forbade him to proceed beyond Khartoum. He asked that 200 British troops might be sent to Berber. They were refused. He begged that a few might be sent to Assuan. None were sent. He proposed to visit the Mahdi himself and try to arrange matters with him personally. Perhaps he recognised a kindred spirit. The Government in this case very naturally forbade him.

At last the quarrel is open. He makes no effort to conceal his disgust. 'I leave you', he says, 'the indelible disgrace of abandoning the garrisons.'[1] He reiterates his determination to abide with the garrison of Khartoum. 'I will not leave these people after all they have gone through.'[2] He tosses his commission contemptuously from him: 'I would also ask her Majesty's Government to accept the resignation of my commission.'[3] The Government 'trust that he will not resign',[4] and his offer remains in abeyance. Finally, in bitterness and vexation, thinking himself abandoned and disavowed, he appeals to Sir Evelyn Baring personally: 'I feel sure, whatever you may feel diplomatically I have your support – and that of every man professing himself a gentleman – in private';[5] and as a last hope he begs Sir Samuel Baker to appeal to 'British and American millionaires' to subscribe two hundred thousand pounds to enable him to carry out the evacuation without, and even in spite of, the Governments of Cairo and London; and Sir

[1] *Major-General Gordon to Sir Evelyn Baring (telegraphic) received at Cairo, 16th April.*
[2] *Major-General Gordon to Sir Evelyn Baring, Khartoum, 30th July; received at Cairo, 15th October.*
[3] *Major-General Gordon to Sir Evelyn Baring (telegraphic) Khartoum, 9th March.*
[4] *Earl Granville to Sir Evelyn Baring, Foreign Office, 13th March.*
[5] *Major-General Gordon to Sir Evelyn Baring (telegraphic) received at Cairo, 16th April.*

Samuel Baker writes a long letter to *The Times* in passionate protest and entreaty.

But meanwhile other and still more stirring events were passing outside the world of paper and ink. The arrival of Gordon at Khartoum had seriously perplexed and alarmed Mohammed Ahmed and his Khalifas. They feared lest the General should be the herald of armies. As the weeks passed without reinforcements arriving, the Mahdi and Abdullah determined to put a brave face on the matter and blockade Khartoum itself. They were assisted in this enterprise by a revival of the patriotic impulse throughout the country and a consequent stimulus to the revolt. To discover the cause it is necessary to look to the Eastern Soudan, where the next tragedy, after the defeat of Hicks, is laid.

The Hadendoa tribe, infuriated by oppression and misgovernment, had joined the rebellion under the leadership of the celebrated Osman Digna. The Egyptian garrisons of Tokar and Sinkat were beleaguered and hard pressed. Her Majesty's Government disclaimed all responsibility. Yet, since these towns were not far from the coast, they did not prohibit an attempt on the part of the Egyptian Government to rescue the besieged soldiers. Accordingly an Egyptian force 3,500 strong marched from Suakin in February 1884 to relieve Tokar, under the command of General Baker, once the gallant colonel of the 10th Hussars. Hard by the wells of Teb they were, on the 5th of February, attacked by about a thousand Arabs.

'On the square being only threatened by a small force of the enemy ... the Egyptian troops threw down their arms and ran, carrying away the black troops with them, and allowing themselves to be killed without the slightest resistance.'[1] The British and European officers in vain endeavoured to rally them. The single Soudanese battalion fired impartially on friend and foe. The General, with that unshaken courage and high military skill

[1] *General Baker to Sir Evelyn Baring, 6th February (official despatch), telegraphic.*

which had already on the Danube gained him a continental reputation, collected some fifteen hundred men, mostly unarmed, and so returned to Suakin. Ninety-six officers and 2,250 men were killed. Krupp guns, machine guns, rifles, and a large supply of ammunition fell to the victorious Arabs. Success inflamed their ardour to the point of madness. The attack of the towns was pressed with redoubled vigour. The garrison of Sinkat, 800 strong, sallied out and attempted to fight their way to Suakin. The garrison of Tokar surrendered. Both were destroyed.

The garrisons they had refused to rescue the British Government now determined to avenge. In spite of their philanthropic professions, and in spite of the advice of General Gordon, who felt that his position at Khartoum would be still further compromised by operations on his only line of retreat,[1] a considerable military expedition consisting of one cavalry and two infantry brigades, was sent to Suakin. The command was entrusted to General Graham. Troops were hurriedly concentrated. The 10th Hussars, returning from India, were stopped and mounted on the horses of the *gendarmerie*. With admirable celerity the force took the field. Within a month of the defeat at Teb they engaged the enemy almost on the very scene of the disaster. On the 4th of March they slew 3,000 Hadendoa and drove the rest in disorder from the ground. Four weeks later a second action was fought at Tamai. Again the success of the British troops was complete; again the slaughter of the Arabs was enormous. But neither victory was bloodless. El Teb cost 24 officers and 168 men; Tamai, 13 officers and 208 men. The effect of these operations was the dispersal of Osman Digna's gathering. That astute man, not for the first or last time, made a good retreat.

Ten thousand men had thus been killed in the space of three months in the Eastern Soudan. By the discipline of their armies the Government were triumphant. The tribes of the Red Sea shore cowered before them. But as they fought without reason, so

---

[1] *Sir Evelyn Baring to Earl Granville, Cairo, 23rd February.*

they conquered without profit.

Gordon's mission was an admitted failure. After that the only question was how to bring him away as quickly as possible. It was certain that he would not come willingly. Force was necessary. Yet it was difficult to know how to apply it. After the victories in the Eastern Soudan the opportunity presented itself. The road was open. The local tribes were crushed. Berber had not then fallen. The Mahdi was himself still on the road from El Obeid to Khartoum. Sir Evelyn Baring saw the chance. With all his influence he urged the despatch of a small flying column to Khartoum. His idea was simple. One thousand or twelve hundred men were to mount on camels and ride thither via Berber. Those who fell ill or whose camels broke down would have to take their chance by the roadside. The plan, however, broke down in the military detail. Only one honourable course remained – a regular expedition. This the British Agent at once began to urge. This the Government obstinately refused to admit; and meanwhile time was passing.

While the British Government was indulging in vengeful operations in the Eastern Soudan, the Mahdi advanced slowly but steadily upon Khartoum with a following variously estimated at from fifteen to twenty thousand men. On the 7th of March Colonel Stewart telegraphed from Khartoum: 'The Mahdi has attempted to raise the people of Shendi by an emissary....We may be cut off';[1] and on the 11th Gordon himself reported: 'The rebels are four hours distant on the Blue Nile.'[2] Thereafter no more telegrams came for on the 15th the wire was cut between Shendi and Berber, and the blockade had commenced.

The long and glorious defence of the town of Khartoum will always fascinate attention. That one man, a European among Africans, a Christian among Mohammedans, should by his genius have inspired the efforts of 7,000 soldiers of inferior race, and by

[1] *Lieut.-Colonel Stewart to Sir Evelyn Baring, 7th March 1884.*
[2] *Major-General Gordon to Sir Evelyn Baring, 11th March 1884.*

his courage have sustained the hearts of 30,000 inhabitants of
notorious timidity, and with such materials and encumbrances
have offered a vigorous resistance to the increasing attacks of an
enemy who, though cruel, would yet accept surrender, during a
period of 317 days, is an event perhaps without parallel in history.
But it may safely be predicted that no one will ever write an
account which will compare in interest with that set forth by the
man himself in the famous *Journals at Khartoum*.

Perhaps it is because he is careless of the sympathy of men that
Charles Gordon so readily wins it. Before the first of the six parts
into which the *Journals* were divided is finished, the reader has
been won. Henceforth he sees the world through Gordon's eyes.
With him he scoffs at the diplomatists; despises the Government;
becomes impatient – unreasonably, perhaps – with a certain Major
Kitchener in the Intelligence Branch, whose information miscar-
ried or was not despatched; is wearied by the impracticable
Shaiggia Irregulars; takes interest in the turkey-cock and his harem
of four wives; laughs at the 'black sluts' seeing their faces for the
first time in the mirror. When the end of the account is reached,
no man of British birth can read the last words, 'Now mark this,
if the Expeditionary Force – and I ask for no more than two hundred men – does not come within ten days, *the town may fall*; and
I have done my best for the honour of our Country. Goodbye',
without being thrilled with vain regrets and futile resolutions.
And then the account stops short. Henceforward Gordon's perils
were unrecorded.

I would select one episode only from the *Journals* as an
example of the peculiarity and the sternness of Charles Gordon's
character – his behaviour towards Slatin. This Austrian officer had
been Governor of Darfur with the rank in the Egyptian service of
Bey. For four years he had struggled vainly against the rebellion.
He had fought numerous engagements with varied success. He
had been several times wounded. Throughout his province and
even beyond its limits he bore the reputation of a brave and capable

soldier, a man of feeling and of honour. He had, however, committed an act which deprived him of Gordon's sympathy and respect. During the fighting in Darfur, after several defeats, his Mohammedan soldiers were discouraged and attributed their evil fortune to the fact that their commander was an infidel under the curse of the Almighty. Slatin therefore proclaimed himself a follower of the Prophet, and outwardly at least adopted the faith of Islam. The troops, delighted at his conversion and cheered by the hope of success, renewed their efforts, and the resistance of the Governor of Darfur was prolonged. The end, however, was deferred, not averted. After the destruction of General Hicks's Army Slatin was compelled to surrender to the Dervishes. The religion he had assumed to secure victory he observed to escape death. The Arab leaders, who admired his courage, treated him at first with respect and kindness, and he was conducted to the Mahdi in his encampment before Khartoum. There during the siege he remained, closely watched but not imprisoned. Thence he wrote letters to Gordon explaining his surrender, excusing his apostasy, and begging that he might be allowed – not even assisted – to escape to Khartoum. The letters are extant, and scarcely anyone who reads them, reflecting on the twelve years of danger and degradation that lay before this man, will refuse their compassion.

Gordon was inflexible. This is the uncompromising minute in the *Journals*: 'Oct. 16. The letters of Slatin have arrived. I have no remarks to make on them, and cannot make out why he wrote them.'[1]

Slatin's position, it should be observed, was not that of an officer released on parole, but of a prisoner of war in durance in the enemy's camp. In such circumstances he was clearly entitled to escape at his own proper risk. If his captors gave him the chance, they had only themselves to blame.

Slatin was, however, in no position to argue his case. His

[1] *Journals at Khartoum.*

35

correspondence with Gordon was discovered. For some days his life hung on a thread. For several months he was heavily chained and fed on a daily handful of uncooked *doura*, such as is given to horses and mules. Tidings of these things were carried to Gordon. 'Slatin', he observes icily, 'is still in chains.' He never doubted the righteousness of the course he had adopted, never for an instant.

Gordon's responsibility was undivided. There was no one to whom he could talk as an equal. There was no one to whom he could reveal his doubts. To some minds the exercise of power is pleasant, but few sensations are more painful than responsibility without control. The General could not supervise the defence. The officers robbed the soldiers of their rations. The sentries slumbered at their posts. The townspeople bewailed their misfortunes, and all ranks and classes intrigued with the enemy in the hope of securing safety when the town should fall. Spies of all kinds pervaded the town. The Egyptian Pashas, despairing, meditated treason. Once an attempt was made to fire the magazine. Once no less than eighty thousand *ardebs* of grain was stolen from the arsenal. From time to time the restless and ceaseless activity of the commander might discover some plot and arrest the conspirators; or, checking some account, might detect some robbery; but he was fully aware that what he found out was scarcely a tithe of what he could not hope to know. The Egyptian officers were untrustworthy. Yet he had to trust them. The inhabitants were thoroughly broken by war, and many were disloyal. He had to feed and inspirit them. The town itself was scarcely defensible. It must be defended to the end. From the flat roof of his palace his telescope commanded a view of the forts and lines. Here he would spend the greater part of each day, scrutinising the defences and the surrounding country with his powerful glass. The *Journals*, the only receptacle of his confidences, display the bitterness of his sufferings no less than the greatness of his character. 'There is no contagion', he writes, 'equal to that of fear. I have been rendered furious when from anxiety I could not eat, I would find those at the same table were in like manner affected.'

To the military anxieties was added every kind of worry which may weary a man's soul. The belief that he was abandoned and discredited, that history would make light of his efforts, would perhaps never know of them, filled his mind with a sense of wrong and injustice which preyed upon his spirits. The miseries of the townsfolk wrung his noble, generous heart. The utter loneliness depressed him. And over all lay the shadow of uncertainty. To the very end the possibility that 'all might be well' mocked him with false hopes. The first light of any morning might reveal the longed-for steamers of relief and the uniforms of British soldiers. He was denied even the numbing anaesthetic of despair.

Yet he was sustained by two great moral and mental stimulants: his honour as a man, his faith as a Christian. The first had put all courses which he did not think right once and for all out of the question, and so allayed many doubts and prevented many vain regrets. But the second was the real source of his strength. He was sure that beyond this hazardous existence, with all its wrongs and inequalities, another life awaited him – a life which, if he had been faithful and true here upon earth, would afford him greater faculties for good and wider opportunities for their use. 'Look at me now', he once said to a fellow-traveller, 'with small armies to command and no cities to govern. I hope that death will set me free from pain and that great armies will be given me, and that I shall have vast cities under my command.'[1]

As the severity of military operations increases, so also must the sternness of discipline. When fortune is dubious or adverse; when supplies fail, arrangements miscarry, and disasters impend, the ugly truth is revealed that fear is the foundation of obedience. It is certain that the influence of General Gordon upon the garrison and townspeople of Khartoum owed its greatest strength to that sinister element. 'It is quite painful', he writes in his *Journals*

[1] *Lieut.-Colonel N. Newnham Davis, 'Some Gordon Reminiscences', published in* The Man of the World *newspaper, 14th December 1898.*

in September, 'to see men tremble so, when they come and see me, that they cannot hold the match to their cigarette.' As the winter drew on, the sufferings of the besieged increased and their faith in their commander and his promises of relief diminished. To preserve their hopes – and, by their hopes, their courage and loyalty – was beyond the power of man. But what a great man in the utmost exercise of his faculties and authority might do, Gordon did.

His extraordinary spirit never burned more brightly than in these last, gloomy days. The money to pay the troops was exhausted. He issued notes, signing them with his own name. The citizens groaned under the triple scourge of scarcity, disease, and war. He ordered the bands to play merrily and discharged rockets. It was said that they were abandoned, that help would never come, that the expedition was a myth – the lie of a General who was disavowed by his Government. Forthwith he placarded the walls with the news of victories and of the advance of a triumphant British Army; or hired all the best houses by the river's bank for the accommodation of the officers of the relieving force. A Dervish shell crashed through his palace. He ordered the date of its arrival to be inscribed above the hole. For those who served him faithfully he struck medals and presented them with pomp and circumstance. Others less laudable he shot. And by all these means and expedients the defence of the city was prolonged through the summer, autumn, and winter of 1884 and on into the year 1885.

All this time the public anxiety in England had been steadily growing. If Gordon was abandoned, he was by no means forgotten. As his mission had been followed with intense interest throughout the whole country, so its failure had caused general despondency. Disappointment soon gave place to alarm. The subject of the personal safety of the distinguished envoy was first raised in the House of Commons on the 16th of March by Lord Randolph Churchill.

'Colonel Coetlogon has stated that Khartoum may be easily captured; we know that General Gordon is surrounded by hostile tribes and cut off from communications with Cairo and London; and under these circumstances the House has a right to ask Her Majesty's Government whether they are going to do anything to relieve him. Are they going to remain indifferent to the fate of the one man on whom they have counted to extricate them from their dilemmas, to leave him to shift for himself, and not make a single effort on his behalf?'[1]

The Government remained impassive. But the subject, once raised, was not allowed to drop. The Opposition were continually growing stronger. Almost every night Ministers were invited to declare whether they would rescue their envoy or leave him to his fate. Mr Gladstone returned evasive answers. The agitation became intense. Even among the supporters of the Government there was dissatisfaction. But the Prime Minister was obdurate and unflinching.

It is usual to look upon Mr Gladstone's conduct in the matter of the relief of Gordon as dictated by benevolent weakness. History may take another view. Strong and stubborn as was the character of the General, that of the Minister was its equal. If Gordon was the better man, Gladstone was incomparably the greater. Few men have feared responsibility less than Gladstone. On the other hand, the expressed desire of the nation was a force to which he had always bowed – to which, indeed, he owed his political existence. Yet, in spite of the growing agitation throughout the land, he remained stern and silent. Most men do what is right, or what they persuade themselves is right; nor is it difficult to believe that Mr Gladstone did not feel justified in involving the nation in operations in the heart of the Soudan for the purpose, not of saving the life of the envoy – for Gordon had but to embark on his steamers and come home – but simply in order to vindicate the personal honour of a man. And it is possible that a feeling of

[1] Hansard's Parliamentary Debates, *16th March 1884.*

resentment against the officer whose intractable nature was bringing such odium upon the Government may have coloured his resolution with a darker tinge.

But for all his power and influence he was forced to give way. The Government which had long ignored the call of honour abroad, was driven to the Soudan by the cries of shame at home. Lord Hartington, at that time Secretary of State for War, must be dissociated from the general censure which his principal colleagues have incurred. He was the first to recognise the obligation which lay upon the Cabinet, and through the Cabinet upon the nation, and it was to his influence that the despatch of the relieving expedition was mainly due. The Commander-in-Chief and the Adjutant-General, who were fully alive to the critical position at Khartoum, added their recommendations. But even at the last moment Mr Gladstone was induced to sanction the advance only by the belief that the scale of the operations would be small, and that only a single brigade would be necessary. The decision was taken forthwith by the Ministry and announced to the nation. The Adjutant-General, however, asked for a very different force from what the Government had anticipated, and the single brigade was expanded into an expedition of ten thousand men, selected from the whole army.

To reverse the decision was now, however, impossible, and the 'Gordon Relief Expedition' began. The commander to whom the conduct of the operations had been entrusted reviewed the situation. He saw himself confronted with a task which was easy and safe if it were undertaken at leisure, and which was doubtful and perilous if begun in haste. Shrewdly estimating the military difficulties, he made his plans for a methodical and deliberate advance which would leave nothing to luck.

Troops and stores were steadily collected at Wady Halfa and along the Nile. The new Camel Corps, consisting of four regiments, practised their drills and evolutions. To pilot the boats up the Cataracts *voyageurs* were brought from Canada. At length, when all preparations were complete, the expedition started. The plan was simple. A strong column of infantry in boats was to work up the river. In case that should not arrive in time, the Camel Corps was to strike across the Bayuda Desert from Korti to Metemma. Having arrived there, a small detachment was to be thrown into Khartoum by Gordon's steamers to sustain the defence until the arrival of the main body in March or even April of 1885, when the town could be regularly relieved.

The Desert Column started from Korti on the 30th of December. Their strength did not exceed 1,100 officers and men, but they were the flower of the army. Dropping their communications, they set forth along the caravan route towards Metemma. The knowledge which we have since gained of the resources of the Mahdists enables the peril of their desperate venture to be fully appreciated. Although the Dervishes were neither so well armed nor trained as at a later date, they were nearly as numerous and equally devoid of fear. Their tactics were more in accordance with modern conditions: their fanaticism was at its height. The British force, on the other hand, was equipped with weapons scarcely comparable with those employed in the concluding campaigns. Instead of the powerful Lee-Metford rifle, with its smokeless powder, its magazine action, and its absence of recoil, they were armed with the Martini-Henry, which possessed none of these advantages. In place of the deadly Maxim there was the Gardner gun – the very gun that jammed at Tamai, and that jammed again at Abu Klea. The artillery was also in every respect inferior to that now in general use. Besides all this, the principles of fire-discipline and of scientific musketry were new, little understood, and hardly admitted. Nevertheless, the Camel Corps went boldly forward, and engaged an enemy whose destruction ultimately required the strength of a better-armed and better-instructed army twelve times as strong.

On the 3rd of January they reached Gakdul Wells. A hundred miles of their march was accomplished. But they were now delayed by the necessity of escorting a second column of supplies to Gakdul, and after that until the arrival of reinforcements which raised their strength to 1,800 of all ranks. The interval was employed in building two small forts and establishing an advanced depot; nor was it until the 13th that the march was resumed. The number of camels was not sufficient for the necessities of the transport. The food of the camels was too poor for the work they had to perform. By the 16th, however, they had made fifty miles, and approached the wells of Abu Klea. Here their further advance was disputed by the enemy.

The news of the advance of the Desert Column had been duly reported to the Mahdi and his Arab generals. A small party of English, it was said, with camels and some cavalry, were coming swiftly to the rescue of the accursed city. Their numbers were few, scarce 2,000 men. How should they hope to prevail against 'the expected Mahdi' and the conquering Ansar who had destroyed Hicks? They were mad; yet they should die; not one should escape. The delay in the advance offered ample opportunity. A great force of Arabs was concentrated. Several thousand men under important Emirs were detached from the army before Khartoum and marched northward eager for the slaughter of the 'enemies of God'. With the reinforcements from Omdurman the total force of the Arabs actually at hand was not less than 10,000, and behind were many thousands more. They permitted the little column to advance until their retreat, if defeated, was impossible, and then, confident of victory, offered battle near the wells of Abu Klea.

The Camel Corps remained halted during the morning of the 16th, and built a small fort, in which they placed their reserve of stores, and made some arrangement for the reception of wounded. At one o'clock they moved leisurely forward, passed through the rocky defile which led into the valley of Abu Klea and bivouacked. Early the next morning the force moved out in square formation and advanced upon the enemy. The most savage and bloody action ever fought in the Soudan by British troops followed. Notwithstanding the numbers and the valour of the Arabs, that they penetrated the square, and that they infilicted on the troops a loss of nine officers and sixty-five men killed and nine officers and eighty-five men wounded – 10 per cent of the entire force – they were driven from the field with great slaughter, and the Desert Column camped at the wells.

On the morning of the 18th they rested, placed their wounded in the small fort they had built, and buried their dead. In the afternoon they continued their advance, marched all through the night, and, having covered twenty-three miles, halted exhausted, almost within sight of the river, at daylight on the 19th. Meanwhile the enemy had again collected in great strength, and an effective rifle fire was opened on the column. Sir Herbert Stewart received the wound of which a few weeks later he died. The command devolved upon Sir Charles Wilson. The position was desperate. Water was running short. The Nile was only four miles away; but the column were impeded by their wounded and stores, and between the river and the thirsty men lay the Dervish Army, infuriated by their losses and fully aware of the sore straits to which their astonishing enemy was now reduced.

It now became necessary to divide the small force. Some must remain to guard the baggage and the wounded; the others must fight their way to the water. At three o'clock in the afternoon of the 19th, 900 men left the hastily made *zeriba* and marched towards the river. Without their camels or those of the transport they appeared insignificant, a mere speck on the broad plain of Metemma. The Dervishes hastened to clinch the matter.

The square advances slowly and painfully over the stony ground, with frequent jerky halts to preserve order and to pick up the wounded. Little puffs of white smoke dot the distant sandhills. Here and there a gaudy flag waves defiantly. In front the green tops of the palm-trees by the Nile tantalise but stimulate the soldiers. On the left the great mud labyrinth of Metemma stretches indefinitely.

Suddenly the firing stops. The low scrub in front is alive with the swarming figures of the enemy. All the flags dance forward together. Ragged white figures spring up in hundreds. Emirs on horses appear as if by magic. Everywhere are men running swiftly forward, waving their spears and calling upon the Prophet of God to speed their enterprise. The square halts. The weary men begin to fire with thoughtful care. The Dervishes drop thickly. On then, children of the desert! you are so many, they are so few. One rush will trample the accursed under the feet of the faithful. The charge continues. A bugle sounds in the waiting square. The firing stops. What is this? They lose heart. Their ammunition is exhausted. On then, and make an end. Again the smoke ripples along the line of bayonets and fire is re-opened, this time at closer range and with far greater effect. The stubborn grandeur of the British soldier is displayed by desperate circumstances. The men shoot to hit. The attack crumples. The Emirs – horse and man – collapse. The others turn and walk – for they will not run – sullenly back towards the town. The square starts forward. The road to the river is open. With dusk the water is reached, and never have victors gained a more longed-for prize. The Nile is won. Gordon remains.

Sir Charles Wilson, having collected his force, remained three days by the bank of the Nile before attempting any further advance on Khartoum. He has explained why this delay was necessary, to the satisfaction of most military critics. On the fourth day he embarked on two of Gordon's steamers, which awaited the relieving column, and taking with him twenty British soldiers and a few blue-jackets set forth towards the Shabluka Gorge and the town that lay beyond. On the 27th of January the rescuers came in sight of Khartoum and under the fire of the enemy. Many of their perilous adventures seem to belong to romance rather than to reality. But the scene that appeals to the imagination above all the others is that where with both banks ablaze with musketry and artillery, the black smoke pouring through the shot-holes in the funnels, the water rising in spurts from the bullets, the men who had come so far and braved so much stared at the palace roof and, seeing no flag flying, knew that all was over and that they had come too late.

The news of the Dervish defeats at Abu Klea and Abu Kru impelled the Mahdi to a desperate venture. The English were but 120 miles away. They were few, but victorious. In spite of the wrath of the true God and the valour of Islam they might prevail. The Mahdi depended on success for existence. The tremendous forces of fanaticism are exerted only in a forward direction. Retreat meant ruin. All must be staked on an immediate assault. Thus the night of the 25th of January arrived.

The band played as usual in the evening. Gradually the shadows fell and it became dark. The hungry inhabitants betook themselves to bed. The anxious but indomitable commander knew that the crisis impended, and knew also that he was powerless to avert it. Perhaps he slept, satisfied that he had done his duty; and in the silence of the night the savage enemy crawled stealthily towards the town. On a sudden the loud explosion of musketry broke the stillness of the night and the slumbers of the people; and with a continual shouting thousands of Dervishes swarmed through the unprotected space and entered Khartoum.

One mob of assailants made their way to the palace. Gordon came out to meet them. The whole courtyard was filled with wild, harlequin figures and sharp, glittering blades. He attempted a parley. 'Where is your master, the Mahdi?' He knew his influence over native races. Perhaps he hoped to save the lives of some of the inhabitants. Perhaps in that supreme moment imagination flashed another picture before his eyes; and he saw himself facing that savage circle with a fanaticism equal to, and a courage greater than, their own; marching in all the pride of faith 'and with retorted scorn' to a martyr's death.

It was not to be. Mad with the joy of victory and religious frenzy, they rushed upon him and, while he disdained even to fire his revolver, stabbed him in many places. The body fell down the steps and lay – a twisted heap – at the foot. There it was decapitated. The head was carried to the Mahdi. The trunk was stabbed again and again by the infuriated creatures, till nothing but a shapeless bundle of torn flesh and bloody rags remained of what had been a great and famous man and the envoy of Her Britannic Majesty. The blood soaked into the ground, and left a dark stain which was not immediately effaced. Slatin mentions that the Arabs used often to visit the place.

With the capture of the city and the death of the envoy the reason for the expedition disappeared. It remained only to withdraw the troops. The stores which had been brought across the desert at a terrible cost were thrown hastily into the Nile. The battered steamers which had waited so long at Metemma were hurriedly dismantled. The Camel Corps, their extraordinary efforts futile and their camels killed, marched back on foot to Korti. Their retreat was pressed by the exultant enemy. The River Column, whose boats after months of labour had just cleared the Cataracts, and who had gained a success at Kirbekan, were carried back swiftly by the strong current against which they had hopefully struggled. The whole Expeditionary Force – Guards, Highlanders, sailors, Hussars, Indian soldiers, Canadian *voyageurs*, mules, camels, and artillery – trooped back forlornly over the desert sands, and behind them the rising tide of barbarism followed swiftly, until the whole vast region was submerged. For several months the garrison of Kassala under a gallant Egyptian maintained a desperate resistance, but at last famine forced them to surrender. The evacuation of the Soudan was thus complete.

CHAPTER 3

THE DERVISH EMPIRE

It might seem at first a great advantage that the peoples of the Soudan, instead of being a multitude of wild, discordant tribes, should unite of their own accord into one strong community, living under fixed laws, and ruled by a single sovereign. But there is one form of centralised government which is almost entirely unprogressive and beyond all other forms costly and tyrannical – the rule of an army. History records many such dominations, ancient and modern, civilised or barbaric; and though education and culture may modify, they cannot change their predominant characteristics. The evil qualities of military hierarchies are always the same. The results of their rule are universally unfortunate. The degree may vary with time and place, but the political supremacy of an army always leads to the formation of a great centralised capital, to the consequent impoverishment of the provinces, to the degradation of the peaceful inhabitants through oppression and want, to the ruin of commerce, the decay of learning, and the ultimate demoralisation even of the military order through overbearing pride and sensual indulgence.

After the fall of Khartoum and the retreat of the British Armies the Mahdi became the absolute master of the Soudan. Whatever pleasures he desired he could command, and, following the example of the founder of the Mohammedan faith, he indulged in what would seem to Western minds gross excesses. He established an extensive harem for his own peculiar use, and immured therein the fairest captives of the war. The conduct of

47

the ruler was imitated by his subjects. The presence of women increased the vanity of the warriors: and it was not very long before the patched smock which had vaunted the holy poverty of the rebels developed into the gaudy *jibba* of the conquerors. Since the unhealthy situation of Khartoum amid swamps and marshes did not commend itself to the now luxurious Arabs, the Mahdi began to build on the western bank of the White Nile a new capital, which, from the detached fort which had stood there in Egyptian days, was called Omdurman.[1] Among the first buildings which he set his subjects to construct were a mosque for the services of religion, an arsenal for the storage of military material, and a house for himself.

In the middle of the month of June, scarcely five months after the completion of his victorious campaigns, the Mahdi fell sick. For a few days he did not appear at the mosque. The people were filled with alarm. They were reassured by remembering the prophecy that their liberator should not perish till he had conquered the earth. Mohammed, however, grew worse. Presently those who attended him could doubt no longer that he was attacked by typhus fever. The Khalifa Abdullah watched by his couch continually. On the sixth day the inhabitants and the soldiers were informed of the serious nature of their ruler's illness, and public prayers were offered by all classes for his recovery. On the seventh day it was evident that he was dying. All those who had shared his fortunes crowded the small room. For some hours he lay unconscious or in delirium, but as the end approached he rallied a little, and, collecting his faculties by a great effort, declared his faithful follower and friend the Khalifa Abdullah his successor, and adjured the rest to show him honour. 'He is of me, and I am of him; as you have obeyed me, so you should deal with him. May God have mercy upon me!'[2] Then he immediately expired.

Grief and dismay filled the city. In spite of the emphatic

[1] *Map, 'The Soudan and the Dervish Empire', p. 54.*
[2] *Slatin*, Fire and Sword.

48

prohibition by law of all loud lamentations, the sound of 'weeping and wailing arose from almost every house'. The whole people, deprived at once of their acknowledged sovereign and spiritual guide, were shocked and affrighted. Only the Mahdi's wives, if we may credit Slatin, 'rejoiced secretly in their hearts at the death of their husband and master', and, since they were henceforth to be doomed to an enforced and inviolable chastity, the cause of their satisfaction is as obscure as its manifestation was unnatural. The body of the Mahdi, wrapped in linen, was reverently interred in a deep grave dug in the floor of the room in which he had died, nor was it disturbed until after the capture of Omdurman by the British forces in 1898, when by the orders of Sir H. Kitchener the sepulchre was opened and the corpse exhumed.

The Khalifa Abdullah had been declared by the Mahdi's latest breath his successor. He determined to have the choice ratified once for all by the popular vote. Hurrying to the pulpit in the courtyard of the mosque, he addressed the assembled multitude in a voice which trembled with intense excitement and emotion. His oratory, his reputation as a warrior, and the Mahdi's expressed desire aroused the enthusiasm of his hearers, and the oath of allegiance was at once sworn by thousands.

As the various provinces had been cleared of the Egyptians, the new Executive had appointed military governors by whom the country was ruled and taxed, subject to the pleasure of Mohammed Ahmed. His death was the signal for a long series of revolts of all kinds – military, political, and religious. Garrisons mutinied; Emirs plotted; prophets preached. Nor was the land torn only by internal struggles. On the east the tremendous power of Abyssinia loomed terrible and menacing. There was war in the north with Egypt and around Suakin with England. The Italians must be confronted from the direction of Massowa. Far to the south Emin Pasha still maintained a troublesome resistance. Yet the Khalifa triumphed over nearly all his enemies; and the greatest spectacle which the Soudan presented from 1885 to 1898 was of this strong, capable ruler bearing up against all reverses, and offering a firm front to every foe.

During the thirteen years of his reign Abdullah tried nearly every device by which Oriental rulers have sought to fortify their perilous sovereignty. The general massacre of all possible claimants usually follows the accession of a usurper to an Oriental throne. The Khalifa was able to avoid this extreme measure. Nevertheless he took precautions. Availing himself of the grief and terror that had followed Mohammed Ahmed's death, he had extorted the oath of allegiance from the two other Khalifas and from the 'Ashraf' or relations of the Prophet.[1] But these complaisant men soon repented of their submission. Both the unsuccessful Khalifas combined against Abdullah. But that sagacious ruler had secured the loyalty of the Baggara tribe, to a section of which he belonged, and of a considerable force of black riflemen. Both parties prepared for war. Abdullah drew up his array without the city, and challenged his rivals to the utmost proof. The combined forces of the ousted Khalifas were the more numerous. But the fierce Baggara waved their swords, and the Soudanese riflemen were famous for their valour. For some hours a bloody struggle appeared imminent. Eventually both bowed to the superior force of the ruler and the superior courage of his followers. Once they had submitted, their power was gone, and they became for the future the useful supporters of a Government they were unable to subvert.

Abdullah knew that to rule the Soudan he must have a great army. To make the great army obedient he must have another separate force; for the influences which keep European armies in subjection were not present among the Dervishes. For some years, indeed, he was compelled to leave much to chance or the loyalty of his officers. But latterly, when he had perfected his organisation, he became quite independent and had no need to

---

[1] *The Mahdi had superseded the original Mohammed as 'the Prophet'. His relations consequently became the 'Ashraf'.*

trust anyone.

He invited his own tribe, the Taaisha section of the Baggara Arabs, to come and live in Omdurman. Allured by the hopes of wealth and wives and the promise of power, the savage herdsmen came to the number of 7,000 warriors. Their path was made smooth and easy. Granaries were erected along the route. Steamers and sailing-vessels waited on the Nile. Arrived at the capital, all were newly clothed at the expense of the State. An entire district of the city was forcibly cleared of its inhabitants for the accommodation of the strangers. What the generosity of the Khalifa forgot or refused, the predatory habits of his clansmen procured; and they robbed, plundered, and swindled with all the arrogance and impunity of royal favourites. The populace of the city returned a bitter hatred for these injuries; and the Khalifa's object was attained. He had created a class in Omdurman who were indissolubly attached to him. Like him, they were detested by the local tribes. Like him, they were foreigners in the land. But, like him, they were fierce and brave and strong. Their lives depended on their loyalty.

Here was the motor muscle which animated the rest. The Taaisha Baggara controlled the black Jehadia, once the irregular troops of the Egyptians, now become the regulars of the Khalifa. The black Jehadia overawed the Arab Army in the capital. The army in the capital dominated the forces in the provinces. The forces in the provinces subdued the inhabitants. The centralisation of power was assured by the concentration of military material. Cannon, rifles, stores of ammunition, all the necessities of war were accumulated in the arsenal. Rifles were issued to the Soudanese whenever safe and necessary; cartridges only when they were about to be used. Thus several millions of warlike and savage people were brought into the firm grip of a single man.

The third principle of government which the Khalifa was compelled to adopt was to keep the relative power of the various tribes and classes conveniently proportioned. If an Emir rose to

51

great influence and wealth, he became a possible rival, and suffered forthwith death, imprisonment, or spoliation. If a tribe threatened the supremacy of the Taaisha it was struck down while its menace was yet a menace. Such was the statecraft of a savage from Kordofan.

His greatest triumph was the Abyssinian war. For some time a harassing and desultory warfare disturbed the border. At length in 1885 a Dervish – half-trader, half-brigand – sacked an Abyssinian church. Ras Adal, the Governor of the Amhara province, demanded that this sacrilegious robber should be surrendered to justice. The Arabs haughtily refused. The response was swift. Collecting an army which may have amounted to 30,000 men, the Abyssinians invaded the district of Gallabat and marched on the town. Against this host the Emir Wad Arbab could muster no more than 6,000 soldiers. But, encouraged by the victories of the previous four years, the Dervishes accepted battle, in spite of the disparity of numbers. Neither valour nor discipline could withstand such odds. The Moslems, broken by the fierce onset and surrounded by the overwhelming numbers of their enemies, were destroyed, together with their intrepid leader. The Abyssinians indulged in all the triumphs of savagery. The wounded were massacred: the slain were mutilated: the town of Gallabat was sacked and burnt. All these tidings came to Omdurman. Under this heavy and unexpected blow the Khalifa acted with prudence. He opened negotiations with King John of Abyssinia for the ransom of the captured wives and children, and at the same time he sent the Emir Yunes with a large force to Gallabat. The immediate necessities having thus been dealt with, Abdullah prepared for revenge.

Of all the Arab leaders which fifteen years of continual war and tumult throughout the Soudan produced, none displayed higher ability, none obtained greater successes, and none were more honourable, than the man whom the Khalifa selected to avenge the destruction of the Gallabat Army. Abu Anga had been a slave in Abdullah's family long before the Mahdi had preached at Abba island and while Egypt yet oppressed the country. After the revolt had broken out, his adventurous master summoned him from the distant Kordofan home to attend him in the war, and Abu Anga came with that ready obedience and strange devotion for which he was always distinguished. Nominally as a slave, really as a comrade, he fought by Abdullah's side in all the earlier battles of the rebellion. The Khalifa was a judge of men. He saw very clearly that the black Soudanese troops, who were surrendering as town after town was taken, might be welded into a powerful weapon. And in Abu Anga he knew a man who could not only fashion the blade, but would hold it ever loyally at his master's disposal. The former slave threw himself into the duties of his command with extraordinary energy. More than any other Emir, Abu Anga contributed to the destruction of Hicks's army. The *Jehadia*, as his soldiers were called — because they had joined in the Jehad, or Holy War — became famous throughout the land for their weapons, their courage, and their cruelty.

At the end of June Abu Anga reached Omdurman with an army variously estimated at from 22,000 to 31,000 men, of whom at least 10,000 were armed with Remington rifles. The Khalifa received him with the utmost honour. After a private interview, which lasted for several hours, a formal entry into the town was arranged. At daybreak on the following morning the whole force marched into the city and camped along the northern suburbs, applauded and welcomed alike by the population and their ruler. A few days after this a great review was held under the Kerreri hills. The whole plain was filled with the throng. Banners of every hue and shape waved gaily in the breeze, and the sunlight glinted from innumerable spear-points. The swarming Dervishes displayed their bright part-coloured *jibbas*. The wild Baggara cavalry circled on the flanks of the array. The brown dome of the Mahdi's tomb, rising above the city, seemed to assure the warriors of supernatural aid. Abdullah was at the summit of his power. The Khalifa

53

THE SOUDAN AND THE DERVISH EMPIRE

had embarked on a great venture in planning the invasion of Abyssinia. The vast strength of the Negus was known to the Dervishes, and the Mahdi had forbidden such a war. An ill-omened prophecy further declared that the King of Abyssinia would tether his horse to a solitary tree by Khartoum, while his cavalry should ride through the city fetlock deep in blood. But Abdullah feared neither God nor man.

The Abyssinians had not watched the extensive hostile preparations apathetically. Ras Adal had collected an army which in numbers actually exceeded that of the Dervishes. But the latter were far superior in rifles, and the black infantry were of invincible valour. Nevertheless, confident in his strength and relying on his powerful cavalry, the Abyssinian general allowed the Arabs to toil through all the mountainous country, to traverse the Mintik Pass, and to debouch unmolested on to the plain of Debra Sin. Abu Anga neglected no precaution. He knew that since he must fight in the heart of Abyssinia, with the mountains behind him, a defeat would involve annihilation. He drew up his army swiftly and with skill. Then the Abyssinians attacked. The rifle fire of the Soudanese repulsed them. The onset was renewed with desperate gallantry. It was resisted with equal valour and superior weapons. After frightful losses the Abyssinians wavered, and the wise Arab seized the moment for a counterstroke. In spite of the devotion of his cavalry Ras Adal was driven from the field. Great numbers of his army were drowned in the river in front of which he had recklessly elected to fight. His camp was captured, and a valuable spoil rewarded the victors, who also gratified their passions with a wholesale slaughter of the wounded – a practice commonly followed by savages. The effect of the victory was great. The whole of the Amhara Province submitted to the invaders, and in the spring of 1887 Abu Anga was able to advance without further fighting to the capture and sack of Gondar, the ancient capital of Abyssinia.

The Dervishes did not long remain in Abyssinia, as they suffered from the climate. In December the army returned to

Gallabat, which they commenced to fortify, and their victorious general followed to Omdurman, where he received the usual welcome accorded by warlike peoples to military heroes. But the famous and faithful slave may have been more gratified by the tears of joy which his master and sovereign shed on beholding him again safe and successful.

The greater struggle was still to come. The whole of Abyssinia was convulsed with fury, and King John in person prepared to take the field and settle the quarrel for ever. He assembled a mighty host, which is said to have amounted to 130,000 foot and 20,000 horsemen. The rumours of this formidable concentration reached Gallabat and Omdurman, and in spite of the recent victory caused deep alarm. The Khalifa saw his frontiers – even his existence – menaced, for King John had declared that he would sweep the Dervishes from off the face of the earth: and in the hour of need the general on whom so much depended died of some poisonous medicine with which he had endeavoured to cure himself of indigestion. Abu Anga was buried in his red-brick house at Gallabat amid the lamentations of his brave black soldiers, and gloom pervaded the whole army. The Khalifa appointed Zeki Tummal, one of Anga's lieutenants, to the command of the forces at Gallabat, which by strenuous exertions he brought up to a total of 85,000 men.

At dawn on the 9th of March 1889, the Abyssinians came within sight of their enemies, and early the next morning the battle began. The Abyssinians, undaunted by the rifle fire of the Soudanese, succeeded in setting the *zeriba* alight. Then, concentrating all their force on one part of the defence, they burst into the enclosure and town. The division of Wad Ali, a fourth part of the entire Dervish Army, which bore the brunt of this attack, was almost completely destroyed. The interior of the *zeriba* was crowded with women and children, who were ruthlessly butchered by the exultant Abyssinians. The assailants scattered in all directions in search of plunder, and they even had time to begin to disinter the body of

Abu Anga, which they were eager to insult in revenge for Gondar. The Dervishes already wavered when suddenly a rumour spread about among the Abyssinians that the King was killed. Seizing what booty they could snatch, the victorious army began a general retreat, and the *zeriba* was soon cleared. The Arabs were too exhausted to pursue, but when on the following day the attack was not renewed they learned, to their surprise, that they were the victors and that their enemy was falling back towards the Atbara River. Zeki Tummal resolved to pursue. Two days after the battle the Dervishes overtook the enemy's rearguard, and, surprising their camp, inflicted severe loss and captured much booty. The temporary Negus who had been appointed to fill the vacancy caused by the death of King John was among the killed. The body of that courageous monarch fell into the hands of the Dervishes, who struck off the head and sent it – a tangible proof of victory – to Omdurman.

The arrival in Omdurman of King John's head intoxicated the Khalifa with joy. Abyssinia was regarded throughout the Soudan as a far greater power than Egypt, and here was its mighty ruler slain and decapitated. But the victory had been dearly purchased. The two great battles had been fought with indescribable ferocity by both sides, and the slaughter was appalling. The flower of the Dervish Army, the heroic blacks of Abu Anga, were almost destroyed. The Khalifa had won a Pyrrhic triumph. Never again was he able to put so great a force in the field.

During the progress of the struggle with Abyssinia the war against Egypt languished. The Mahdi, counting upon the support of the population, had always declared that he would free the Delta from 'the Turks', and was already planning its invasion when he and his schemes were interrupted by death. His successor inherited all the quarrel, but not all the power. The success of the Abyssinian war encouraged and enabled the Khalifa to resume the offensive on his northern frontier, and he immediately ordered Wad-el-Nejumi, who commanded in Dongola, to march with his scanty force to the invasion of Egypt. The mad enterprise ended, as might have been foreseen, in the destruction of both Emir and army at Toski. The Khalifa received the news with apparent grief, but it is difficult to avoid suspecting him of dark schemes. He was far too clever to believe that Egypt could be conquered by five thousand men. He knew that besides the Egyptians there was a strange white tribe of men, the same that had so nearly saved Khartoum. 'But for the English', he exclaimed on several occasions, 'I would have conquered Egypt.' Yet, knowing of the British occupation, he deliberately sent an army to its inevitable ruin. It is difficult to reconcile such conduct with the character for sagacity and intelligence which Abdullah has deserved.

The terrible slaughter of the Abyssinian war had fallen mainly on the Jehadia and the eastern Arabs. The jealous tribes in the north had not suffered. The balance of power was in need of re-adjustment. The Jaalin and Barabra were fast becoming dangerous. Nejumi's army was recruited almost entirely from these sources. The reinforcements sent from Omdurman consisted of men selected from the flag of the Khalifa Sherif, who was growing too powerful, and of the Batahin tribe, who had shown a mutinous spirit.[1] The success of such an army in Egypt would be glorious. Its destruction anywhere would be convenient. Whatever Abdullah's motives may have been, his advantage was certain.

Other forces were soon added to the work of exhaustion. The year following the end of the Abyssinian war was marked by a fearful famine. Slatin and Ohrwalder vie with each other in relating its horrors – men eating the raw entrails of donkeys; mothers devouring their babies; scores dying in the streets, all the more ghastly in the bright sunlight; hundreds of corpses floating down the Nile. The depopulation caused by the scarcity was even greater than that produced by the fighting. The famine area extended over the whole Soudan and ran along the banks of the river as far as Lower Egypt. Entire districts between Omdurman and Berber

[1] *Ohrwalder*, Ten Years' Captivity.

became wholly depopulated. The camel-breeding tribes ate their she-camels. The riverain peoples devoured their seed-corn. The population of Gallabat, Gedaref, and Kassala was reduced by nine-tenths, and the frightful mortality, general throughout the whole country, may be gauged by the fact that Zeki Tummal's army, which before the famine numbered not fewer than 87,000, could scarcely muster 10,000 men in the spring of 1890.

The new harvest came only in time to save the inhabitants of the Soudan from becoming extinct. The remnant were preserved for further misfortunes. In 1890 innumerable swarms of locusts descended on the impoverished soil. The multitude of their red or yellow bodies veiled the sun and darkened the air, and although their flesh, tasting when roasted like fried shrimps, might afford a delicate meal to the natives, they took so heavy a toll of the crops that the famine was prolonged and scarcity became constant. Since their first appearance the locusts are said to have returned annually.[1] Their destructive efforts were aided by millions of little red mice, who destroyed the seeds before they could grow. So vast and immeasurable was the number of these tiny pests that after a heavy rain the whole country was strewn with, and almost tinted by, the squirrel-coloured corpses of the drowned.

Yet, in spite of all the strokes of fate, the Khalifa maintained his authority unshaken. The centralisation which always occurs in military States was accelerated by the famine. The provincial towns dwindled; thousands and tens of thousands perished; but Omdurman continually grew, and its ruler still directed the energies of a powerful army. Thus for the present we leave the Dervish Empire.

[1] *Ohrwalder*, Ten Years' Captivity.

CHAPTER 4

THE YEARS OF PREPARATION

In the summer of 1886, when all the troops had retreated to Wady Halfa and all the Soudan garrisons had been massacred, the British people averted their eyes in shame and vexation from the valley of the Nile. Besides the pain produced by the death of General Gordon, the heavy losses in officers and men, and the serious expenditure of public money, the nation smarted under failure and disappointment, and were, moreover, deeply sensible that they had been humiliated before the whole world. The situation in Egypt was scarcely more pleasing. The reforms initiated by the British Administrators had as yet only caused unpopularity. Baring's interference galled the Khedive and his Ministers. Vincent's parsimony excited contempt. Moncrieff's energy had convulsed the Irrigation Department. Wood's army was the laughing-stock of Europe. Among and beneath the rotten weeds and garbage of old systems and abuses the new seed was being sown. But England saw no signs of the crop; saw only the stubborn husbandmen begrimed with the dust and dirt, and herself hope-lessly involved in the Egyptian muddle: and so in utter weariness and disgust, stopping her ears to the gibes and cat-calls of the Powers, she turned towards other lands and other matters.

The regeneration of Egypt is not a theme which would fall within the limits of this account. But the reorganisation of the Egyptian Army, the forging of the weapon of reconquest, is an essential feature. On the 20th of December 1882, the old Egyptian Army – or, rather, such parts as had escaped destruction

– was disbanded by a single sentence of a British decree, and it was evident that some military body must replace that which had been swept away. All sorts of schemes for the employment of foreign legions or Turkish janissaries were devised. But Lord Dufferin adhered firmly to the principle of entrusting the defence of a country to its inhabitants, and it was determined to form a new Egyptian Army. The force was intended only for the preservation of internal order and the defence of the southern and western frontiers of Egypt against the Bedouin Arabs. Six thousand men was the number originally drawn by conscription – for there are no volunteers in Egypt - from a population of more than 6,000,000. Twenty-six British officers – either poor men attracted by the high rates of pay, or ambitious allured by the increased authority – and a score of excellent drill-sergeants undertook the duty of teaching the recruits to fight. Sir Evelyn Wood directed the enterprise, and became the first British Sirdar of the Egyptian Army. The work began and immediately prospered. Within three months of its formation the army had its first review. The whole 6,000 paraded in their battalions and marched past the Khedive and their country's flag. Their bearing and their drill extorted the half-contemptuous praise of the indifferent spectators. Indeed, the new army differed greatly from the old. In the first place, it was paid. The recruits were treated with justice. Their rations were not stolen by the officers. The men were given leave to go to their villages from time to time. When they fell sick, they were sent to hospital instead of being flogged. In short, the European system was substituted for the Oriental.

It was hardly possible that the fertile soil and enervating climate of the Delta would have evolved a warrior race. Ages of oppression and poverty rarely produce proud and warlike spirits. The *fellah* soldier lacks the desire to kill. Even the Mohammedan religion has failed to excite his ferocity. He may be cruel. He is never fierce. Yet he is not without courage – a courage which bears pain and hardship in patience, which confronts ill-fortune with indifference, and which looks on death with apathetic composure. He has other military virtues. He is obedient, honest, sober, well-behaved, quick to learn, and, above all, physically strong. Generations of toiling ancestors, though they could not brace his nerves, have braced his muscles. Under the pressure of local circumstances there has been developed a creature who can work with little food, with little incentive, very hard for long hours under a merciless sun.

Such was the material out of which the British officers have formed the new Egyptian Army. At first, indeed, their task was embittered by the ridicule of their comrades in the British and Indian Services; but as the drill and bearing of the force improved, the thoughtless scorn would have been diverted from the Englishmen to fall only upon the Egyptian soldiers. But the British officers identified themselves with their men. Those who abused the *fellah* soldier were reminded that they insulted English gentlemen. Thus a strange bond of union was established between the officers and soldiers of the Egyptian Service; and although material forces may have accomplished much, without this moral factor the extraordinary results would never have been achieved.

The numbers of the army grew with its responsibilities. Up to the end of 1883 the infantry still consisted of eight *fellahin* battalions. In 1884 the first Soudanese battalion was raised. The black soldier was of a very different type from the *fellahin*. The Egyptian was strong, patient, healthy, and docile. The negro was in all these respects his inferior. His delicate lungs, slim legs, and loosely knit figure contrasted unfavourably with the massive frame and iron constitution of the peasant of the Delta. Always excitable and often insubordinate, he required the strictest discipline. But he possessed two tremendous military virtues. To the faithful loyalty of a dog he added the heart of a lion. He loved his officer, and feared nothing in the world. With the introduction of this element the Egyptian Army became a formidable military machine. In Lord Kitchener's campaigns on the Nile the losses in the six

Soudanese battalions exceeded the aggregate of the whole of the rest of the army.

The service was hard and continual. Though the operations were petty, an untiring vigilance was imperative. A pitiless economy was everywhere enforced. The British officer was deprived of his leave and the Egyptian private of his rations, that a few pounds might be saved to the Egyptian Treasury. The clothing of the battalions wore thin and threadbare, and sometimes their boots were so bad that the soldiers' feet bled from the cutting edges of the rocks, and the convoy escorts left their trails behind them. But the army improved in efficiency, and the constant warfare began to produce, even among the *fellahin* infantry, experienced soldiers. The sword of reconquest was gradually sharpened; and when the process was almost complete, the man who was to wield it presented himself.

Horatio Herbert Kitchener, the eldest son of a lieutenant-colonel, was born in 1850 and entered in 1869 the Royal Military Academy at Woolwich as a cadet of the Royal Engineers. In the spring of 1871 he obtained his commission, and for the first ten years of his military service remained an obscure officer, performing his duties with regularity, but giving no promise of the talents and character which he was afterwards to display. One powerful weapon, however, he acquired in this time of waiting. In 1874 accident or instinct led him to seek employment in the surveys that were being made of Cyprus and Palestine, and in the latter country he learned Arabic. For six years the advantage of knowing a language with which few British officers were familiar brought him no profit. For procuring military preferment Arabic was in 1874 as valueless as Patagonian. All this was swiftly changed by the unexpected course of events. The year 1882 brought the British fleet to Alexandria, and the connection between England and Egypt began to be apparent. Kitchener did not neglect his opportunity. Securing leave of absence, he hurried to the scene of crisis. Alexandria was bombarded. Detachments from the fleet were landed to restore order. The British Government decided to send an army to Egypt.

Lord Wolseley soon found employment for the active officer who could speak Arabic. Kitchener served through the campaign of 1882 as a major. He joined the new army which was formed at the conclusion of the war, as one of the original twenty-six officers. In the Nile expedition of 1885 Arabic again led him to the front, and in the service of the Intelligence Department he found ample opportunity for his daring and energy. His efforts to communicate with Gordon in Khartoum did not, however, meet with much success, and the *Journals* bristle with so many sarcastic comments that their editor has been at pains to explain in his preface that there was really no cause for complaint. Major Kitchener, however, gave satisfaction to his superiors in Cairo, if not to the exacting General at Khartoum, and in 1886 he was appointed Governor of Suakin. This post, always one of responsibility and danger, did not satisfy Kitchener. Eager for more responsibility and more danger, he harried and raided the surrounding tribes; he restricted and almost destroyed the slender trade which was again springing up, and in consequence of his measures the neighbourhood of Suakin was soon in even greater ferment than usual. This culminated at the end of 1887 in the reappearance and advance of Osman Digna. The defences of the town had been greatly strengthened and improved by the skill and activity of its new Governor.[1] Osman Digna retreated. The 'friendlies' were incited to follow, and Kitchener, although he had been instructed not to employ British officers or Egyptian regulars in offensive operations, went out in support. At Handub on the morning of the 17th of January 1888, the friendlies attacked the camp of Osman Digna. They were at first successful; but while they dispersed to plunder the enemy rallied

---

[1] *See despatch from Major-General Dormer to War Office, Cairo, 22nd April 1888: 'With regard to the military works and defences of the town, I was much struck with the great improvement that has been effected by Colonel Kitchener since my last visit to Suakin in the autumn of 1884.'*

and, returning, drove them back with loss. Kitchener arrived on the field with the support, to find a defeat instead of a victory awaiting him. He bravely endeavoured to cover the retreat of the friendlies, and in so doing was severely – as it first seemed dangerously – wounded in the jaw. The loss among the friendlies and the support amounted to twenty men killed and two British officers and twenty-eight men wounded. The Governor returned in great pain and some discomfiture to Suakin. In spite of his wound and his reverse he was impatient to renew the conflict, but this was definitely forbidden by the British Government. 'The policy which it is desirable to follow ... in the Eastern Soudan', wrote Sir Evelyn Baring on the 17th of March, in measured rebuke, 'should consist in standing purely on the defensive against any hostile movement or combination of the Arab tribes, in avoiding any course of action which might involve the ultimate necessity of offensive action, and in encouraging legitimate trade by every means in our power.'[1]

The Governor could scarcely be expected to carry out a policy so much at variance with his views and inclinations, and in the summer of 1888 he was transferred to a purely military appointment and became Adjutant-General of the Egyptian Army. For the next four years he worked busily in the War Office at Cairo, effecting many useful reforms and hard economies, and revealing powers of organisation which were noticed by one vigilant eye. In 1892 Sir F. Grenfell resigned the post of Sirdar, and the chief command of the Egyptian Army was vacant. Two men stood out prominently as candidates – Colonel Wodehouse, who held the command of the Halfa Field Force, and the Adjutant-General. Colonel Wodehouse had undoubtedly the greater claims. He had been for several years in command of a large force in continual contact with the enemy. He had conducted the civil administration of the frontier province with conspicuous success,

[1] *Sir Evelyn Baring to Consul Cameron, 14th March 1888.*

and he was popular with all ranks of the Egyptian Army. Kitchener had little to set against this. He had shown himself a brave and active soldier. He was known to be a good official. But he had not been in accord with the Government in his civil administration, and was, moreover, little known to his brother officers. Sir Evelyn Baring's influence, however, turned the scale. Somewhat, therefore, to the astonishment of the Egyptian Army, Kitchener was promoted Sirdar. Lord Cromer had found the military officer whom he considered capable of reconquering the Soudan when the opportunity should come.

The years of preparation, wasted by no one in Egypt, were employed by no department better than by the Intelligence Branch. The greatest disadvantage from which Lord Wolseley had suffered was the general ignorance of the Soudan and its peoples. The Intelligence Branch of the Egyptian Army rose under the direction of Colonel (now Sir Reginald) Wingate to an extraordinary efficiency. For ten years the history, climate, geography, and inhabitants of the Soudan were the objects of a ceaseless scrutiny. The sharp line between civilisation and savagery was drawn at Wady Halfa; but beyond that line, up the great river, within the great wall of Omdurman, into the arsenal, into the treasury, into the mosque, into the Khalifa's house itself, the spies and secret agents of the Government – disguised as traders, as warriors, or as women – worked their stealthy way. By whatever route it came, information – whispered at Halfa, catalogued at Cairo – steadily accumulated, and the diaries of the Intelligence Department grew in weight and number, until at last every important Emir was watched and located, every garrison estimated, and even the endless intrigues and brawls in Omdurman were carefully recorded.

The reports of the spies were at length confirmed and amplified by two most important witnesses. At the end of 1891 Father Ohrwalder made his escape from Omdurman and reached the Egyptian territory. Besides giving the Intelligence Department much valuable information, he published a thrilling account of his captivity,[1] which created a wide and profound impression in England. In 1895 a still more welcome fugitive reached Assuan. Early on the 16th of March a weary, travel-stained Arab, in a tattered *jibba* and mounted on a lame and emaciated camel, presented himself to the Commandant. He was received with delighted wonder, and forthwith conducted to the best bathroom available. Two hours later a little Austrian gentleman stepped forth, and the telegraph hastened to tell the news that Slatin, sometime Governor of Darfur, had escaped from the Khalifa's clutches. Here at last was a man who knew everything that concerned the Dervish Empire. Slatin, the Khalifa's trusted and confidential servant, almost his friend, who had lived with him, who was even permitted to dine with him alone, who had heard all his counsels, who knew all his Emirs, and moreover Slatin, the soldier and administrator, who could appreciate all he had learned, was added with the rank of Pasha to the Staff of the Intelligence Department. While his accurate knowledge confirmed the belief of the Egyptian authorities that the Dervish power was declining, his tale of 'Fire and Sword in the Soudan' increased the horror and anger of thoughtful people in England at the cruelties of the Khalifa. Public opinion began to veer towards the policy of reconquest.

The year 1895 brought in a Conservative and Unionist Administration, supported by a majority which was so strong that there seemed little reason to expect a transference of power for five or six years. Ministers belonged chiefly to that party in the State which had consistently assailed Mr Gladstone's Egyptian policy. Here was an opportunity of repairing the damage done by their opponents. The idea of reconquering the Soudan presented itself indefinitely, but not unpleasingly, alike to the Government and the people of Great Britain. The unforeseen course of events crystallised the idea into a policy.

On the 1st of March 1896, the Battle of Adowa was fought,

[1] *Ohrwalder*, Ten Years' Captivity.

and Italy at the hands of Abyssinia sustained a crushing defeat. Two results followed. First, a great blow had been struck at European prestige in North Africa. It seemed probable that the Abyssinian success would encourage the Dervishes to attack the Italians at Kassala. It was possible that they might also attack the Egyptians at Suakin or on the Wady Halfa frontier. Secondly, the value of Italy as a factor in European politics was depreciated. The fact that her defeat had been assisted by the arms and munitions of war which had been supplied to the Abyssinians from French and Russian sources complicated the situation. The Triple Alliance was concerned. The third partner had been weakened. The balance might be restored if Great Britain would make some open sign of sympathy.

In these circumstances the British Government determined to assist Italy by making a demonstration on the Wady Halfa frontier. They turned to Egypt. It had always been recognised that the recovery of the lost provinces was a natural and legitimate aspiration. 'The doubtful point was to decide the time when the military and financial resources of the country were sufficiently developed to justify an assumption of the offensive.'[1] From a purely Egyptian point of view the best possible moment had not yet arrived. A few more years of recuperation were needed. The country would fight the Soudan campaigns more easily if first refreshed by the great reservoirs which were projected. For more than two years both projects had been pressed upon the Government of his Highness the Khedive – or, to write definitely, upon Lord Cromer. At regular intervals Sir Herbert Kitchener and Sir William Garstin would successively visit the British Agency (it would be treason to call it 'Government House') – the one to urge the case for a war, the other to plead for a reservoir. The reservoir had won. Only a few weeks before the advance to Dongola was ordered Garstin met Kitchener returning

[1] *Lord Cromer's Reports: Egypt, No.2, 1896.*

from the Agency. 'I'm beaten,' said Kitchener abruptly; 'you've got your dam' – and Garstin went on his way rejoicing.

The decision of the British Government came therefore as a complete surprise to the Cairene authorities. The season of the year was unfavourable to military operations. The hot weather was at hand. The Nile was low. With the exception of a small raid on a village in the Wady Halfa district and an insignificant incursion into the Tokar Delta the Dervish forces had during the year maintained 'a strictly defensive attitude'.[1] Lord Cromer, however, realised that while the case for the reservoirs would always claim attention, the re-conquest of the Soudan might not receive the support of a Liberal Government. The increasing possibility of French intrigues upon the Upper Nile had also to be considered. All politics are series of compromises and bargains, and while the historian may easily mark what would have been the best possible moment for any great undertaking, a good moment must content the administrator.

It will be convenient, before embarking upon the actual chronicle of the military operations, to explain how the money was obtained to pay for the war. About half the revenue of Egypt is devoted to the development and government of the country, and the other half to the payment of the interest on the debt and other external charges; and the London Convention in 1885 prescribed that the annual expenditure of Egypt shall not exceed a certain sum. When the expenditure exceeds this amount, for every pound that is spent on the government or development of Egypt another pound must be paid to the Commissioners of the Debt; so that, after the limit is reached, for every pound that is required to promote Egyptian interests two pounds must be raised by taxation from an already heavily taxed community. But the working of the law was found to be so severe that, like all laws which exceed the human conception of justice, it has been somewhat modified. By an arrangement which was effected in 1888, the

[1] *Egypt, No. I, 1896.*

Caisse de la Dette are empowered, instead of devoting *their* surplus pound to the sinking fund, to pay it into a general reserve fund, from which the Commissioners may make grants to meet 'extra-ordinary expenses'; those expenses, that is to say, which may be considered 'once for all' (capital) expenditure and not ordinary annual charges.

The Dongola expedition was begun, as has been said, without reference to the immediate internal condition of Egypt. It was obviously impossible for Egypt to provide for the extraordinary expenses of the military operations out of revenue. The Ministry of Finance therefore appealed to the Caisse de la Dette for a grant from the general reserve fund. Here was an obvious case of 'extra-ordinary expenses'. The Egyptian Government asked for £E500,000.

The Caisse met in council. Six Commissioners – representing England, France, Russia, Germany, Austria, and Italy – duly discussed the application. Four Commissioners considered that the grant should be made. Two Commissioners, those representing France and Russia, voted against it. The majority decided. The grant was made. The money was handed to the Egyptian Government and devoted to the prosecution of the war.

Egypt as a sovereign power had already humbly begged to be allowed to devote part of the surplus of her own revenues to her own objects. A greater humiliation remained. The Commissioners of France and Russia, who had been out-voted, brought an action against their colleagues on the grounds that the grant was *ultra vires*; and against the Egyptian Government for the return of the money thus wrongly obtained. Other actions were brought at French instigation by various people purporting to represent the bondholders, who declared that their interests were threatened. The case was tried before the Mixed Tribunals, an institution which exists in Egypt superior to and independent of the sovereign rights of that country.

The Mixed Tribunals, an international institution, delivered its judgement on strictly political grounds, the judges taking their orders from the different countries they represented. It was solemnly pronounced that war expenses were not 'extraordinary expenses'. A state of war was apparently regarded as usual in Egypt. On this wise and sensible ground the Egyptian Government were condemned to pay back £E500,000, together with interest and costs. After a momentary hesitation as to whether the hour had not come to join issue on the whole subject of the financial restrictions of Egypt, it was decided to bow to this iniquitous decision. The money had now to be refunded. It had already been spent. More than that, other sums were needed for the carrying on of the war. It was impossible to stop; yet without money it seemed impossible to go on; and, besides, it appeared that Egypt would be unable to repay the £E500,000 which she had been granted, and of which she was now deprived.

At this period France still exercised a considerable force on Egyptian politics. One Egyptian party, the weaker, but still by no means insignificant, looked towards her for support. The news of the French success cheered their hearts and raised their spirits. Orientals appreciate results. The result was a distinct reverse to the British. The conclusion to the native mind was obvious. Great Britain had been weighed in the European balances and found wanting.

But meanwhile the Consul-General telegraphed to Lord Salisbury, asking that he might be 'authorised to state directly that Her Majesty's Government will be prepared to advance the money on conditions to be hereafter arranged'. The reply was prompt, though guarded. 'You are authorised', said Lord Salisbury, 'by the Chancellor of the Exchequer to state that though of course the primary liability for the payment of the £E500,000 rests with the Egyptian Government, Her Majesty's Government will hold themselves prepared to advance, on conditions to be decided hereafter, such a sum as they feel satisfied that the Egyptian

Treasury is powerless to provide.'[1] This obvious development does not seem to have been foreseen by the French diplomatists, and when, on the 3rd of December, it was rumoured in Cairo that Great Britain was prepared to pay the money, a great feeling of astonishment and of uncertainty was created. But the chances of the French interference proving effective still seemed good. It was believed that the English Government would not be in a position to make an advance to the Egyptian Government until funds had been voted by Parliament for the purpose. It was also thought that Egypt would be utterly unable to find the money immediately. A complete disillusionment, however, awaited the French Government. The taxes in Egypt, as in other countries, are not collected evenly over the whole year. During some months there is a large cash balance in the Exchequer. In others the money drains in slowly. It happened at this period of the year, after the cotton crop had been gathered, that a considerable balance had accumulated in the Treasury, and on the guarantee of the English Government being received, to the effect that they would ultimately assist Egypt with regard to the expenses of the expedition, Lord Cromer determined to repay the money at once.

On the 5th of December the Egyptian Council of Ministers, presided over by the Khedive in person, decided on their own initiative to despatch an official letter expressing in warm terms their gratitude for the financial help offered them by her Majesty's Government.

On the 6th of December £E500,000, together with £E15,600 interest and costs, in gold, was conveyed in boxes in a cart from the Egyptian Treasury to the offices of the Caisse de la Dette. The effect was tremendous. The reverse of the French diplomacy was far greater even than its success had appeared.

---

[1] *The original £500,000 was afterwards increased to £800,000; which sum was paid by the British Exchequer to the Egyptian Government, at first as a loan, and later as a gift.*

CHAPTER 5

THE BEGINNING OF THE WAR

Shortly before midnight on the 12th of March 1896, the Sirdar received instructions from Lord Cromer authorising an expedition into the Dongola Province and directing him to occupy Akasha. The next morning the news was published in *The Times*, ostensibly as coming from its correspondent in Cairo: and the Egyptian Cabinet was convened to give a formal assent by voting the decree.

On Sunday, the 15th of March, three days after the Sirdar had received his orders, and before the first reinforcements had started from Cairo, Colonel Hunter, who commanded on the frontier, formed a small column of all arms to seize and hold Akasha. At dawn on the 18th the column started, and the actual invasion of the territory which for ten years had been abandoned to the Dervishes began. The route lay through a wild and rocky country – the debatable ground, desolated by years of war – and the troops straggled into a long procession, and had several times for more than an hour to move in single file over passes and through narrow defiles strewn with the innumerable boulders from which the 'Belly of Stones' has derived its name. The right of their line of march was protected by the Nile, and although it was occasionally necessary to leave the bank, to avoid difficult ground, the column camped each night by the river. The cavalry and the Camel Corps searched the country to the south and east; for it was expected that the Dervishes would resist the advance. Creeping along the bank, and prepared at a moment's notice to stand at bay at the water's edge, the small force proceeded on its way. Wady Atira was reached on the 18th, Tanjore on the 19th, and on the 20th the column marched into Akasha.

Akasha was now converted into a strong entrenched camp, in which an advanced base was formed. Its garrison of three battalions, a battery, and the mounted troops, drew their supplies by camel transport from Sarras. The country to the south and east was continually patrolled, and the communications were further strengthened by the establishment of fortified posts at Semna, Wady Atira, and Tanjore. The friendly Arab tribes – Bedouin, Kabbabish, and Foggara – ranged still more widely in the deserts and occupied the scattered wells. All this time the Dervishes watched supinely from their position at Firket, and made no attempt to disturb the operations.

Meanwhile the concentration of the Egyptian Army on the frontier was proceeding. The line of communications from Cairo, the permanent base, to the advanced post at Akasha was 825 miles in length. But of this distance only the section lying south of Assuan could be considered as within the theatre of war. The ordinary broad-gauge railway ran from Cairo to Balliana, where a river base was established. From Balliana to Assuan reinforcements and supplies were forwarded by Messrs Cook's fleet of steamers, by barges towed by small tugs, and by a number of native sailing craft. A stretch of seven miles of railway avoids the First Cataract, and joins Assuan and Shellal. Above Shellal a second flotilla of gunboats, steamers, barges, and Nile boats was collected to ply between Shellal and Halfa. The military railway ran from Halfa to Sarras. South of Sarras supplies were forwarded by camels. To meet the increased demands of transport, 4,500 camels were purchased in Egypt and forwarded in boats to Assuan, whence they marched via Korosko to the front. The British Government had authorised the reconstruction of the military railway to Akasha, and a special railway battalion was collected at Assuan, through which place sleepers and other material at once began to pass to Sarras. The strategic railway construction will form the subject of a later chapter.

By the 1st of April, less than three weeks from the commencement of the advance, the whole line of communications had been organised and was working efficiently, although still crowded with the concentrating troops.

As soon as the 16th Battalion of reservists arrived at Suakin, the IXth Soudanese were conveyed by transports to Kossier, and marched thence across the desert to Kena. The distance was 120 miles, and the fact that in spite of two heavy thunderstorms – rare phenomena in Egypt – it was covered in four days is a notable example of the marching powers of the black soldiers. It had been determined that the Xth Soudanese should follow at once, but circumstances occurred which detained them on the Red Sea littoral and must draw the attention of the reader thither.

The aspect and history of the town and port of Suakin might afford a useful instance to a cynical politician. Most of the houses stand on a small barren island which is connected with the mainland by a narrow causeway. At a distance the tall buildings of white coral present an imposing appearance, and the prominent chimneys of the condensing machinery – for there is scarcely any fresh water – seem to suggest manufacturing activity. But a nearer view reveals the melancholy squalor of the scene. A large part of the town is deserted. The narrow streets wind among the tumbled-down and neglected houses. The soil exhales an odour of stagnation and decay. The traveller who lands on Quarantine Island is first confronted with the debris of the projected Suakin-Berber Railway. Huge piles of railway material rot, unguarded and neglected, on the shore. Rolling stock of all kinds – carriages, trucks, vans, and ballast wagons – are strewn or heaped near the sheds. The Christian cemetery alone shows a decided progress, and the long lines of white crosses which mark the graves of British soldiers and sailors increase the depression of the visitor. The numerous graves of Greek traders protest that the climate of the island is pestilential.

The island on which the town stands is joined to the mainland by a causeway, at the further end of which is an arched gateway of curious design called 'the Gate of the Soudan'. Upon the mainland stands the crescent-shaped suburb of El Kaff. It comprises a few mean coral-built houses, a large area covered with mud huts inhabited by Arabs and fishermen, and all the barracks and military buildings. The whole is surrounded by a strong wall a mile and a half long, fifteen feet high, six feet thick, with a parapet pierced for musketry and strengthened at intervals by bastions armed with Krupp guns.

Three strong detached posts complete the defences of Suakin. Ten miles to the northward, on the scene of Sir H. Kitchener's unfortunate enterprise, is the fort of Handub. Tambuk is twenty-five miles inland and situate upon a high rock, and consisting only of a store, a formidable blockhouse, and a lookout tower, is safe from any enemy unprovided with artillery. Both Handub and Tambuk were at the outset of the campaign provisioned for four months. The third post, Tokar Fort, lies fifty miles along the coast to the south. Its function is to deprive the Arabs of a base in the fertile delta of the Tokar River. The fort is strong, defended by artillery, and requires for its garrison an entire battalion of infantry.

No description of Suakin would be complete without some allusion to the man to whom it owes its fame. Osman Digna had been for many years a most successful and enterprising Arab slave dealer. The attempted suppression of his trade by the Egyptian Government drove him naturally into opposition. He joined in the revolt of the Mahdi, and by his influence roused the whole of the Hadendoa and other powerful tribes of the Red Sea shore. Year after year, at a horrid sacrifice of men and money, the Imperial Government and the old slaver fought like wolves over the dry bone of Suakin. Often defeated, but never crushed, the wily Arab might justly boast to have run further and fought more than any Emir in the Dervish armies.

It had scarcely seemed possible that the advance on Dongola

could influence the situation around Kassala, yet the course of events encouraged the belief that the British diversion in favour of Italy had been effective; for at the end of March – as soon, that is to say, as the news of the occupation of Akasha reached him – Osman Digna separated himself from the army threatening Kassala, and marched with 300 cavalry, 70 camelry, and 2,500 foot towards his old base in the Tokar Delta.

The state of affairs in the Eastern Soudan has always been turbulent. The Hadendoa and other tribes who lived under the walls of Suakin professed loyalty to the Egyptian Government, not from any conviction that their rule was preferable to that of Osman Digna, but simply for the sake of a quiet life. As their distance from Suakin increased, the loyalty of the tribesmen became even less pronounced, and at a radius of twenty miles all the Sheikhs oscillated alternately between Osman Digna and the Egyptian Government, and tried to avoid open hostilities with either. Omar Tita, Sheikh of the district round about Erkowit, found himself situated on this fringe of intriguing neutrality. Although he was known to have dealings with Osman, it was believed that if he had the power to choose he would side with the Egyptian Government. Early in April Omar Tita reported that Osman Digna was in the neighbourhood of Erkowit with a small force, and that he, the faithful ally of the Government, had on the 3rd of the month defeated him with a loss of four camels. He also said that if the Egyptian Government would send up a force to fight Osman, he, the aforesaid ally, would keep him in play until it arrived.

After a few days of hesitation and telegraphic communication with the Sirdar, Colonel Lloyd, the Governor of Suakin, who was then in very bad health, decided that he had not enough troops to justify him in taking the risk of going up to Erkowit to fight Osman. Around Suakin, as along the Indian frontier, a battle was always procurable on the shortest notice. In the present instance it was determined to have only a small-scale operation. The

Governor therefore arranged a plan for a demonstration at the foot of the hills near Khor Wintri by means of combined movements from Suakin and Tokar. The garrison of Suakin consisted of the 1st and half the 5th Egyptian Battalions; the 16th Egyptian Reservists, who had just replaced the IXth Soudanese, and were as yet hardly formed into a military body; one squadron of cavalry, one company of Camel Corps, and some detachments of artillery. The garrison of Tokar consisted of the Xth Soudanese and a few gunners. From these troops there was organised in the second week in April, with all due ceremony, a 'Suakin Field Force'.

The plan of campaign was simple. Colonel Lloyd was to march out from Suakin and effect a junction with the 'Tokar Column' at Khor Wintri, where the Erkowit road enters the hills. It was then hoped that Osman Digna would descend and fight a battle of the required dimensions in the open; after which, if victorious, the force would return to Suakin and Tokar.

In order to make the Suakin Column as mobile as possible, the whole force was mounted on camels, of which more than 1,000 were requisitioned, as well as 60 mules and 120 donkeys. Six days' forage and rations, one day's reserve of water, 200 rounds per man, and 100 shell per gun were carried. At five o'clock on the afternoon of Tuesday, the 14th of April, the troops paraded outside the walls of Suakin, and bivouacked in the open ready to march at daylight.

The next morning the column, which numbered about 1,200 men of all arms, started. After marching for four or five hours in the direction of Khor Wintri the cavalry, who covered the advance, came in contact with the Dervish scouts. The force thereupon assumed an oblong formation: the mixed Soudanese company and the two guns in front, three Egyptian companies on each flank, the Camel Corps company in the rear, and the transport in the centre. The pace was slow, and, since few of the camels had ever been saddled or ridden, progress was often interrupted by their behaviour and by the broken and difficult nature of the country. Nevertheless at about four o'clock in the afternoon, Teroi Wells, eight miles from Khor Wintri, were reached; and here, having marched nineteen miles, Colonel Lloyd determined to halt. While the infantry were making the *zeriba*, the cavalry were sent on under Captain Fenwick (an infantry officer employed on the Staff) to gain touch with the Tokar force, who were expected to have already reached the rendezvous. Apparently under the belief that Omar Tita and his Arabs would give timely notice of an attack, the cavalry seem to have neglected many of the usual pre-cautions, and in consequence at about five o'clock, when approaching Khor Wintri, they found themselves suddenly con-fronted with a force of about 200 Dervish horsemen supported by a large body of infantry. The squadron wheeled about with promptitude, and began to retire at a trot. The Dervish horsemen immediately pursued. The result was that the Egyptians began a disorderly flight at a gallop through the thick and treacherous scrub and over broken, dangerous ground. Sixteen horses fell; their riders were instantly speared by the pursuers. Rallying thirty-eight troopers, Captain Fenwick seized a rocky hillock, and dismounting with the natural instinct of an infantry soldier, prepared to defend himself to the last. The remainder of the squadron continued their flight, and thirty-two troopers, under an Egyptian officer (whose horse is said to have bolted), arrived at the Teroi *zeriba* with the news that their comrades had been destroyed, or had perhaps 'returned to Suakin', and that they themselves had been closely followed by the enemy. The news caused the gravest anxiety, which was aggra-vated towards midnight, when the Dervishes began to approach the *zeriba*. In the darkness what was thought to be a body of horsemen was seen moving along a shallow *khor* opposite the right face of the defence. At the same moment a loud yell was raised by the enemy on the other side. An uncontrolled musketry fire immediately broke out. The guns fired blindly up the valley; the infantry wildly on all sides. The fusillade continued furiously for some time, and when by the efforts of the British officers the

81

troops were restrained, it was found that the Dervishes had retired, leaving behind them a single wounded man.

Meanwhile Captain Fenwick maintained his solitary and perilous position on the hillock. He was soon surrounded by considerable bodies of the enemy, and as soon as it became dark he was sharply attacked. But the Dervishes fortunately possessed few rifles, and the officers and troopers, by firing steady volleys, succeeded in holding their ground and repulsing them. The sound of the guns at Teroi encouraged the Egyptians and revealed the direction of their friends. With the daylight the Dervishes, who seem throughout the affair to have been poor-spirited fellows, drew off, and the detachment, remounting, made haste to rejoin the main body.

The force, again united, pursued their way to Khor Wintri, where they found the column from Tokar already arrived. Marching early on the 15th, Major Sidney with 250 men of the Xth Soudanese, the only really trustworthy troops in the force, had reached Khor Wintri the same afternoon.

Up to this point Colonel Lloyd's plan had been successfully carried out. The columns from Suakin and Tokar had effected a junction at Khor Wintri on the Erkowit road. It now remained to await the attack of Osman Digna, and inflict a heavy blow upon him. It was decided, however, in view of what had occurred, to omit this part of the scheme, and both forces returned together without delay to Suakin, which they reached on the 18th, having lost in the operations eighteen Egyptian soldiers killed and three wounded.

After the affair of Khor Wintri it was evident that it would not be possible to leave Suakin to the defence only of the 16th Battalion of Reservists. On the other hand, Sir H. Kitchener required every soldier the Egyptian Army could muster to carry out the operations on the Nile. It was therefore determined to send Indian troops to Suakin to garrison the town and forts, and thus release the Xth Soudanese and the Egyptian battalions for the

Dongola Expedition. Accordingly early in the month of May the Indian Army authorities were ordered to prepare a brigade of all arms for service in Egypt.

The troops selected were as follows: 26th Bengal Infantry, 35th Sikhs, 1st Bombay Lancers, 5th Bombay Mountain Battery, two Maxim guns, one section Queen's Own (Madras) Sappers and Miners – in all about 4,000 men. The command was entrusted to Colonel Egerton, of the Corps of Guides.

On the 30th of May the dreary town of Suakin was enlivened by the arrival of the first detachments, and during the following week the whole force disembarked at the rotten piers and assumed the duties of the defence.

The Indian contingent landed in the full expectation of being immediately employed against the enemy. After a week, when all the stores had been landed, officers and men spent their time speculating when the order to march would come. It was true that there was no transport in Suakin, but that difficulty was easily overcome by rumours that 5,000 camels were on their way from the Somali coast to enable the force to move on Kassala or Berber. As these did not arrive, General Egerton sent in a proposed scheme to the Sirdar, in which he undertook to hold all the advanced posts up to the Kokreb range, if he were supplied with 1,000 camels for transport. A characteristic answer was returned, to the effect that it was not intended to use the Indian contingent as a mobile force. They had come as a garrison for Suakin, and a garrison for Suakin they should remain. This information was not, however, communicated to the troops, who continued to hope for orders to advance until the fall of Dongola.

The heat when the contingent arrived was not great, but as the months wore on the temperature rose steadily, until in August and September the thermometer rarely fell below 103° during the night, and often rose to 115° by day. Dust storms were frequent. A veritable plague of flies tormented the unhappy soldiers. The unhealthy climate, the depressing inactivity, and the scantiness of fresh meat or the use of condensed water, provoked an outbreak of scurvy. At one time nearly all the followers and 50 per cent of the troops were affected. Several large drafts were invalided to India. All the Europeans suffered acutely from prickly heat. Malarial fever was common. There were numerous cases of abscess on the liver. Twenty-five per cent of the British officers were invalided to England or India, and only six escaped a stay in hospital. The experiences of the battalion holding Tokar Fort were even worse than those of the troops in Suakin. At length the longed-for time of departure arrived. With feelings of relief and delight the Indian contingent shook the dust of Suakin off their feet and returned to India. It is a satisfaction to pass from the dismal narrative of events in the Eastern Soudan to the successful campaign on the Nile.

By the middle of April the concentration on the frontier was completed. Eleven thousand troops had been massed at and beyond Wady Halfa. But no serious operations could take place until a strong reserve of stores had been accumulated at the front. Meanwhile the army waited, and the railway grew steadily. The battalions were distributed in three principal fortified camps – Halfa, Sarras, and Akasha – and detachments held the chain of small posts which linked them together.

Including the North Staffordshire Regiment, the garrison of Wady Halfa numbered about 3,000 men. The town and cantonment, nowhere more than 400 yards in width, straggle along the river-bank, squeezed in between the water and the desert, for nearly three miles. The houses, offices, and barracks are all built of mud, and the aspect of the place is brown and squalid. The whole town is protected towards the deserts by a ditch and mud wall; and heavy Krupp field-pieces are mounted on little bastions where the ends of the rampart rest upon the river. Five small detached forts strengthen the land front, and the futility of an Arab attack at this time was evident. Halfa had now become the terminus of a railway, which was rapidly extending; and the continual arrival and despatch of tons of material, the building of sheds, workshops, and storehouses lent the African slum the bustle and activity of a civilised city.

Sarras Fort is an extensive building, perched on a crag of black rock rising on the banks of the Nile about thirty miles south of Halfa. During the long years of preparation it had been Egypt's most advanced outpost and the southern terminus of the military railway. The beginning of the expedition swelled it into an entrenched camp, holding nearly 6,000 men. From each end of the black rock on which the fort stood a strong stone wall and wire entanglement ran back to the river. The space thus enclosed was crowded with rows of tents and lines of animals and horses; and in the fort Colonel Hunter, commanding the district known as 'Sarras and the South', had his headquarters.

The railway reconstruction followed the old track which had been prepared through the desert in 1885. The convoy route wound along by the river. Both were protected from attack. The 7th Egyptians guarded Railhead, while the chain of small posts secured the road by the Nile to Akasha. The advanced base grew during the months of April and May into a strong position.

The Sirdar, accompanied by Colonel Rundle, his Chief of Staff, had left Cairo on the 22nd of March, and after a short stay at Assuan reached Wady Halfa on the 29th. Here he remained during the month of April, superintending and pressing the extension of the railroad and the accumulation of supplies. On the 1st of May he arrived at Akasha, with a squadron of cavalry, under Major Burn-Murdoch, as his escort.

During May the preparations for the advance on the Dervish position at Firket continued, and towards the end of the month it became evident that they were nearly complete. The steady accumulation of stores at Akasha had turned that post into a convenient base from which the force might operate for a month without drawing supplies of any kind from the north. The railway, which had progressed at the rate of about half a mile a day, had reached and was working to Ambigole Wells, where a four-gun fort and entrenchment had been built. The distance over which convoys must plod was reduced by half, and the business of supply was doubly accelerated. By degrees the battalions and squadrons began to move forward towards Akasha. Sarras, deprived of its short-lived glory, became again the solitary fort on a crag. Wady Halfa was also deserted, and, except for the British battalion in garrison, could scarcely boast a soldier. Both the Egyptian battalions from Suakin had arrived on the Nile. The Xth Soudanese were on their way. The country beyond Akasha had been thoroughly reconnoitred and mapped to within three miles of the Dervish position. Everything was ready.

The actual concentration may be said to have begun on the 1st of June. Construction work on the railway came to a full stop. The railway battalions, dropping their picks and shovels, shouldered their Remington rifles and became the garrisons of the posts on the line of communications. On the 2nd of June the correspondents were permitted to proceed to Akasha. On the 3rd the Xth Soudanese passed through Ambigole and marched south. The Horse battery from Halfa followed. The Egyptian battalions and squadrons which had been camped along the river at convenient spots from Ambigole to Akasha marched to a point opposite Okma. Between this place and the advanced post an extensive camp, stretching three miles along the Nile bank, arose with magic swiftness. On the 4th the 7th Egyptians moved from Railhead, and with these the last battalion reached the front. Nine thousand men, with ample supplies, were collected within striking distance of the enemy.

CHAPTER 6

FIRKET
7th June 1896

Since the end of 1895 the Dervish force in Firket had been under the command of the Emir Hammuda, and it was through the indolence and neglect of this dissipated Arab that the Egyptian Army had been able to make good its position at Akasha without any fighting. Week after week the convoys had straggled unmolested through the difficult country between Sarras and the advanced base. No attack had been made upon the brigade at Akasha. No enterprise was directed against its communications. This fatal inactivity did not pass unnoticed by Wad Bishara, the Governor of Dongola; but although he was normally in supreme command of all the Dervish forces in the province he had hardly any means of enforcing his authority. His rebukes and exhortations, however, gradually roused Hammuda, and during May two or three minor raids were planned and executed, and the Egyptian position at Akasha was several times reconnoitred.

Bishara remained unsatisfied, and at length, despairing of infusing energy into Hammuda, he ordered his subordinate Osman Azrak to supersede him. Osman was a Dervish of very different type. He was a fanatical and devoted believer in the Mahdi and a loyal follower of the Khalifa. For many years he had served on the northern frontier of the Dervish Empire, and his name was well known to the Egyptian Government as the contriver of the most daring and the most brutal raids. His cruelty to the wretched inhabitants of the border villages had excluded him from all hope of mercy should he ever fall into the hands of the enemy. Among the Emirs gathered at Firket there was none whose death would have given greater satisfaction to the military authorities than the man who was now to replace Hammuda.

The force which the Sirdar had concentrated for the capture of Firket amounted to about nine thousand men, and was organised as follows:

Commander-in-Chief: THE SIRDAR
The Infantry Division: COLONEL HUNTER *Commanding*

1st Brigade	*2nd Brigade*	*3rd Brigade*
MAJOR LEWIS	MAJOR MACDONALD	MAJOR MAXWELL
3rd Egyptians	IXth Soudanese	2nd Egyptian
4th	XIth	7th
Xth Soudanese	XIIth	8th
	XIIIth	

Mounted Forces: MAJOR BURN-MURDOCH

Egyptian Cavalry	7 squadrons
Camel Corps	8 companies

Artillery

Horse Artillery	1 battery
Field Artillery	2 batteries
Maxim Guns	1 battery

Two roads led from Akasha to Firket – one by the bank of the river, the other inland and along the projected railway line. The Sirdar determined to avail himself of both. The force was therefore divided into two columns. The main column, under command of the Sirdar, was to move by the river road, and consisted of the infantry division, the Field Artillery, and the Maxim guns. The Desert Column, under command of Major Burn-Murdoch, consisted of the mounted forces, the Horse Artillery, and one battalion of infantry (the XIIth Soudanese) drawn from MacDonald's brigade and mounted upon camels: in all about two thousand men.

The infantry column began to march out of Akasha at 3.30 in the afternoon of the 6th, and trailed southwards along the track by the river in the following order: Lewis's brigade, with the Xth Soudanese leading; two Maxim guns and the artillery; MacDonald's brigade; Maxwell's brigade; and lastly, the field hospitals and a half-battalion forming rearguard. The Sirdar marched behind the artillery. The rear of the long column was clear of the camp by 4.30, and about two hours later the mounted force started by the desert road. The River Column made good progress till dark, but thereafter the advance was slow and tedious. The track was so narrow that it nowhere allowed a larger front to be formed than of four men abreast. In some places the sharp rocks and crumbling heaps of stone almost stopped the gun-mules altogether, while the infantry tripped and stumbled painfully. The moon had not risen, and the darkness was intense. Still the long procession of men, winding like a whiplash between the jagged hills, toiled onward through the night, with no sound except the tramping of feet and the rattle of accoutrements. At half past ten the head of Lewis's brigade debouched into a smooth sandy plain about a mile to the north of Sarkamatto village. This was the spot – scarcely three miles from the enemy's position – where the Sirdar had decided to halt and bivouac.

Meanwhile the mounted force were also on their way. Like the River Column, they were disordered by the broken ground, and the XIIth Soudanese, who were unused to camel riding and mounted only on transport saddles, were soon wearied. After one o'clock many men, both in the Camel Corps and in the battalion, fell asleep on their camels, and the officers had great difficulty in keeping them awake. However, the force reached their point of concentration – about three miles to the south-east of Firket – at a quarter to three.

The Sirdar moved on again with the infantry at 2.30. The moon had risen over the rocks, but it was only a thin crescent and did not give much light. The very worst part of the whole track was encountered immediately the bivouac was left, and the column of nearly six thousand men had to trickle through one narrow place in single file. There were already signs of the approach of dawn; the Dervish camp was near; the Sirdar and his Staff began to look anxious. He sent many messages to the leading battalions to hurry; and the soldiers, although now very weary, ran and scrambled through the difficult passage like sheep crowding through a gate. By four o'clock the leading brigade had cleared the obstacle, and the most critical moment seemed to have passed.

The great mass of Firket mountain, still dark in the half-light, now rose up on the left of the line of march. Between it and the river stretched a narrow strip of scrub-covered ground; and here, though obstructed by the long grass, bushes, palm-trees, and holes, the leading brigade was ordered to deploy. There was, however, as yet only room for the Xth Soudanese to form line, and the 3rd and 4th Egyptians contented themselves with widening to column of companies – the 3rd in rear of the right of the Xth, the 4th in rear of the centre. The force now began to emerge from the narrow space between the hills and the river, and debouch into open country. As the space widened No.1 Field Battery came into line on the left, and No.2 on the right of the Xth Soudanese. A swell of ground hid Firket village, though it was known to be within a mile, and it was now daylight. Still there was no sign that the Dervishes were prepared. It seemed scarcely possible to believe that the advance had not yet been discovered. The silence seemed to forbode some unexpected attack. The leading brigade and guns halted for a few minutes to allow MacDonald to form his battalions from 'fours' into column of companies. Then at five o'clock the advance was resumed, and at this moment from the shoulder of Firket mountain there rang out a solitary shot. The Dervish outposts had at last learned their danger. Several other shots followed in quick succession, and were answered by a volley from the Xth, and then from far away to the south-east came the report of a field-gun. The Horse Artillery Battery had come into action. The operation of the two columns was simultaneous: the surprise of the enemy was complete.

The great object was now to push on and deploy as fast as possible. The popping of musketry broke out from many points, and the repeated explosions of the Horse Battery added to the eager excitement of the troops. The Xth Soudanese had now reached the top of the rise which had hidden Firket, and the whole scene came into view. To the right front the village of Firket stretched by the side of the river – a confusion of mud houses nearly a mile in length and perhaps 300 yards broad. On the landward side the tents and straw shelters of the Dervish force showed white and yellow. A system of mud walls and loopholed houses strengthened the northern end of the village. Behind it as a background stood lines and clusters of palm-trees, through which the broad river and the masts of the Arab boats might be seen. In front of the troops, but a little to their left, rose a low rocky ridge surmounted with flags and defended by a stone breastwork running along its base. Across the open space between the village and the hill hundreds of Dervishes on horse and on foot were hurrying to man their defences, and others scrambled up the rocks to see for themselves the numbers of the enemy.

The attack developed very rapidly. The narrow passage between the mountain and the river poured forth its brigades and battalions, and the firing-line stretched away to the right and left with extraordinary speed. The Xth Soudanese opened fire on the village as soon as they topped the rise. The 3rd and 4th Egyptians deployed on the right and left of the leading regiment, two companies of the 4th extending down on to the foreshore below the steep river-bank. Peake's battery (No. 1) and the Maxim guns, coming into action from a spur of Firket mountain, began to fire over the heads of the advancing infantry.

The whole of Lewis's brigade now swung to the right and attacked the village; MacDonald's, coming up at the double in line of battalion columns, deployed to the left, inland, round the shoulder of the mountain, and, bearing away still more to the left, advanced swiftly upon the rocky ridge. The ground in MacDonald's front was much broken by boulders and scrub, and a deep *khor* delayed the advance. The enemy, though taken at obvious disadvantage, maintained an irregular fire; but the Soudanese, greatly excited, pressed on eagerly towards the breastworks. When the brigade was still 200 yards from the ridge, about fifty Dervish horsemen dashed out from among the rocks and charged the left flank. All were immediately shot down by a wild but heavy independent fire. With joyful yells the blacks broke into a run and carried the breastworks at the bayonet. The Dervishes did not await the shock. As soon as they saw their horsemen – among whom was the Emir Hammuda himself and Yusef Angar, Emir of the Jehadia – swept away, they abandoned the first ridge and fell back on another which lay behind. The Soudanese followed closely, and pursued the outnumbered enemy until at last the hills were cleared of all except the dead, and the fugitives were running towards the river-bank.

While MacDonald's brigade was storming the hills, Lewis's had advanced on the village and the Dervish camp. The Arabs made a stubborn resistance, and the 4th battalion by the river-bank were sharply engaged. Encouraged by their enormous superiority in number and weapons, the Egyptians showed considerable zeal in the attack, and their conduct on this occasion was regarded as a very happy augury for the war.

As Lewis's brigade had swung to its right, and MacDonald's had borne away to the left, a wide gap had opened in the centre of the attack. This was immediately filled by Maxwell's brigade, so that the whole force was now formed in one line, which curved and wheeled continually to the right until, by the time the rocky hills had been taken, all three brigades practically faced west and were advancing together towards the Nile. The Dervishes – penned between the river and the enemy, and unable to prevent the remorseless advance – now thought only of flight, and they could be seen galloping hither and thither seeking for some means of escape. The position of the Desert Column would have enabled the XIth Soudanese, by moving down to the river, to cut off this line of retreat; but the foreshore of the river at the southern end of Firket is concealed from a landward view by the steep bank, and by this sandy path the greater number of the fugitives found safety.

The three brigades now closed upon the village and, clearing it step by step, advanced to the water's edge. MacDonald's brigade did not indeed stop until they had crossed the swampy isthmus and occupied the island. The Arabs, many of whom refused quarter, resisted desperately, and more than eighty corpses were afterwards found in one group of buildings. By 7.20 all firing had ceased; the entire Dervish camp was in the hands of the Egyptian troops, and the engagement of Firket was over.

The local inhabitants, tired of the ceaseless war which had desolated the frontier province for so long, welcomed their new masters with an appearance of enthusiasm. The main pursuit stopped at Suarda, but a week later two squadrons and sixteen men of the Camel Corps, under Captain Mahon, were pushed out twenty miles further south, and an Arab store of grain was captured.

The Dervish loss in action was severe. More than 800 dead were left on the field, and there were besides 500 wounded and 600 prisoners. The casualties in the Egyptian Army were 1 British officer – Captain Legge – wounded, 20 native soldiers killed and 83 wounded.

Firket is officially classed as a general action: special despatches were written, and a special clasp struck. The whole operation was well and carefully planned, and its success in execution was complete. The affair caused great satisfaction in England, and the further prosecution of the campaign was looked for with increasing interest.

CHAPTER 7

THE RECOVERY OF THE DONGOLA PROVINCE

Countless and inestimable are the chances of war. Those who read the story, and still more those who share the dangers, of a campaign feel that every incident is surrounded with a host of possibilities, any one of which, had it become real, would have changed the whole course of events.

The 'Sirdar's luck' became almost proverbial in the Soudan. As the account progresses numerous instances will suggest themselves. But after Firket all things were contrary. One unexpected misfortune succeeded another. Difficulties were replaced by others as soon as they had been overcome. The autumn of 1896 was marked by delay and disappointment. The state of the Nile, the storms, the floods, the cholera, and many minor obstacles, vexed but did not weary the commander. The army had made one spring forward; it must now gather energy for another. A strong camp was formed at Firket. MacDonald's brigade occupied Suarda two days after the fight, and this place now became the advanced post, just as Akasha had been in the first phase of the campaign. The accumulation of stores at Firket and Suarda began forthwith. Owing to the arrangements which had been made before the engagement it was possible to collect within one week of the action two months' supplies at Suarda for the garrison of 2,000 men, and one month's at Firket for the 7,000 troops encamped there. Thereafter, however, the necessity of hurrying the railway construction and the considerable daily demands of 9,000 men only allowed this margin to be increased very gradually.

The army had now passed beyond the scope of a pack-animal system of supply, except for very short distances, and it was obvious that they could only advance in future along either the railway or a navigable reach of the river, and preferably along both. From the Dal Cataract near Kosheh there is a clear waterway at high Nile to Merawi. To Kosheh, therefore, the railway must be extended before active operations could recommence. A third condition had also to be observed. For the expulsion of the Dervishes from Kerma and Dongola it was desirable that a flotilla of gunboats should co-operate with the land forces. Four of these vessels – the *Tamai*, *El Teb*, the *Metemma*, and the *Abu Klea*; and three steamers – the *Kaibar*, *Dal*, and *Akasha*, which it was proposed to arm – had, since 1885, patrolled the river from Assuan to Wady Halfa, and assisted in protecting the frontier from Dervish raids. All seven were now collected at the foot of the Second Cataract, and awaited the rise of the river to attempt the passage. To strengthen the flotilla three new and very powerful gunboats had been ordered in England. These were to be brought in sections over the railway to a point above the Second Cataract, and be fitted together there. It was thus necessary to wait, firstly, for the railway to reach Kosheh; secondly, for the Nile to rise; thirdly, for the old gunboats to ascend the Cataract; fourthly, for the new gunboats to be launched on the clear waterway; and, fifthly, for the accumulation of supplies. With all these matters the Sirdar now busied himself.

The reconstruction of the railway to Akasha and its extension beyond this place towards Kosheh was pressed forward. Kosheh is six miles south of Firket, and consists, like most places in the 'Military Soudan', of little more than a name and a few ruined mud-huts which were once a village. On the 5th of July the whole camp was moved thither from the scene of the action. The reasons were clear and apparent. Kosheh is a point on the river above the Dal Cataract whence a clear waterway runs at high Nile to beyond Dongola. The camp at Firket had become foul and insanitary. The dysentery which had broken out was probably due

to the 'green' water of the Nile; for during the early period of the
flood what is known as 'the false rise' washes the filth and sewage
off the foreshore all along the river, and brings down the green
and rotting vegetation from the spongy swamps of Equatoria. The
water is then dangerous and impure. There was nothing else for
the army to drink; but it was undesirable to aggravate the evil by
keeping the troops in a dirty camp.

The earliest freight which the railway carried to Kosheh was
the first of the new stern-wheel gunboats. Train after train arrived
with its load of steel and iron, or with the cumbrous sections of
the hull, and a warship in pieces – engines, armaments, fittings,
and stores – soon lay stacked by the side of the river. An impro-
vised dockyard, equipped with powerful twenty-ton shears and
other appliances, was established, and the work of fitting and riv-
eting together the hundreds of various parts proceeded swiftly.
The new gunboats were in every way remarkable. The old vessels
had been 90 feet long. These were 140 feet. Their breadth was 24
feet. They steamed twelve miles an hour. They had a command of
30 feet. Their decks were all protected by steel plates, and prepared
by loopholed shields for musketry. Their armament was formidable.
Each carried one twelve-pounder quick-firing gun forward, two
six-pounder quick-firing guns in the central battery, and four
Maxim guns. Every modern improvement – such as ammunition
hoists, telegraphs, search-lights, and steam-winches – was added.
Yet with all this they drew only thirty-nine inches of water.

The vessels and machinery had been constructed and erected
in the works in London; they were then marked, numbered, and
taken to pieces, and after being transported to the front were finally
put together at Kosheh. Although in a journey of 4,000 miles they
were seven times transhipped, not a single important piece was
lost.

The convenience of Kosheh on the clear waterway, and the
dirty condition of Firket, were in themselves sufficient reasons for
the change of camp; but another and graver cause lay behind.

During the month of June an epidemic of cholera began to creep up the Nile from Cairo. On the 29th there were some cases at Assuan. On the 30th it reached Wady Halfa. In consequence of this the North Staffordshire Regiment marched into camp at Gemai. During the sixteen-mile march along the railway track to Gemai the first fatal case occurred, and thereafter the sickness clung to the regiment until the middle of August, causing continual deaths.

The cholera spread steadily southward up the river, claiming successive victims in each camp. In the second week of July it reached the new camp at Kosheh, whence all possible precautions to exclude it had proved vain. The epidemic was at first of a virulent form. Of the first thousand cases between Assuan and Suarda nearly eight hundred proved fatal. Nor were the lives thus lost to be altogether measured by the number.[1] To all, the time was one of trial, almost of terror. The Egyptians, in spite of their fatalistic creed, manifested profound depression. The English soldiers were moody and ill-tempered. Even the light-hearted Soudanese lost their spirits.

At length the epidemic was stamped out, and by the middle of August it had practically ceased to be a serious danger. But the necessity of enforcing quarantine and other precautions had hampered movement up and down the line of communications, and so delayed the progress of the preparations for an advance.

Other unexpected hindrances arose. Sir H. Kitchener had clearly recognised that the railway, equipped as it then was, would be at the best a doubtful means for the continual supply of a large force many miles ahead of it. He therefore organised an auxiliary

[1] *The attacks and deaths from cholera in the Dongola Expeditionary Force were as follows*:

	Attacks	Deaths
British troops	24	19
Native troops	406	260
Followers	788	640

boat service and passed *gyassas* and *nuggurs*[2] freely up the Second Cataract. During the summer months, in the Soudan, a strong north wind prevails, which not only drives the sailing-boats up against the stream – sometimes at the rate of twenty miles a day – but also gratefully cools the air. This year, for forty consecutive days, at the critical period of the campaign, the wind blew hot and adverse from the south. The whole auxiliary boat service was thus practically arrested. But in spite of these aggravating obstacles the preparations for the advance were forced onwards, and it soon became necessary for the gunboats and steamers to be brought on to the upper reach of the river.

The Second Cataract has a total descent of sixty feet, and is about nine miles long. For this distance the Nile flows down a rugged stairway formed by successive ledges of black granite. The flood river deeply submerges these steps, and rushes along above them with tremendous force, but with a smooth though swirling surface. As the Nile subsides, the steps begin to show, until the river tumbles violently from ledge to ledge, its whole surface for miles churned to the white foam of broken water, and thickly studded with black rocks. At the Second Cataract, moreover, the only deep channel of the Nile is choked between narrow limits, and the stream struggles furiously between stern walls of rock. These dark gorges present many perils to the navigator. The most formidable, the Bab-el-Kebir, is only thirty-five feet wide. The river here takes a plunge of ten feet in seventy yards, and drops five feet at a single bound. An extensive pool above, formed by the junction of two arms of the river, increases the volume of the water and the force of the stream, so that the 'Gate' constitutes an obstacle of difficulty and danger.

Everything depended upon the rise of the river, and in the perversity of circumstances the river this year rose much later and slower than usual. By the middle of August, however, the attempt

---

[2] *Native sailing craft.*

appeared possible. On the 14th the first gunboat, the *Metemma*, approached the Cataract. The North Staffordshire Regiment from Gemai, and the 6th and 7th Egyptian Battalions from Kosheh, marched to the 'Gate' to draw the vessel bodily up in spite of the current. The best native pilots had been procured. Colonel Hunter and the naval officers under Commander Colville directed the work. The boat had been carefully prepared for the ordeal. To reduce, by raising the free-board, the risk of swamping, the bows were heightened and strengthened, and stout wooden bulwarks were built running from bow to stern. Guns and ammunition were then removed, and the vessel lightened by every possible means. A strop of wire rope was passed completely round the hull, and to this strong belt the five cables were fastened – two on each side and one at the bow. So steep was the *slope of the water* that it was found necessary to draw all the fires, and the steamer was thus de-pendent entirely upon external force. It was luckily possible to obtain a direct pull, for a crag of black rock rose above the surface of the pool opposite the 'Gate'. On this a steel block was fixed, and the hawser was led away at right angles until it reached the east bank, where a smooth stretch of sand afforded a convenient place for the hauling parties. Two thousand men were then set to pull at the cables, yet such was the extraordinary force of the cur-rent that, although the actual distance in which these great efforts were necessary was scarcely one hundred yards, the passage of each steamer occupied an hour and a half, and required the most strenuous exertions of the soldiers. No accident, however, occurred, and the six other vessels accomplished the ascent on successive days. In a week the whole flotilla steamed safely in the open water of the upper reach.

And now for a moment it seemed that the luck of the expe-dition had returned. The cholera was practically extinct. All the seven steamers which had passed the Cataract arrived in a stately procession opposite the camp. Almost at the same time the wind changed to the north, and a cool and delicious breeze refreshed the weary men and bore southward to Suarda a whole fleet of sailing boats laden with supplies, which had been lying weather-bound during the previous six weeks at the head of the rapids. At last the miserable delay was over.

From Kosheh to Kerma, the first Dervish position, the distance by river is 127 miles. By land marches this can be shortened by nearly forty-one miles; thirty miles being saved by cutting across the great loop of the Nile from Kosheh to Sadin Fanti, and eleven miles by avoiding the angle from Fereig to Abu Fatmeh. From Kerma to Dongola, which latter town was the objective of the expedition, a further distance of thirty-five miles must be traversed, making a total of 120 miles by land or 161 by river. The long desert march from Kosheh to Sadin Fanti was the only natural difficulty by land. Although the river from Kosheh to Kerma is broken by continual rapids, it is, with one interval, freely navigable at half Nile. At Hannek the three miles of islands, rocks, rapids, and broken water which are called the Third Cataract are, except at high Nile, a formidable barrier. Once this is passed, there is open water for more than 200 miles at all seasons to Merawi. The banks of the river, except near Sadin Fanti, where the hills close in, are flat and low. The eastern bank is lined with a fringe of palm-trees and a thin strip of cultivation, which constitutes what is called 'the fertile province of Dongola'. On the other side the desert reaches the water's edge. Along the right bank of this part of the river the army was now to move.

The first act of the advance was the occupation of Absarat, and on the 23rd of August MacDonald's brigade marched thither from Suarda, cutting across the desert to Sadin Fanti, and then following the bank of the Nile. The occupation of Absarat covered the next movement. On the 26th Lewis's brigade was ordered to march across the loop from Kosheh to Sadin Fanti, and reinforce the brigade at Absarat. The distance of thirty-seven miles was far too great to be accomplished without a system of watering-places. This the Sirdar rapidly organised. Water-depôts were formed by carrying tanks and water-skins on camels to two points in the desert, and replenishing them by daily convoys. But now a heavy calamity descended on the arrangements of the General and the hopes of the troops.

During the afternoon of the 25th the wind veered suddenly to the south, and thereupon a terrific storm of sand and rain, accompanied by thunder and lightning, burst over the whole of the Nubian desert, and swept along the line of communications from Suarda to Halfa. On the next day a second deluge delayed the march of Lewis's brigade. Late on the 27th they started. Before they had reached the first watering place a third tempest, preceded by its choking sandstorm, overtook them. Nearly 300 men fell out during the early part of the night, and crawled and staggered back to Kosheh. Before the column reached Sadin Fanti 1,700 more sank exhausted to the ground. Out of one battalion 700 strong, only sixty men marched in. Nine deaths and eighty serious cases of prostration occurred, and the movement of the brigade from Kosheh to Absarat was grimly called 'The Death March'.

The violent rains produced floods such as had not been seen in the Soudan for fifty years. The water, pouring down the broad valleys, formed furious torrents in the narrower gorges. More than twelve miles of the railway was washed away. The rails were twisted and bent; the formation entirely destroyed. The telegraph wires were broken. The work of weeks was lost in a few hours. The advance was stopped as soon as it had been begun.

In this time of crisis the success of the whole campaign hung in the balance. Public opinion was still undecided on the general question of the war. All the croakers were ready. 'A Jingo Government' – 'An incapable general' – 'Another disaster in the Soudan' – such were the whispers. A check would be the signal for an outcry. The accounts of 'The Death March' had not yet reached England; but the correspondents, irritated at being 'chained to headquarters', were going to see about that. And, besides all this, there were the army to feed and the Dervishes to fight. In this serious emergency, which threatened to wreck his schemes, the Sirdar's organising talents shone more brilliantly than at any other moment in this account. Travelling swiftly to Moghrat, he possessed himself of the telephone, which luckily still worked. He knew the exact position of every soldier, coolie, camel, or donkey at his disposal. In a few hours, in spite of his crippled transport, he concentrated 5,000 men on the damaged sections of the line, and thereafter fed them until the work was finished. In seven days traffic was resumed. The advance had been delayed, but it was not prevented.

On the 5th of September the 1st (Lewis) and 2nd (MacDonald) Brigades moved to Dulgo, and at the same time the remainder of the army began to march across the loop from Kosheh by Sadin Fanti to Absarat. Every available soldier had been collected for the final operation of the campaign.

The Expeditionary Force was organised as follows:

Commander-in-Chief: THE SIRDAR
The Infantry Division: COLONEL HUNTER *Commanding*

1st Brigade	2nd Brigade	3rd Brigade	4th Brigade
MAJOR LEWIS	MAJOR MACDONALD	MAJOR MAXWELL	MAJOR DAVID
3rd Egyptians	XIth Soudanese	2nd Egyptian	1st Egyptians
4th	XIIth	7th	5th
IXth Soudanese	XIIIth	8th	15th
Xth			

Cavalry Brigade and Mounted Forces: MAJOR BURN-MURDOCH

Cavalry	8 squadrons
Camel Corps	6 companies
Horse Artillery	1 battery

Artillery: MAJOR PARSONS

Field Artillery   2 batteries

Maxims   1 battery (British)

Divisional Troops: MAJOR CURRIE

North Staffordshire Regiment 1st Battalion

The Flotilla: COMMANDER COLVILLE

Gunboats   *Zafir, Tamai, Abu Klea, Metemma, El Teb*

Armed Steamers   *Kaibar, Dal, Akasha*

Total: 15,000 men, 8 war-vessels, and 36 guns

Thus thirteen of the sixteen battalions of the Egyptian Army were employed at the front. Two others, the 6th and XIVth, were disposed along the line of communication, holding the various fortified posts. The 16th Battalion of Reservists remained at Suakin. The whole native army was engaged in the war, and the preservation of domestic order in the capital and throughout the Khedive's dominions was left entirely to the police and to the British Army of Occupation. By the 9th all four brigades had reached the rendezvous at Dulgo; on the 10th the British regiment, which it was determined to send up in the steamers, was moved to Kosheh by rail from Sarras and Gemai. The Sirdar prepared to start with the flotilla on the 12th.

But a culminating disappointment remained. By tremendous exertions the gunboat *Zafir* had been finished at Kosheh in time. On the afternoon of the 11th of September many officers and men came to witness her trial trip. The bank was lined with spectators. Colville took command. The Sirdar and his Staff embarked. Flags were hoisted and amid general cheering the moorings were cast off. But the stern paddle had hardly revolved twice when there was a loud report, like that of a heavy gun, clouds of steam rushed up from the boilers, and the engines stopped. Sir H. Kitchener and Commander Colville were on the

104

upper deck. The latter rushed below to learn what had happened, and found that she had burst her low-pressure cylinder, a misfortune impossible to repair until a new one could be obtained from Halfa and fitted.

In spite of this, however, the advance was not delayed. On the 13th the 1st, 2nd, and 3rd Brigades occupied Kaderma. Here the flotilla overtook them, and henceforward the boats on the river kept pace with the army on the bank. Fareig was reached on the 14th, and on the 16th the 4th Brigade arrived, and the concentration of the force was then complete.

After the annihilation of his strong advanced post at Firket, the Dervish Emir, Wad Bishara, concentrated his remaining forces in Dongola. Here during the summer he had waited, and in the middle of August some small reinforcements under one Emir of low rank reached him from Omdurman. The Khalifa, indeed, promised that many more should follow, but his promises long remained unfulfilled, and the greatest strength that Bishara could muster was 900 Jehadia, 800 Baggara Arabs, 2,800 spearmen, 450 camelmen, 650 cavalry – in all 5,600 men, with six small brass cannon and one mitrailleuse gun.

The first sign that the forces were drawing closer was the cutting of the telegraph-wire by a Dervish patrol on the 6th of September. On the 10th the Sirdar heard that Kerma was strongly held. On the 15th of September the Egyptian cavalry first established contact with the Dervish scouts, and a slight skirmish took place. On the 18th the whole force advanced to Sardek, and as Bishara still held his position at Kerma it looked as if an action was imminent. It was resolved to attack the Dervish position at Kerma at dawn. With the first light the army began to move, and when the sun rose the spectacle of the moving masses of men and artillery, with the gunboats on the right, was inspiring. The soldiers braced themselves for the expected action. But no sooner were the village and fort of Kerma visible than the report passed along the ranks that they were deserted. On reaching Kerma it was found that the Dervishes had evacuated the place, and only the strong, well-built mud fort attested the recent presence of Bishara. Whither had he gone?

Half a mile to the southward, on the opposite bank of the river, ran a long and continuous line of shelter trenches and loop-holed walls. The flanks of this new position rested on the deep morasses which extend from the river both on the north and south sides of Hafir. A small steamer, a fleet of large *gyassas* and other sailing vessels moored to the further shore explained what had happened. Conscious of his weakness, the prudent Emir had adroitly transported himself across the river, and had thus placed that broad flood between his troops and their destruction.

The Dervish position was about half a mile in length. As the gunboats approached the northern end they opened fire with their guns, striking the mud entrenchments at every shot, and driving clouds of dust and splinters into the air. Now, as on other occasions throughout the war, the Dervishes by their military behaviour excited the admiration of their enemies. Encouraged by the arrival in the morning of a reinforcement from Omdurman of 1,000 Black Jehadia and 500 spearmen under Abdel Baki, the Dervish gunners stood to their guns and the riflemen to their trenches, and, although suffering severely, maintained a formidable fire.

The gunboats continued to advance, beating up slowly against the strong current. As they came opposite Hafir, where the channel narrows to about 600 yards, they were received by a very heavy fire from guns placed in cleverly screened batteries, and from the rifle-men sheltered in deep pits by the water's edge or concealed amid the foliage of the tops of the palm-trees. These aerial skirmishers commanded the decks of the vessels, and the shields of the guns were thus rendered of little protection. All the water round the gunboats was torn into foam by the projectiles. The bullets pattered against their sides, and, except where they were protected by steel plates, penetrated. So hot was the fire that it was thought doubtful whether to proceed with the bombardment, and the *Tamai* swung round, and hurried down the river with the current and at full steam to report to the Sirdar. The other gunboats remained in action, and continued to shell the Dervish defences. The *Tamai* soon returned to the fight, and, steaming again up the river, was immediately hotly re-engaged.

The sight which the army witnessed was thrilling. Beyond the flood waters of the river, backed against a sky of staring blue and in the blazing sunlight, the whole of the enemy's position was plainly visible. Behind the entrenchments and among the mud houses and enclosures strong bodies of the *jibba*-clad Arabs were arrayed. Still further back in the plain a large force of cavalry – conspicuous by the gleams of light reflected from their broad-bladed spears – wheeled and manoeuvred. By the Nile all the tops of the palm-trees were crowded with daring riflemen, whose positions were indicated by the smoke-puffs of their rifles, or when some tiny black figure fell, like a shot rook, to the ground. In the foreground the gunboats, panting and puffing up the river, were surrounded on all sides by spouts and spurts of water, thrown up by the shells and bullets. Again the flotilla drew near the narrow channel; again the watching army held their breath; and again they saw the leading boat, the *Metemma*, turn and run down stream towards safety, pursued by the wild cheers of the Arabs. It was evident that the gunboats were not strong enough to silence the Dervish fire.

The firing had lasted two hours and a half and the Sirdar saw that his flotilla could not hope to silence the Dervishes. He therefore ordered De Rougemont – who had assumed the command after Colville was wounded – to run past the entrenchments without trying to crush their fire, and steam on to Dongola. To support and cover the movement, the three batteries of artillery under Major Parsons were brought into action from the swampy island of Artagasha, which was connected at this season with the right bank by a shoal. At the same time three battalions of infantry were moved along the river until opposite the Arab position. At 9 a.m. the eighteen guns on the island opened a tremendous bombardment at 1,200 yards range on the entrenchments, and at the same time the infantry and a rocket detachment concentrated their fire on the tops of the palm-trees. The artillery now succeeded in silencing three of the five Dervish guns and in sinking the little Dervish steamer *Tahra*, while the infantry by a tremendous long-range fire drove the riflemen out of the palms. Profiting by this, the gunboats at ten o'clock moved up the river in line, and, disregarding the fusillade which the Arabs still stubbornly maintained, passed by the entrenchment and steamed on towards Dongola. After this the fight may be said to have ended.

It is doubtful whether Bishara would have retreated, if he had not feared being cut off. He seems to have believed that the Sirdar would march along the right bank at once to Dongola, and cross there under cover of his gunboats. Like all Moslem soldiers, he was nervous about his line of retreat. Nor, considering the overwhelming force against him, can we wonder. There was, besides this strategic reason for retiring, a more concrete cause. All his supplies of grain were accumulated in the *gyassas* which lay moored to the west bank. These vessels were under the close and accurate fire of the artillery and Maxim guns on Artagasha island. Several times during the night the hungry Dervishes attempted to reach their store; but the moon was bright and the gunners watchful. Each time they were driven back. When morning dawned, it was found that Hafir was evacuated, and that the enemy had retreated on Dongola.

Wad Bishara's anxiety about his line of retreat was unnecessary, for the Sirdar could not advance on Dongola with a strong Dervish force on his line of communications: and it was not desirable to divide the army and mask Hafir with a covering force. But as soon as the Dervishes had left their entrenchments the situation was simplified. At daybreak all the Arab boats were brought over to the right bank by the villagers, who reported that

Bishara and his soldiers had abandoned the defence and were retreating to Dongola. Thereupon the Sirdar, relieved of the necessity of forcing the passage, transported his army peacefully to the other bank.

The casualties on the 19th were not numerous, and in a force of nearly 15,000 men they appear insignificant. The total – fourteen – amounted to less than one per thousand of the troops engaged. Nevertheless this picturesque and bloodless affair has been solemnly called the 'Battle of Hafir'. It is officially counted in records of service as a 'general action'. Telegrams of congratulation were received from Her Majesty and the Khedive. A special clasp was struck. Of all the instances of cheaply bought glory which the military history of recent years affords, Hafir is the most remarkable.

Bishara continued his retreat during the 20th, and, marching all day, reached Dongola in the evening. Wounded as he was, he reoccupied the town and began forthwith to make preparations for the defence of its considerable fortifications.

Notwithstanding that the army did not finish crossing the river until the afternoon of the 21st, the Sirdar determined to continue his advance without delay, and the force accordingly marched twelve miles further south and camped opposite the middle of the large island of Argo. At daybreak the troops started again, and before the sun had attained its greatest power reached Zowarat. This place was scarcely six miles from Dongola, and, as it was expected that an action would be fought the next day, the rest of eighteen hours was welcomed by the weary soldiers. All day long the army remained halted by the palms of the Nile bank. Looking through their glasses up the river, the officers might watch the gunboats methodically bombarding Dongola, and the sound of the guns was clearly heard. At intervals during the day odd parties of Dervishes, both horse and foot, approached the outpost line and shots were exchanged.

All these things, together with the consciousness that the culmination of the campaign was now at hand, raised the excitement of the army to a high pitch. An atmosphere of unrest hung over the bivouac, and few slept soundly. At three o'clock the troops were aroused, and at half past four the final advance on Dongola had begun.

It was still night. The full moon, shining with tropical brilliancy in a cloudless sky, vaguely revealed the rolling plains of sand and the huge moving mass of the army. Presently the warmer, yellower light of dawn began to grow across the river and through the palms, and gradually, as the sun rose and it became daylight, the dense formation of the army was extended to an array more than two miles long. On the left, nearest the river, marched Lewis's brigade – three battalions in line and the fourth in column as a reserve. Next in order Maxwell's three battalions prolonged the line. The artillery were in the centre, supported by the North Staffordshire Regiment. MacDonald's brigade was on the right. David's brigade followed in rear of the centre as a reserve. The cavalry, the Camel Corps, and the Horse Artillery watched the right flank; and on the left the gunboats steamed along the river.

For two hours the army were the only living things visible on the smooth sand, but at seven o'clock a large body of Dervish horses appeared on the right flank. The further advance of half a mile discovered the Arab forces. Their numbers were less than those of the Egyptians, but their white uniforms, conspicuous on the sand, and the rows of flags of many colours lent an imposing appearance to their array. Their determined aspect, no less than the reputation of Bishara, encouraged the belief that they were about to charge.

The disparity of the forces was, however, too great; and as the Egyptian Army steadily advanced, the Dervishes slowly retired. Their retreat was cleverly covered by the Baggara horse, who, by continually threatening the desert flank, delayed the progress of the troops. Bishara did not attempt to re-enter the town, on which

Churchill as an officer of the 4th Queen's Own Hussars, 1896

Lord Cromer (formerly Sir Evelyn Baring), 1841-1917,
British Consul-General in Egypt, 1883-1907.

Mohammed Ahmed 1848-1885, known as the Mahdi, leader of the revolt against Egyptian rule in the Sudan.

Baron Rudolf Karl von Slatin, Austrian soldier in Egyptian government service, and author of *Fire and Sword in the Soudan*.

Charles George Gordon, 1833-1885, known as "Chinese Gordon" for his years leading Chinese imperial forces against the Taiping rebellion. Governor of the Sudan in 1877, he returned in 1884 to attempt the relief of Egyptian garrisons in territory conquered by the Mahdi.

Kitchener of Khartoum

Horatio Herbert Kitchener, later Earl Kitchener of Khartoum, 1850-1916.
Born in County Kerry, Ireland, he became Sirdar (Commander) of the
Egyptian army in 1890 and won back the Sudan from Mahdist forces.
Became Secretary of War in the British Government in 1914 but was lost at
sea in 1916.

The Charge of the 21st Lancers at Omdurman in which Churchill took part.
From a painting by Caton Woodville

Colonel R.H. Martin leading the 21st Lancers against the Dervishes at Omdurman. *An artist's impression.*

Jean-Baptiste Marchand and his staff at Fashoda. Marchand, 1863-1934, was a French soldier and explorer who caused a Franco-British crisis in 1898 by claiming the Sudan for France.

the gunboats were now concentrating their fire, but continued to retire in excellent order towards the south and Debba.

The Egyptian infantry halted in Dongola, which when they arrived they found already in the hands of detachments from the flotilla. The red flag with the crescent and star waved once again from the roof of the Mudiria. The garrison of 400 Black Jehadia had capitulated, and were already fraternising with their Soudanese captors, whose comrades in arms they were soon to be. While the infantry occupied the town the cavalry and Camel Corps were despatched in pursuit. Wad Bishara, Osman Azrak, and the Baggara horse made good their flight across the desert to Metemma, and, in spite of terrible sufferings from thirst, retained sufficient discipline to detach a force to hold Abu Klea Wells in case the retreat was followed. The Dervish infantry made their way along the river to Abu Hamed, and were much harassed by the gunboats until they reached the Fourth Cataract, when the pursuit was brought to an end.

The Egyptian losses in the capture of Dongola and in the subsequent pursuit were: British, *nil*. Native ranks: killed, 1; wounded 25. Total, 26.

The occupation of Dongola terminated the campaign of 1896. About 900 prisoners, mostly the Black Jehadia, all the six brass cannon, large stores of grain, and a great quantity of flags, spears, and swords fell to the victors, and the whole of the province, said to be the most fertile in the Soudan, was restored to the Egyptian authority. The existence of a perpetual clear waterway from the head of the Third Cataract to Merawi enabled the gunboats at once to steam up the river for more than 200 miles, and in the course of the following month the greater part of the army was established in Merawi below the Fourth Cataract, at Debba, or at Korti, drawing supplies along the railway, and from Railhead by a boat service on the long reach of open water. The position of a strong force at Merawi – only 120 miles along the river bank from Abu Hamed, the northern Dervish post – was, as will be seen, convenient to the continuance of the campaign whenever the time should arrive. But a long delay in the advance was now inevitable, and nearly a year was destined to pass without any collision between the forces of the Khedive and those of the Khalifa.

CHAPTER 8

THE DESERT RAILWAY

It often happens that in prosperous public enterprises the applause of the nation and the rewards of the sovereign are bestowed on those whose offices are splendid and whose duties have been dramatic. Others whose labours were no less difficult, responsible, and vital to success are unnoticed. If this be true of men, it is also true of things.

It cannot be denied that a battle, the climax to which all military operations tend, is an event which is not controlled by strategy or organisation. In savage warfare in a flat country the power of modern machinery is such that flesh and blood can scarcely prevail, and the chances of battle are reduced to a minimum. Fighting the Dervishes was primarily a matter of transport. The Khalifa was conquered on the railway.

Throughout the Dongola campaign in 1896 the Nile was the main channel of communication between the Expeditionary Force and its base in Egypt. All supplies were brought to the front as far as possible by water transport. Wherever the Nile was navigable, it was used. But the Nile is not always available. Frequent cataracts obstruct its course for many miles. Other long reaches are only navigable when the river is in flood. To join the navigable reaches, and thus preserve the continuity of the communications, a complex system of railways and caravans was necessary.

In the expedition to Dongola a line of railway was required to connect the two navigable reaches of the Nile which extend from Assuan to Wady Halfa, and from Kerma to Merawi. Before the capture of Dongola, however, this distance was shortened by the fact that the river at high Nile is navigable between the Third Cataract and Kerma. In consequence it was at first only necessary to construct the stretch of 108 miles between Wady Halfa and Kosheh. During the years when Wady Halfa was the southernmost garrison of the Egyptian forces a strong post had been maintained at Sarras. In the Nile expeditions of 1885 the railway from Halfa had been completed through Sarras and as far as Akasha, a distance of eighty-six miles. After the abandonment of the Soudan the Dervishes destroyed the line as far north as Sarras. The position in 1896 may, in fact, be summed up as follows: The section of thirty-three miles from Wady Halfa to Sarras was immediately available and in working order. The section of fifty-three miles from Sarras to Akasha required partial reconstruction. The section of thirty-two miles from Akasha to Kosheh must, with the exception of ten miles of embankment completed in 1885, at once be newly made. And, finally, the section from Kosheh to Kerma must be completed before the Nile flood subsided.

The first duty, therefore, which the Engineer officers had to perform was the reconstruction of the line from Sarras to Akasha. The lack of men with technical knowledge was doubtfully supplied by the enlistment of a 'Railway Battalion' 800 strong. These men were drawn from many tribes and classes. Their only qualification was capacity and willingness for work. They presented a motley appearance. Dervish prisoners, released but still wearing their *jibbas*, assisted stalwart Egyptians in unloading rails and sleepers. Dinkas, Shillooks, Jaalin, and Barabras shovelled contentedly together at the embankments. One hundred civilian Soudanese – chiefly time-expired soldiers – were also employed; and these, since they were trustworthy and took an especial pride in their work, soon learned the arts of spiking rails and sleepers, fishing rails together, and straightening. To direct and control the labours of these men of varied race and language, but of equal inexperience, some civilian foremen platelayers were obtained at high rates of pay from Lower Egypt. These, however, with very few exceptions were not satisfactory, and they were gradually replaced by intelligent men of the 'Railway Battalion', who had learned their trade as the line progressed. The projection, direction, and execution of the whole work were entrusted to a few subalterns of Engineers, of whom the best known was Edouard Girouard.

As the line grew longer, native officers and non-commissioned officers from the active and reserve lists of the Egyptian Army were appointed stationmasters. Intelligent non-commissioned officers and men were converted into shunters, guards, and pointsmen. Traffic was controlled by telephone. To work the telephone, men were discovered who could read and write – very often who could read and write only their own names, and even that with such difficulty that they usually preferred a seal. To improve their education, and to train a staff in the office work of a railway, two schools were instituted at Halfa. In these establishments, which were formed by the shade of two palm-trees, twenty pupils received the beginnings of knowledge.

The rolling stock of the Halfa-Sarras line was in good order and sufficient quantity but the eight locomotives were out of all repair, and had to be patched up again and again with painful repetition. The regularity of their breaks-down prevented the regularity of the road, and the Soudan military railway gained a doubtful reputation during the Dongola expedition and in its early days. Nevertheless the work went on continually.

The initial difficulties of the task were aggravated by an unexpected calamity. On the 26th of August the violent cyclonic rain-storm of which some account has been given in the last chapter broke over the Dongola province.

A writer on the earlier phases of the war[1] has forcibly explained why the consequences were so serious:

[1] *A. Hilliard Atteridge*, Towards Khartoum.

'In a country where rain is an ordinary event the engineer lays his railway line, not in the bottom of a valley, but at a higher level on one slope or the other. Where he passes across branching side valleys, he takes care to leave in all his embankments large culverts to carry off flood-water. But here, in what was thought to be the rainless Soudan, the line south of Sarras followed for mile after mile the bottom of the long valley of Khor Ahrusa, and no provision had been made, or had been thought necessary, for culverts in the embankments where minor hollows were crossed. Thus, when the flood came, it was not merely that the railway was cut through here and there by the rushing deluge. It was covered deep in water, the ballast was swept away, and some of the banks so destroyed that in places rails and sleepers were left hanging in the air across a wide gap.'

Nearly fourteen miles of track were destroyed. The camp of the construction gangs was wrecked and flooded. Some of the rifles of the escort – for the conditions of war were never absent – were afterwards recovered from a depth of three feet of sand. In one place, where the embankment had partly withstood the deluge, a great lake several miles square appeared. By extraordinary exertions the damage was repaired in a week.

As soon as the line as far as Kosheh was completed, the advance towards Dongola began. After the army had been victorious at Hafir the whole province was cleared of Dervishes, and the Egyptian forces pushed on to Merawi. Here they were dependent on river transport. But the Nile was falling rapidly, and the army were soon in danger of being stranded by the interruption of river traffic between the Third Cataract and Kerma. The extension of the line from Kosheh to Kerma was therefore of vital importance. Of the ninety-five miles of extended track, fifty-six were through the desert, and the constructors here gained the experience which was afterwards of value on the great Desert Railway from Wady Halfa to the Atbara. Track-laying commenced south of Kosheh on the 9th of October, and the whole work was carried forward with feverish energy. As it progressed, and before

RAIL AND RIVER

it was completed, the reach of the river from the Third Cataract to Kerma ceased to be navigable. The army were now dependent for their existence on the partly finished railway, from the head of which supplies were conveyed by an elaborate system of camel transport. Every week the line grew. Railhead moved forward, and the strain upon the pack animals diminished. The carrying capacity of the line was strictly limited. The worn-out engines frequently broke down. Three times the construction had to be suspended to allow the army to be revictualled. Every difficulty was, however, overcome. By the beginning of May the line to Kerma was finished.

In the first week in December the Sirdar returned from England with permission to continue the advance towards Khartoum, and the momentous question of the route to be followed arose. It may at first seem that the plain course was to continue to work along the Nile, connecting its navigable reaches by sections of railway. But from Merawi to Abu Hamed the river is broken by continual cataracts, and the broken ground of both banks made a railway nearly an impossibility. The movements of the French expeditions towards the Upper Nile counselled speed. The poverty of Egypt compelled economy. The Nile route, though sure, would be slow and very expensive. A short cut must be found. Three daring and ambitious schemes presented themselves: (1) the line followed by the Desert Column in 1884 from Korti to Metemma; (2) the celebrated, if not notorious, route from Suakin to Berber; (3) across the Nubian desert from Korosko or Wady Halfa to Abu Hamed.

The question involved the whole strategy of the war. The known strength of the Khalifa made it evident that a powerful force would be required for the destruction of his army and the capture of his capital. The use of railway transport to some point on the Nile whence there was a clear waterway was therefore imperative. Berber and Metemma were known, and Abu Hamed was believed, to fulfil this condition. But both Berber and

Metemma were important strategic points. It was improbable that the Dervishes would abandon these keys to Khartoum and the Soudan without severe resistance. It seemed likely, indeed, that the Khalifa would strongly reinforce both towns, and desperately contest their possession. The deserts between Korti and Metemma, and between Suakin and Berber, contained scattered wells, and small raiding parties might have cut the railway and perhaps have starved the army at its head. It was therefore too dangerous to project the railway towards either Berber or Metemma until they were actually in our hands. The argument is circular. The towns could not be taken without a strong force; so strong a force could not advance until the railway was made; and the railway could not be made till the towns were taken.

Both the Korti-Metemma and the Suakin-Berber routes were therefore rejected. The resolution to exclude the latter was further strengthened by the fact that the labour of building a railway over the hills behind Suakin would have been very great.

The route *via* Abu Hamed was selected by the exclusion of the alternatives. But it had distinct and apparent advantages. Abu Hamed was within striking distance of the army at Merawi. It was not a point essential to the Dervish defences, and not, therefore, likely to be so strongly garrisoned as Berber or Metemma. It might, therefore, be captured by a column marching along the river, and sufficiently small to be equipped with only camel transport. The deserts through which the railway to Abu Hamed would pass contain few wells, and therefore it would be difficult for small raiding parties to cut the line or attack the construction gangs; and before the line got within reach of the Dervish garrison at Abu Hamed, that garrison would be dislodged and the place seized.

The plan was perfect, and the argument in its favour conclusive. It turned, however, on one point: Was the Desert Railway a possibility? The General appealed to expert opinion. Eminent railway engineers in England were consulted. They replied with unanimity that, having due regard to the circumstances, and remembering the conditions of war under which the work must be executed, it was impossible to construct such a line. Distinguished soldiers were approached on the subject. They replied that the scheme was not only impossible, but absurd. Having received this advice, and reflected on it duly, the Sirdar ordered the railway to be constructed, without more delay.

A further question immediately arose: Should the railway to Abu Hamed start from Korosko or from Wady Halfa? There were arguments on both sides. The adoption of the Korosko line would reduce the river stage from Assuan by forty-eight hours up stream. The old caravan route, by which General Gordon had travelled to Khartoum on his last journey, had been from Korosko *via* Murat Wells to Abu Hamed. On the other hand, many workshops and appliances for construction were already existing at Wady Halfa. It was the northern terminus of the Dongola railway. This was an enormous advantage. Both routes were reconnoitred: that from Wady Halfa was selected. The decision having been taken, the enterprise was at once begun.

Lieutenant Girouard, to whom everything was entrusted, was told to make the necessary estimates. Sitting in his hut at Wady Halfa, he drew up a comprehensive list. Nothing was forgotten. Every want was provided for; every difficulty was foreseen; every requisite was noted. The questions to be decided were numerous and involved. The answers to all these questions were set forth by Lieutenant Girouard in a ponderous volume several inches thick; and such was the comprehensive accuracy of the estimate that the working parties were never delayed by the want even of a piece of brass wire.

In any circumstances the task would have been enormous. It was, however, complicated by five important considerations: It had to be executed with military precautions. There was apparently no water along the line. The feeding of 2,000 platelayers in a barren desert was a problem in itself. The work had to be completed before the winter. And, finally, the money voted was not to be outrun. The Sirdar attended to the last condition.

Girouard was sent to England to buy the plant and rolling stock. Fifteen new engines and two hundred trucks were ordered. The necessary new workshops were commenced at Halfa. Experienced mechanics were procured to direct them. Fifteen hundred additional men were enlisted in the Railway Battalion and trained. Then the water question was dealt with. The reconnoitring surveys had reported that though the line was certainly 'good and easy' for 110 miles – and, according to Arab accounts, for the remaining 120 miles – no drop of water was to be found, and only two likely spots for wells were noted. Camel transport was, of course, out of the question. Each engine must first of all haul enough water to carry it to Railhead and back, besides a reserve against accidents. It was evident that the quantity of water required by any locomotive would continually increase as the work progressed and the distance grew greater, until finally the material trains would have one-third of their carrying power absorbed in transporting the water for their own consumption. The amount of water necessary is largely dependent on the grades of the line. The 'flat desert' proved to be a steady slope up to a height of 1,600 feet above Halfa, and the calculations were further complicated. The difficulty had, however, to be faced, and a hundred 1,500-gallon tanks were procured. These were mounted on trucks and connected by hose; and the most striking characteristic of the trains of the Soudan military railway was the long succession of enormous boxes on wheels, on which the motive power of the engine and the lives of the passengers depended.

The first spadeful of sand of the Desert Railway was turned on the first day of 1897; but until May, when the line to Kerma was finished, no great efforts were made, and only forty miles of track had been laid. In the meanwhile the men of the new Railway Battalion were being trained; the plant was steadily accumulating; engines, rolling stock, and material of all sorts had arrived from England. All this was preparation; nor was it until the

8th of May that track-laying into the desert was begun in earnest. The whole of the construction gangs and railroad staff were brought from Kerma to Wady Halfa, and the daring pioneers of modern war started on their long march through the wilderness, dragging their railway behind them.

It is scarcely within the power of words to describe the savage desolation of the regions into which the line and its constructors plunged. A smooth ocean of bright-coloured sand spread far and wide to distant horizons. The tropical sun beat with senseless perseverance upon the level surface until it could scarcely be touched with a naked hand, and the filmy air glittered and shimmered as over a furnace. Here and there huge masses of crumbling rock rose from the plain, like islands of cinders in a sea of fire. Alone in this vast expanse stood Railhead – a canvas town of 2,500 inhabitants, complete with station, stores, post office, telegraph office, and canteen, and only connected with the living world of men and ideas by two parallel iron streaks, three feet six inches apart, growing dim and narrower in a long perspective until they were twisted and blurred by the mirage and vanished in the indefinite distance.

Every morning in the remote nothingness there appeared a black speck growing larger and clearer, until with a whistle and a welcome clatter, amid the aching silence of ages, the 'material' train arrived, carrying its own water and 2,500 yards of rails, sleepers, and accessories. At noon came another speck, developing in a similar manner into a supply train, also carrying its own water, food and water for the half-battalion of the escort and the 2,000 artificers and platelayers, and the letters, newspapers, sausages, jam, whisky, soda-water, and cigarettes which enable the Briton to conquer the world without discomfort. And presently the empty trains would depart, reversing the process of their arrival, and vanishing gradually along a line which appeared at last to turn up into the air and run at a tangent into an unreal world.

So, week in, week out, the work went on. Every few days saw

a further advance into the wilderness. As Wady Halfa became more remote and Abu Hamed grew near, an element of danger, the more appalling since it was peculiar, was added to the strange conditions under which the inhabitants of Railhead lived. What if the Dervishes should cut the line behind them? They had three days' reserve of water. After that, unless the obstruction were removed and traffic restored, all must wither and die in the sand, and only their bones and their cooking-pots would attest the folly of their undertaking.

By the 20th of July a hundred and thirty miles of line had been finished, and it became too dangerous to advance further until Abu Hamed had been cleared of the Dervish force. They were still a hundred miles away, but camels travel fast and far, and the resources of the enemy were uncertain. It appeared that progress would be checked, but on the 7th of August General Hunter, marching from Merawi along the river bank, attacked and took Abu Hamed – an operation which will be described here-after. Work was at once resumed with renewed energy. The pace of construction now became remarkable. As much as 5,300 yards of track was surveyed, embanked, and laid in a single day. On the 1st of November Abu Hamed was reached, and by the banks of the Nile the men who had fought their way across the desert joined hands with those who had fought their way along the river.

The strain and hardship had not, however, been without effect on the constructors. Two of the Engineer subalterns – Polwhele and Cator – out of the eight concerned in the laying of the Dongola and the Desert railways had died. Their places were eagerly filled by others.

The completion of the line was accelerated by nearly a month through the fortunate discovery of water. At the beginning of July a well was sunk in what was thought to be a likely place at 'No. 4 Station', seventy-seven miles from Halfa. After five weeks' work water was found in abundance at a depth of ninety feet. A steam-pump was erected, and the well yielded a continual supply. In

October a second well was sunk at 'No.6 Station', fifty-five miles further on, whence water was obtained in still greater quantity. These discoveries modified, though they did not solve, the water question. They substantially increased the carrying capacity of the line, and reduced the danger to which the construction gangs were exposed.

As the railway had been made, the telegraph-wire had, of course, followed it. Every consignment of rails and sleepers had been accompanied by its proportion of telegraph-poles, insulators, and wire. Another subaltern of Engineers, Lieutenant Manifold, who managed this part of the military operations against the Arabs, had also laid a line from Merawi to Abu Hamed, so that immediate correspondence was effected round the entire circle of rail and river.

The labours of the Railway Battalion and its officers did not end with the completion of the line to Abu Hamed. The Desert Railway was made. It had now to be maintained, worked, and rapidly extended. The terminus at Halfa had become a busy town. A mud village was transformed into a miniature Crewe. The great workshops that had grown with the line were equipped with diverse and elaborate machines. Plant of all kinds purchased in Cairo or requisitioned from England, with odds and ends collected from Ismail's scrap heaps, filled the depôts with an extraordinary variety of stores. Foundries, lathes, dynamos, steam-hammers, hydraulic presses, cupola furnaces, screw-cutting machines, and drills had been set up and were in continual work. They needed constant attention. Every appliance for repairing each must be provided. To haul the tonnage necessary to supply the army and extend the line nearly forty engines were eventually required. Purchased at different times and from different countries, they included ten distinct patterns; each pattern needed a special reserve of spare parts. Some of the engines were old and already worn out. These broke down periodically. The frictional parts of all were affected by the desert sand, and needed ceaseless attention and repair. The workshops were busy night and day for seven days a week.

To the complication of machinery was added the confusion of tongues. Natives of various races were employed as operatives. Foremen had been obtained from Europe. No fewer than seven separate languages were spoken in the shops. Wady Halfa became a second Babel. Yet the undertaking prospered. The Engineer officers displayed qualities of tact and temper: their director was cool and indefatigable. Over all the Sirdar exercised a regular control. The sympathy of common labour won him the affection of the subalterns. Nowhere in the Soudan was he better known than on the railroad. Nowhere was he so ardently believed in.

It is now necessary to anticipate the course of events. As soon as the railway reached Abu Hamed, General Hunter's force, which was holding that place, dropped its slender camel communications with Merawi and drew its supplies along the new line direct from Wady Halfa. After the completion of the desert line there was still left seventeen miles of material for construction, and the railway was consequently at once extended to Dakhesh, sixteen miles south of Abu Hamed. Meanwhile Berber was seized, and military considerations compelled the concentration of a larger force to maintain that town. The four battalions which had remained at Merawi were floated down stream to Kerma, and, there entraining, were carried by Halfa and Abu Hamed to Dakhesh – a journey of 450 miles.

When the railway had been begun across the desert, it was believed that the Nile was always navigable above Abu Hamed. In former campaigns it had been reconnoitred and the waterway declared clear. But as the river fell it became evident that this was untrue. With the subsidence of the waters cataracts began to appear, and to avoid these it became necessary first of all to extend the railway to Bashtinab, later on to Abadia, and finally to the Atbara. To do this more money had to be obtained, and the usual financial difficulties presented themselves. Finally, however, the matter was settled, and the extension began at the rate of about a mile a day. From Bashtinab to Abadia another desert section of fifty miles was necessary to avoid some very difficult ground by the Nile bank. From Abadia to the Atbara the last stretch of the line runs across a broad alluvial expanse from whose surface plane-trees of mean appearance, but affording welcome shade, rise, watered by the autumn rains. The fact that the railway was approaching regions where rain is not an almost unknown phenomenon increased the labour of construction. To prevent the embankments from being washed away in the watercourses, ten bridges and sixty culverts had to be made; and this involved the transport over the railway of more than 1,000 tons of material in addition to the ordinary plant.

By the arrival of the reinforcements at Berber the fighting force at the front was doubled: doubled also was the business of supply. The task of providing the food of an army in a desert, a thousand miles from their base, and with no apparent means of subsistence at the end of the day's march, is less picturesque, though not less important, than the building of railways along which that nourishment is drawn to the front. Supply and transport stand or fall together; history depends on both. The Sirdar exercised a direct and personal supervision over the whole department of supply, but his action was restricted almost entirely to the distribution of the rations. Their accumulation and regular supply were the task of Colonel Rogers, and this officer, by three years of exact calculation and unfailing allowance for the unforeseen, has well deserved his high reputation as a feeder of armies.

The first military necessity of the war was, as has been described, to place the bulk of the Egyptian Army at Akasha. In ordinary circumstances this would not have been a serious commissariat problem. The frontier reserves of food were calculated to meet such an emergency. But in 1895 the crops in Egypt had been much below the average. At the beginning of

1896 there was a great scarcity of grain. When the order for the advance was issued, the frontier grain stores were nearly exhausted. The new crops could not be garnered until the end of April. Thus while the world regarded Egypt as a vast granary, her soldiers were obliged to purchase 4,000 tons of *doura* and 1,000 tons of barley from India and Russia on which to begin the campaign.

The chief item of a soldier's diet in most armies is bread. In several of our wars the health, and consequently the efficiency, of the troops has been impaired by bad bread or by the too frequent substitution of hard biscuit. For more than a year the army up the river ate twenty tons of flour daily, and it is easy to imagine how bitter amid ordinary circumstances would have been the battle between the commissariat officers, whose duty it was to insist on proper quality, and the contractors – often, I fear, meriting the epithet 'rascally' – intent only upon profit. But the War Department had in 1892 converted one of Ismail Pasha's gun factories near Cairo into a victualling-yard. Here were set up their own mills for grinding flour, machinery for manufacturing biscuit to the extent of 60,000 rations daily, and even for making soap. Three great advantages sprang from this wise arrangement. Firstly, the good quality of the supply was assured. Secondly, all risk of contractors failing to deliver in time was avoided. Lastly, the funds resulting from the economy had been utilised to form a useful corps of 150 bakers. And thus, although the purchase of foreign grain added to the expense, the beginning of the war found the commissariat of the Egyptian Army in a thoroughly efficient state.

Vast reserves of stores were quickly accumulated at Assuan. From these not an ounce of food was issued without the Sirdar's direct sanction. At the subsidiary depôt, formed at Wady Halfa, the same rule prevailed. The man who was responsible to no one took all the responsibility; and the system whereby a Chief of the Staff is subjected to the continual bombardment of heads of departments was happily avoided. Sufficient supplies having been accumulated at Akasha to allow of a forward movement, Firket was fought. After Firket the situation became difficult, and the problem of the supply officers was to keep the troops alive without delaying the progress of the railway with the carriage of their food. A small quantity of provisions was painfully dragged, with an average loss of fifty per cent from theft and water damage, up the succession of cataracts which obstruct the river-way from Halfa to Kosheh. Camel convoys from Railhead carried the rest. But until the line reached Kosheh the resources of the transport were terribly strained, and at one time it was even necessary to send the mounted troops north to avoid actual famine. The apparent inadequacy of the means to the end reached a climax when the army moved southward from Dulgo. The marches and halts to Dongola were estimated to take ten days, which was the utmost capacity of camel and steam transport. A few boat-loads of grain might be captured; a few handfuls of dates might be plucked; but scarcely any local supplies would be available. The sailing-boats, which were the only regular means of transport, were all delayed by the adverse winds. Fortune returned at the critical moment. By good luck on the first day of the march the north wind began to blow, and twelve days' supplies, over and above those moved by camel and steamer, reached Dongola with the troops. With this reserve in hand, the occupation of the province was completed, and although the army only existed from hand to mouth until the railway reached Kerma, no further serious difficulty was experienced in supplying them.

The line continued to grow rapidly, and as it grew the weight was shifted from the backs of the camels and the bottoms of the sailing-boats to the trucks of the iron road. The strong hands of steam were directed to the prosecution of the war, and the swiftness of the train replaced the toilsome plodding of the caravan. The advance of the Dervishes towards Berber checked the progress of the railway. Military precautions were imperative. Construction was delayed by the passage of the 1st British Brigade from Cairo to the front, and by the consequently increased volume

of daily supplies. By the 10th of March, however, the line was completed to Bashtinab. On the 5th of May it had reached Abadia. On
the 3rd of July the whole railway from Wady Halfa to the Atbara
was finished, and the southern terminus was established in the
great entrenched camp at the confluence of the rivers. The
question of supply was then settled once and for all. In less than
a week stores sufficient for three months were poured along the
line, and the exhausting labours of the commissariat officers
ended. Their relief and achievement were merged in the greater
triumph of the Railway Staff. The director and his subalterns had
laboured long, and their efforts were crowned with complete
success. On the day that the first troop train steamed into the
fortified camp at the confluence of the Nile and the Atbara rivers
the doom of the Dervishes was sealed.

CHAPTER 9

ABU HAMED

The news of the fall of Dongola created a panic in Omdurman. Great numbers of Arabs, believing that the Khalifa's power was about to collapse, fled from the city. All business was at a standstill. For several days there were no executions. Abdullah himself kept his house. On the fifth day, he proceeded to the mosque, and after the morning prayer ascended his small wooden pulpit and addressed the assembled worshippers. After admitting the retreat of the Dervishes under Wad Bishara, he enlarged on the losses the 'Turks' had sustained and described their miserable condition. He bewailed the lack of faith in God which had allowed even the meanest of the Ansar to abandon the *Jehad* against the infidel. But he proclaimed his confidence in the loyalty of his subjects and his enjoyment of the favour of God and the counsels of the late Mahdi; and having by his oratory raised the fanatical multitude to a high pitch of excitement, he thus concluded: 'It is true that our chiefs have retired from Dongola. Yet they are not defeated. Only they that disobeyed me have perished. I instructed the faithful to refrain from fighting and return to Metemma. For the angel of the Lord and the spirit of the Mahdi have warned me in a vision that the souls of the accursed Egyptians and of the miserable English shall leave their bodies between Dongola and Omdurman, at some spot which their bones shall whiten. Thus shall the infidels be conquered.' Then, drawing his sword, he cried with a loud voice: '*Ed din mansur!* The religion is victorious! Islam shall triumph!' Whereupon the worshippers, who to the number of 20,000 filled

131

the great quadrangle, saw his sword flashing in the sunlight, and with one accord imitated him, waving their swords and spears, and raising a mighty shout of fury and defiance.

In order that the divine favour might be assisted by human effort, Abdullah adopted every measure or precaution that energy or prudence could suggest. At first he seems to have apprehended that the Sirdar's army would advance at once upon Omdurman, following the route of the Desert Column in 1885 from Korti to Metemma. He therefore ordered Osman Azrak – in spite of his severe wound – to hold Abu Klea Wells with the survivors of his flag. Bishara, who had rallied and reorganised the remains of the Dongola army, was instructed to occupy Metemma, the head-quarters of the Jaalin. Emir Ibrahim Khalil was recalled from the Ghezira, or the land between the Blue and White Niles, and with his force of about 4,000 Jehadia and Baggara soon reached the city. Another chief, Ahmed Fedil, who was actually on his way to Gedaref, was ordered to return to the capital. Thither also Osman Digna repaired from Adarama. But it appears that the Khalifa only required the advice of that wily councillor, for he did not reduce the number of Dervishes in the small forts along the line of the Atbara – Ed Damer, Adarama, Asubri, El Fasher – and after a short visit and a long consultation Osman Digna returned to his post at Adarama. Last of all Mahmud, who commanded the 'Army of the West', was ordered to leave very reduced garrisons in Kordofan and Darfur, and march with his whole remaining force, which may have numbered 10,000 fighting men, to the Nile, and so to Omdurman. Mahmud, who was as daring and ambitious as he was conceited and incapable, received the summons with delight, and began forthwith to collect his troops.

The Khalifa saw very clearly that he could not trust the riverain tribes. The Jaalin and Barabra were weary of his rule and of war. In proportion as the Egyptian Army advanced, so their loyalty and the taxes they paid decreased. He therefore aban-doned all idea of making a stand at Berber. The Emir Yunes –

who, since he had been transferred from Dongola in 1895, had ruled the district – was directed to collect all the camels, boats, grain, and other things that might assist an invading army and send them to Metemma. The duty was most thoroughly performed. The inhabitants were soon relieved of all their property and of most of their means of livelihood.

The power of the gunboats and their effect in the Dongola campaign were fully appreciated by the Arabs; and the Khalifa, in the hopes of closing the Sixth Cataract, began to construct several forts at the northern end of the Shabluka Gorge. But the prophecy of the Mahdi exercised a powerful effect on the Khalifa's mind, and while he neglected no detail he based his hopes on the issue of a great battle on the plains of Kerreri, when the invaders should come to the walls of the city.

But after a while it became apparent that the 'Turks' were not advancing. They tarried on the lands they had won. The steamers went no further than Merawi. The iron road stopped at Kerma. Why had they not followed up their success? Obviously because they feared the army that awaited them at Omdurman. At this the Khalifa took fresh courage, and in January 1897 he began to evolve schemes for taking the offensive and expelling the invaders from the Dongola Province. The army drilled and manoeuvred continually on the plains of Kerreri; great numbers of camels were collected at Omdurman; large stores of dried *kisru* or 'Soudan biscuit', the food of Dervishes on expeditions, were prepared.

At the end of May, Mahmud with his army arrived at Omdurman. The Khalifa received him with delight, and several imposing reviews were held outside the city. Mahmud himself was eager to march against the 'Turks'. He had no experience of modern rifles, and felt confident that he could easily destroy or at least roll back the invading forces. Partly persuaded by the zeal of his lieutenant, and partly by the wavering and doubtful attitude of the Jaalin, the Khalifa determined early in June to send the Kordofan army to occupy Metemma, and thereby either to awe the tribe into loyalty, or force them to revolt while the Egyptian troops were still too distant to assist them. He summoned the chief of the Jaalin, Abdalla–Wad–Saad, to Omdurman, and informed him that the Jaalin territories were threatened by the Turks. In the goodness of his heart, therefore, and because he knew that they loved the Mahdi and practised the true religion, he was resolved to protect them from their enemies. The trusty Mahmud with his army would be sent for that purpose; Abdalla might show his loyalty in furnishing them with all supplies and accommodation. But the Jaalin chief had the temerity to protest. He assured the Khalifa of his loyalty, and of the ability of his tribe to repel the enemy. He implored him not to impose the burden of an army upon them. He exaggerated the poverty of Metemma; he lamented the misfortunes of the times. Finally he begged forgiveness for making his protest.

The Khalifa was infuriated. Forgetting his usual self-control and the forms of public utterance, he broke out into a long and abusive harangue. Abdalla–Wad–Saad crept from the presence, and returned in fury and disgust to Metemma. Having collected the head men of his tribe, he informed them of his reception and the Khalifa's intent. They did not need to be told that the quartering upon them of Mahmud's army meant the plunder of their goods, the ruin of their homes, and the rape of their women. It was resolved to revolt and join the Egyptian forces. As a result of the council the Jaalin chief wrote two letters. The first was addressed to the Sirdar, and reached General Rundle at Merawi by messenger on the 24th of June. It declared the Jaalin submission to the Government, and begged for help, if possible in men, or, failing that, in arms. The second letter – a mad and fatal letter – carried defiance to the Khalifa.

Rundle, who was at Merawi when the Jaalin messenger found him, lost no time. A large amount of ammunition and 1,100 Remington rifles were speedily collected and hurried on camels across the desert by the Korti–Metemma route, escorted by a strong detachment of the Camel Corps. The Khalifa did not receive his letter until the 27th of June. But he acted with even greater promptitude. Part of Mahmud's army had already started for the north. Mahmud and the rest followed on the 28th. On the 30th the advanced guard arrived before Metemma. The Jaalin prepared to resist desperately. Nearly the whole tribe had responded to the summons of their chief, and more than 2,500 men were collected behind the walls of the town. But in all this force there were only eighty serviceable rifles, and only fifteen rounds of ammunition each.

On the morning of the 1st of July, Mahmud, with a force variously estimated at 10,000 or 12,000 men, began his assault. The first attack fell, as the chief had anticipated, on the southern face. It was repulsed with severe loss by the Jaalin riflemen. A second attack followed immediately. The enemy had meanwhile surrounded the whole town, and just as the Jaalin ammunition was exhausted a strong force of the Dervishes penetrated the northern face of their defences, which was held only by spearmen. The whole of Mahmud's army poured in through the gap, and the garrison, after a stubborn resistance, were methodically exterminated. An inhuman butchery of the children and some of the women followed. Abdalla-Wad-Saad was among the killed.

But while the attention of the Khalifa was directed to these matters, a far more serious menace offered from another quarter. Unnoticed by the Dervishes, or, if noticed, unappreciated, the railway was stretching farther and farther into the desert. By the middle of July it had reached the 130th mile. The Nile was rising fast. Very soon steamers would be able to pass the Fourth Cataract. It should have been evident that the next movement in the advance of the 'Turks' impended. The Khalifa seems, indeed, to have understood that the rise of the river increased his peril, for throughout July he continued to send orders to the Emir in Berber – Yunes – that he should advance into the Monassir district, harry such villages as existed, and obstruct the frequent reconnaissances from Merawi. Yunes, however, preferred to do otherwise, and remained on the left bank opposite Berber until, at length, his master recalled him to Omdurman to explain his conduct.

At the end of July preparations were made, as secretly as possible, to despatch a flying column against Abu Hamed. The Dervish garrison, under Mohammed-ez-Zein, was not believed to exceed 600 men, but in order that there should be no doubt as to the result it was determined to employ a strong force.

A brigade of all arms was formed as follows:

Commanding: MAJOR-GENERAL HUNTER		
Cavalry		One troop
Artillery		No.2 Field Battery [1]
		3rd Egyptians
Infantry	MACDONALD'S Brigade	IXth Soudanese
		Xth
		XIth

Major-General Sir Archibald Hunter, the officer to whom the operation was entrusted, was from many points of view the most imposing figure in the Egyptian Army. He had served through the Nile Expedition of 1884-85, with some distinction, in the Khedive's service. Thenceforward his rise was rapid, even for an Egyptian officer, and in ten years he passed through all the grades from Captain to Major-General. Foremost in every action, twice wounded – once at the head of his brigade – always distinguished for valour and conduct, Hunter won the admiration of his comrades and superiors. During the River War he became, in spite of his hard severity, the darling of the Egyptian Army. All the personal popularity which great success might have brought to the Sirdar focused itself on his daring, good-humoured subordinate, and it

---

[1] *This battery consisted of six Krupp guns, two Maxims, one Gardner gun, and one Nordenfeldt - an effective medley.*

was to Hunter that the soldiers looked whenever there was fighting to be done. The force now placed under his command for the attack upon Abu Hamed amounted to about 3,600 men. Until that place was taken all other operations were delayed. The Sirdar awaited the issue at Merawi. The railway paused in mid-desert.

The troops composing the 'flying column' concentrated at Kassingar, a small village a few miles above Merawi, on the right (or Abu Hamed), bank of the Nile. General Hunter began his march on the 29th of July. The total distance from Kassingar to Abu Hamed is 146 miles. Speed was essential; for if the Dervish garrison in Abu Hamed were reinforced from Berber, the flying column might not be strong enough to take the village. On the other hand, the great heat and the certainty that the troops would have to fight an action at the end of the march imposed opposite considerations on the commander. To avoid the sun, the greater part of the distance was covered at night.

Throughout the whole length of the course of the Nile there is no more miserable wilderness than the Monassir Desert. The stream of the river is broken and its channel obstructed by a great confusion of boulders, among which the water rushes in dangerous cataracts. The line of advance lay along the river; but no road relieved the labour of the march. Sometimes trailing across a broad stretch of white sand, in which the soldiers sank to their ankles; sometimes winding over a pass or through a gorge of sharp-cut rocks – always in a long, jerky, and interrupted procession of men and camels, often in single file – the column toiled painfully like the serpent to whom it was said, 'On thy belly shalt thou go, and dust shalt thou eat.'

The column started at 5.30 in the evening, and by a march of sixteen and a half miles reached Mushra-el-Obiad at about midnight. Here a convenient watering-place, not commanded by the opposite bank, and the shade of eight or ten thorny bushes afforded the first suitable bivouac. At 3.30 p.m. on the 30th the march was continued eight and a half miles to a spot some little distance beyond Shebabit. It was after dark when the halting-place was reached. General Hunter had proposed to push on the next day to Hosh-el-Geref, but the fatigues of his troops in the two night marches had already been severe, and as, after Abu Haraz, the track twisted away from the river so that there was no water for five miles, he resolved to halt for the day and rest. Hosh-el-Geref was therefore not reached until the 1st of August – a day later than had been expected; but the rest had proved of such benefit to the troops that the subsequent acceleration of progress fully compensated for the delay.

On the 5th, the force reached Khula. Here they were joined by Sheikh Abdel-Azim with 150 Ababda camel-men from Murat Wells. Up to this point three Egyptians had died and fifty-eight men had been left behind exhausted in depôts. A double ration of meat was issued to the whole force. The column moved on during the night, and arrived at Ginnifab at eight in the morning of the 6th. Here startling news of the enemy was received. It was known that Mohammed-ez-Zein was determined to fight, and a trustworthy report was now received that a large force was coming down from Berber to support the Abu Hamed garrison. In spite of the long marches and the fatigues of the troops, General Hunter resolved to hurry on. He had already made up the day spent at Abu Haraz. He now decided to improve on the prescribed itinerary, accelerate his own arrival and anticipate that of the Dervish reinforcements. Accordingly the troops marched all through the night of the 6-7th with only a short halt of an hour and a half, so as to attack Abu Hamed at dawn.

The village of Abu Hamed straggles along the bank of the Nile, and consists of a central mass of mud houses, intersected by a network of winding lanes and alleys, about 500 yards long by perhaps 100 yards wide. To the north and south are detached clusters of ruined huts, and to the south there rises a large, ragged pile of rocks. The ground slopes gradually up from the river, so that at a distance of 300 yards the village is surrounded on three sides by a low plateau. Upon this plateau stand three stone watch-towers, which were erected by General Gordon. The Dervish garrison were strongly posted in shelter trenches and loopholed houses along the eastern face of the village. The towers were held by their outposts.

Making a wide circuit to their left, and then swinging round to the right, so as to front facing the river, the brigade silently moved towards the enemy's position, and at a quarter past six occupied the plateau in a crescent-shaped formation; the XIth Soudanese on the right, opposite the north-east corner of the village; the battery, escorted by the remaining half-battalion of the 3rd Egyptians, next; then the IXth in the centre, and the Xth Soudanese on the left flank. As the troops approached the watch-towers the Dervish outposts fell back, and the force continued to advance until the edge of the plateau was reached.

The day was just breaking, and the mist hung low and white over the steel-grey surface of the river. The Dervish riflemen crouched in the shelter trench that ran round the village. Their cavalry, perhaps a hundred strong, were falling in hurriedly on the sandy ground to the south near the ragged rocks.

At half past six the battery came into action, and after a few shells had been fired at the loopholed houses in the left centre of the position, a general advance was ordered. In excellent order the three Soudanese battalions, with General Hunter, Lieut.-Colonel MacDonald, and the other British officers on horseback in front of their line, advanced slowly down the hill, opening a destructive fire on the entrenchment. The distance was scarcely three hundred yards; but the crescent formation of the attack made the lines of advance converge, and before half the distance was covered the Xth were compelled to halt, lest the XIth Soudanese on the right flank should fire into them. The Dervishes remained silent until the troops were within a hundred yards, when they discharged two tremendous volleys, which were chiefly effective upon the halted battalion. Major Sidney, Lieutenant Fitzclarence, and a dozen men were shot dead. More than fifty men were wounded. All the Soudanese thereupon with a loud shout rushed upon the entrenchment, stormed it, and hunted the Dervishes into the houses. In the street-fighting which followed, the numbers of the troops prevailed. The advance scarcely paused until the river bank was reached, and by 7.30 Abu Hamed was in the possession of the Egyptian forces.

The Dervish horsemen, who had remained spectators near the southern crag during the attack, fled towards Berber as soon as they saw the attack successful. Scarcely any of the infantry escaped.

In this action, besides the two British officers, Major H. M. Sidney and Lieutenant E. Fitzclarence, 21 native soldiers were killed; 61 native soldiers were wounded.

The news of the capture of Abu Hamed was carried swiftly by camel and wire. The Sirdar, anticipating the result, had already ordered the gunboats to commence the passage of the Fourth Cataract. The Dervishes who were hurrying from Berber were only twenty miles from Abu Hamed when they met the fugitives. They immediately turned back, and retired to the foot of the Fifth Cataract, whence after a few days' halt they continued their retreat. Their proximity to the captured village shows how little time the column had to spare, and that General Hunter was wise to press his marches. The Emir who commanded at Berber heard of the loss of the outpost on the 9th. He sent the messenger on to Metemma. Mahmud replied on the 11th that he was starting at once with his whole army to reinforce Berber. Apparently, however, he did not dare to move without the Khalifa's permission.

On the 4th of August the gunboats *El Teb* and *Tamai* approached the Fourth Cataract to ascend to the Abu Hamed-Berber reach of the river. Major David was in charge of the operation. Lieutenants Hood and Beatty (Royal Navy) commanded the vessels. Two hundred men of the 7th Egyptians were towed in barges to assist in hauling the steamers in the difficult places. The current was, however, too strong, and it was found necessary to leave three barges, containing 160 soldiers, at the foot of the rapids. Nevertheless, as the cataract was not considered a very formidable barrier, Major David determined to make the attempt. Early on the 5th, therefore, the *Tamai* tried the ascent. The steamer, with her engines working at full speed, succeeded in mounting half the distance. But the rush of water was then so great that her bows were swept round, and, after a narrow escape of capsizing, she was carried swiftly down the stream.

The officers thought that this failure was due to the accidental fouling of a rope at a critical moment, and to the fact that there were not enough local tribesmen pulling at the hawsers. Four hundred more Shaiggia were therefore collected from the neighbouring villages, and in the afternoon *El Teb* attempted the passage. Her fortunes were far worse than those of the *Tamai*. Owing to the lack of co-operation and discipline among the local tribesmen, and the want of proper supervision, the hauling power was again too weak. Again the bows of the steamer were swept round, and, as the hawsers held, a great rush of water poured over the bulwarks. In ten seconds *El Teb* heeled over and turned bottom upwards. The hawsers parted under this new strain, and she was swept down stream with only her keel showing. Lieutenant Beatty and most of the crew were thrown, or glad to jump, into the foaming water of the cataract, and, being carried down the river, were picked up below the rapids by the *Tamai*, which was luckily under steam. Their escape was extraordinary, for of the score who were flung into the water only one Egyptian was drowned.

Search was now made for another passage. This was found on the 6th, nearer the right bank of the river. On the 8th the *Metemma* arrived with 300 more men of the 7th Egyptians. Three days were spent in preparations and to allow the Nile to rise a little more. On the 13th, elaborate precautions being observed, the *Metemma* passed the cataract safely, and was tied up to the bank on the higher reach. The *Tamai* followed the next day. On the 19th and 20th the new gunboats, *Fateh*, *Naser* and *Zafir*, the most powerful vessels on the river, accomplished the passage. Meanwhile the *Metemma* and *Tamai* had already proceeded up stream. On the 23rd the unarmed steamer *Dal* made the ascent, and by the 29th the whole flotilla reached Abu Hamed safely.

The sudden dart upon Abu Hamed had caused the utmost consternation among the Dervishes. Finding that Mahmud was not going to reinforce him, and fearing the treachery of the local tribes, Zeki Osman, the Emir in Berber, decided to fall back, and on the 24th he evacuated Berber and marched south. On the 27th General Hunter at Abu Hamed heard that the Dervish garrison had left the town. The next day he despatched Abdel-Azim, the chief of Irregulars, and Ahmed Bey Khalifa, his brother, with forty Ababda tribesmen, to reconnoitre. These bold fellows pushed on recklessly, and found the inhabitants everywhere terrified or acquiescent. Spreading extraordinary tales of the strength of the army who were following them, they created a panic all along the river, and, in spite of a sharp fight with a Dervish patrol, reached Berber on the 31st. As there was no armed force in the town, the enterprising allies rode into the streets and occupied the grain store – the only public building – in the name of the Government. They then sent word back to Abu Hamed of what they had done, and sat down in the town, thus audaciously captured, to await developments.

The astonishing news of the fall of Berber reached General Hunter on the 2nd of September. He immediately telegraphed to Merawi. Sir Herbert Kitchener was confronted with a momentous question: should Berber be occupied or not? It may at first seem that there could be little doubt about the matter. The objective of the expedition was Omdurman. The occupation of Berber by an Egyptian garrison would settle at once the difficulties near Suakin. The moral effect of its capture upon the riverain tribes and throughout the Soudan would be enormous. Berber was, in fact, the most important strategic point on the whole line of advance.

The opposite considerations were, however, tremendous. Abu Hamed marked a definite stage in the advance. As long as Merawi and the other posts in Dongola were strongly held, the line from Abu Hamed to Debba was capable of easy defence. Abu Hamed could soon be made impregnable to Dervish attack. The forces in Dongola could be quickly concentrated on any threatened point. At this moment in the campaign it was possible to stop and wait with perfect safety. In the meantime the Khalifa would steadily weaken and the railway might steadily grow. When the line reached the angle of the river, it would be time to continue the systematic and cautious advance. Until then to occupy Berber was to risk much. Mahmud, with a large and victorious army, lay at Metemma. Osman Digna, with 2,000 men, held Adarama almost within striking distance. The railway still lagged in the desert. The Dongola garrisons must be weakened to provide a force for Berber. The Dervishes had the advantage of occupying the interior of the angle which the Nile forms at Abu Hamed. The troops in Berber would have to draw their supplies by a long and slender line of camel communication, winding along all the way from Merawi, and exposed throughout its whole length to attack. More than all this: to advance to Berber must inevitably force the development of the whole war.

The Sirdar and the Consul-General faced the responsibility together. On the 3rd of September General Hunter received orders to occupy Berber. He started at once with 350 men of the IXth Soudanese on board the gunboats *Tamai*, *Zafir*, *Naser*, and *Fateh*. Shortly after daybreak on the 5th the Egyptian flag was hoisted over the town. Having disembarked the infantry detachment, the flotilla steamed south to try to harass the retreating Emir. On the next day they caught him, moving along the bank in considerable disorder, and, opening a heavy fire, soon drove the mixed crowd of fugitives, horse and foot, away from the river into the desert. Meanwhile the Sirdar had started for the front himself, and reached Berber on the 10th of September. Having inspected the immediate arrangements for defence, he withdrew to Abu Hamed, and there busily prepared to meet the developments which he knew must follow.

CHAPTER 10

BERBER

The town of Berber stands at a little distance from the Nile, on the right bank of a channel which is full only when the river is in flood. Between this occasional stream and the regular waterway there runs a long strip of rich alluvial soil, covered during the greater part of the year with the abundant crops which result from its annual submersion and the thick coating of Nile mud which it then receives. The situation of Berber is fixed by this fertile tract, and the houses stretch for more than seven miles along it and the channel by which it is caused. The town, as is usual on the Nile, is comparatively narrow, and in all its length it is only at one point broader than three-quarters of a mile. The Berber of Egyptian days lies in ruins at the southern end of the main road. The new town built by the Dervishes stands at the north. Both are foul and unhealthy. The houses of both were constructed by a simple method. A hole was dug in the ground. The excavated mud formed the walls of the building. The roof consisted of palm-leaves and thorn-bushes. The hole became a convenient cesspool. Such was Berber, and it contained at the time of its recapture by the Egyptian forces a miserable population of 5,000 males and 7,000 females, as destitute of property as their dwellings were of elegance.

The Egyptian garrison of Berber at first consisted only of the 350 men of the IXth Soudanese, and two companies of the Camel Corps, who arrived on the 16th of September, having marched across the desert from Merawi. But the proximity of Osman

Digna at Adarama made it necessary speedily to strengthen the force.

The effect of the occupation of Berber upon the tribes around Suakin was decisive. Osman Digna's influence was destroyed. The friendly villages were no longer raided. The Governor of the town became in reality, as well as in name, the Governor of the Red Sea Littoral. The route from Suakin to Berber was opened; and a Camel Corps patrol, several small caravans of traders, and a party of war correspondents – the first Europeans to make the journey for thirteen years – passed safely along it.

It is now necessary to look to the enemy. Had the Khalifa allowed the Emir Mahmud to march north immediately after the destruction of the Dervish outpost in Abu Hamed, the course of the operations would have been very different. Mahmud would certainly have defended Berber with his whole army. But, as the last chapter has described, the sudden seizure of Abu Hamed, the defection of the riverain tribes, and the appearance of the gunboats above the Fourth Cataract persuaded Abdullah that the climax of the war approached, and that he was about to be attacked in his capital. He accordingly devoted himself to his preparations for defence, and forbade his lieutenant to advance north of Metemma or attempt any offensive operations. An elaborate system of forts armed with artillery was constructed outside the great wall of Omdurman along the river-bank. The concentration of Arab and black soldiery from Gedraef, Kordofan, and Darfur continued. Large quantities of grain, of camels and other supplies, were requisitioned from the people of the Ghezira (the country lying between the Blue and White Niles) and stored or stabled in the city. The Khalifa Sherif, who had been suspected of sympathising with the Jaalin, was made a prisoner at large. The direst penalties attended the appearance of sedition, and the Khalifa was able to muster all the remaining force of the Dervish Empire to meet the expected onslaught of his enemies.

As soon as Berber had been strongly occupied by the Egyptian troops, Osman Digna realised that his position at Adarama was not only useless but very dangerous. Mahmud had long been imperiously summoning him to join the forces at Metemma; and although he hated the Kordofan general, and resented his superior authority, the wary and cunning Osman decided that in this case it would be convenient to obey. Accordingly he withdrew with his two thousand Hadendoa from Adarama, moved along the left bank of the Atbara until the tongue of desert between the rivers became sufficiently narrow for it to be crossed in a day, and so made his way by easy stages to Shendi.

When the Sirdar heard of the evacuation of Adarama he immediately determined to assure himself of the fact, to reconnoitre the unmapped country in that region, and to destroy any property that Osman might have left behind him. On the 23rd of October, therefore, a flying column started from Berber under the command of General Hunter. The report that Osman Digna had returned to the Nile proved to be correct. His former headquarters were deserted, and although a patrol of sixty of the Camel Corps and the Arab irregulars scouted for forty miles further up the river, not a single Dervish was to be seen.

It was now November. The Nile was falling fast, and an impassable rapid began to appear at Um Tiur, four miles north of the confluence. The Sirdar had a few days in which to make up his mind whether he would keep his gunboats on the upper or lower reach. As in the latter case their patrolling limits would have been restricted, and they would no longer have been able to watch the army at Metemma, he determined to leave them on the enemy's side of the obstruction. This involved the formation of a depôt at Dakhila, where simple repairs could be executed and wood and other necessities stored. To guard this little dockyard half the 3rd Egyptian battalion was moved from Berber and posted in a small entrenchment. The other half-battalion followed in a

147

few weeks. The post at the confluence was gradually growing into the great camp of a few months later.

A regular system of gunboat patrolling was established on the upper reach, and on the 1st of November the *Zafir*, *Naser*, and *Metemma*, under Commander Keppel, again steamed south to reconnoitre Mahmud's position. The next day they were joined by the *Fateh*, and on the 3rd the three larger boats ran the gauntlet of the forts. A brisk artillery duel ensued, but the Dervish aim was, as usual, erratic, and the vessels received no injury. It was observed that the position of the Dervish force was unchanged, but that three new forts had been constructed to the south of the town.

No other incident enlivened the monotony of November. The Khalifa continued his defensive preparations. Mahmud remained motionless at Metemma; and although he repeatedly begged to be allowed to advance against the force near Berber he was steadily refused, and had to content himself with sending raiding parties along the left bank of the Nile, and collecting large stores of grain from all the villages within his reach. Meanwhile the railway was stretching further and further to the south, and the great strain which the sudden occupation of Berber had thrown upon the transport was to some extent relieved. The Sirdar, delighted that he was neither attacked nor harassed in any way, journeyed to Kassala to arrange the details of its retrocession.

The convenient situation of Kassala – almost equally distant from Omdurman, Berber, Suakin, Massowa, and Rosaires – and the fertility of the surrounding region raise it to the dignity of the most important place in the Eastern Soudan. The soil is rich; the climate, except in the rainy season, not unhealthy. A cool night breeze relieves the heat of the day, and the presence of abundant water at the depth of a few feet below the surface supplies the deficiency of a river. In the year 1883 the population is said to have numbered more than 60,000. The Egyptians considered the town of sufficient value to require a garrison of 3,900 soldiers. A cotton mill adequately fitted with machinery and a factory chimney gave promise of the future development of manufacture. But in 1885, after a long siege and a stubborn resistance, Kassala was taken by the Dervishes. The garrison were massacred, enslaved, or incorporated in the Mahdi's army. The town was plundered and the trade destroyed. For nearly ten years an Arab force occupied the ruins and a camp outside them. Kassala became a frontier post of the Dervish Empire. Its population perished or fled to the Italian territory. This situation might have remained unaltered until after the Battle of Omdurman if the Dervishes had been content with the possession of Kassala. But in 1893 the Emir in command of the garrison, being anxious to distinguish himself, disobeyed the Khalifa's instructions to remain on the defensive and attacked the Europeans at Agordat. The Arab force of about 8,000 men were confronted by 2,300 Italian troops, protected by strong entrenchments, under Colonel Arimondi. After a fierce but hopeless attack the Dervishes were repulsed with a loss of 3,000 men, among whom was their rash leader. The engagement was, however, as disastrous to Italy as to the Khalifa. The fatal African policy of Signor Crispi received a decided impetus, and in the next year, agreeably to their aspirations in Abyssinia, the Italians under General Baratieri advanced from Agordat and captured Kassala. The occupation was provisionally recognised by Egypt without prejudice to her sovereign rights, and 900 Italian regulars and irregulars established themselves in a well-built fort. The severe defeat at Adowa in 1896, the disgrace of Baratieri, the destruction of his army, and the fall of the Crispi Cabinet rudely dispelled the African ambitions of Italy. Kassala became an encumbrance. Nor was that all. The Dervishes, encouraged by the victory of the Abyssinians, invested the fort, and the garrison were compelled to fight hard to hold what their countrymen were anxious to abandon. In these circumstances the Italian Government offered to retrocede Kassala to Egypt. The offer was accepted, and an arrangement made. The advance of the Khedivial forces into the Dongola Province relieved, as has been described, the pressure of the Dervish attacks. The Arabs occupied various small posts along the Atbara and contented themselves with raiding. The Italians remained entirely on the defensive, waiting for the moment when the fort could be handed over to the Egyptian troops.

The Sirdar had no difficulty in coming to a satisfactory arrangement with General Caneva, the Italian commander. The fort was to be occupied by an Egyptian force, the stores and armament to be purchased at a valuation, and a force of Italian Arab irregulars to be transferred to the Egyptian service. Kitchener then returned to the Nile, where the situation had suddenly become acute. During November Colonel Parsons, the 16th Egyptian Battalion, and a few native gunners marched from Suakin, and on the 20th of December arrived at Kassala. The Italian irregulars – henceforth to be known as the Arab battalion – were at once despatched to the attack of the small Dervish posts at El Fasher and Asubri, and on the next day these places were surprised and taken with scarcely any loss. The Italian officers, although a little disgusted at the turn of events, treated the Egyptian representatives with the most perfect courtesy, and the formal transference of Kassala fort was arranged to take place on Christmas Day.

Here, then, for a year we leave Colonel Parsons and his small force to swelter in the mud fort. The reader, like the Sirdar, must return in a hurry to the Upper Nile.

Towards the end of November the Khalifa had begun to realise that the 'Turks' did not mean to advance any further till the next flood of the river. As soon as he had come to this conclusion, he no longer turned a deaf ear to Mahmud's solicitations. He knew that the falling Nile would restrict the movements of the gunboats. He knew that there were only 2,000 men in Berber – a mere handful. He did not realise the tremendous power of rapid concentration which the railway had given his enemies; and he began to think of offensive operations. But Mahmud should not go alone. The whole strength of the Dervish Army should be exerted to drive back the invaders. All the troops in Omdurman were ordered north. A great camp was again formed near Kerreri. At the beginning of December he sent his own secretary to Mahmud to explain the plan, and to assure him of early reinforcements and supplies. Lastly, Abdullah preached a new *Jehad*, and it is remarkable that, while all former exhortations had been directed against 'the infidel' – i.e. those who did not believe in the Mahdi – his letters and sermons on this occasion summoned the tribes to destroy not the Egyptians but the Christians. There were at this time scarcely 150 Europeans in the Soudan; but they had made their presence felt.

Kitchener's reply to the Khalifa's open intent was to order a general concentration of the available Egyptian Army towards Berber, to telegraph to Lord Cromer asking for a British brigade, and to close the Suakin-Berber route.

The gunboat depôt at the confluence, with only a half-battalion escort, was now in an extremely exposed position. The gunboats could not steam north, for the cataract four miles below the confluence was already impassable. Since they must remain on the enemy's side, so must their depôt; and the depôt must be held by a much stronger force. Although the Sirdar felt too weak to maintain himself even on the defensive without reinforcements, he was now compelled to push still further south. On the 22nd of December Lewis's brigade of four battalions and a battery were hurried along the Nile to its junction with the Atbara, and began busily entrenching themselves in an angle formed by the rivers. The Atbara fort sprang into existence.

Meanwhile the concentration was proceeding. All the troops in Dongola, with the exception of scanty garrisons in Merawi, Korti, and Debba, were massed at Berber. The infantry and guns, dropping down the river in boats, entrained at Kerma, were carried back to Halfa, then hustled across the invaluable Desert Railway, past Abu Hamed, and finally deposited at Railhead, which then (1st January) stood at Dakhesh. The whole journey by rail from

151

Merawi to Dakhesh occupied four days, whereas General Hunter with his flying column had taken eight. The Egyptian cavalry at Merawi received their orders on the 25th of December, and the British officers hurried from their Christmas dinners to prepare for their long march across the bend of the Nile to Berber. Of the eight squadrons, three were pushed on to join Lewis's force at the position which will hereinafter be called 'the Atbara encampment', or more familiarly 'the Atbara'; three swelled the gathering forces at Berber; and two remained for the present in the Dongola Province, looking anxiously out towards Gakdul Wells and Metemma.

The War Office, who had been nervous about the situation in the Soudan since the hasty occupation of Berber, and who had a very lively recollection of the events of 1884 and 1885, lost no time in the despatch of British troops. The 1st Battalions of the Royal Warwickshire Regiment, of the Lincoln Regiment, and of the Cameron Highlanders were formed into a brigade and moved from Cairo into the Soudan. The 1st Battalion of the Seaforth Highlanders was brought from Malta to Egypt, and held in immediate readiness to reinforce the troops at the front.

The officer selected for the command of the British brigade was a man of high character and ability. General Gatacre had already led a brigade in the Chitral expedition. He left India, leaving behind him golden opinions, just before the outbreak of the great Frontier rising, and was appointed to a brigade at Aldershot. Thence we now find him hurried to the Soudan – a spare, middle-sized man, of great physical strength and energy, of marked capacity and unquestioned courage, but disturbed by a restless irritation, which often left him the exhausted victim of his own vitality.

By the end of January a powerful force lay encamped along the river from Abu Hamed to the Atbara. Meanwhile the Dervishes made no forward movement. Their army was collected at Kerreri; supplies were plentiful; all preparations had been made.

THE NILE FROM ATBARA TO KHARTOUM

Yet they tarried. The burning question of the command had arisen. When the whole army was regularly assembled, the Khalifa announced publicly that he would lead the faithful in person; but at the same time he arranged privately that many Emirs and notables should beg him not to expose his sacred person. After proper solicitation, therefore, he yielded to their appeals. Then he looked round for a subordinate. The Khalifa Ali-Wad-Helu presented himself. In the Soudan every advantage and honour accrues to the possessor of an army, and the rival chief saw a chance of regaining his lost power. This consideration was not, however, lost upon Abdullah. He accepted the offer with apparent delight, but he professed himself unable to spare any rifles for the army which Ali-Wad-Helu aspired to lead. 'Alas!' he cried, 'there are none. But that will make no difference to so famous a warrior.' Ali-Wad-Helu, however, considered that it would make a great deal of difference, and declined the command. Osman Sheikh-ed-Din offered to lead the army, if he might arm the riverain tribes and use them as auxiliaries to swell his force. This roused the disapproval of Yakub. Such a policy, he declared, was fatal. The riverain tribes were traitors – dogs – worthy only of being destroyed. The squabble continued, until at last the Khalifa, despairing of any agreement, decided merely to reinforce Mahmud, and accordingly ordered the Emir Yunes to march to Metemma with about 5,000 men. But it was then discovered that Mahmud hated Yunes, and would have none of him. At this the Khalifa broke up his camp, and the Dervish Army marched back for a second time, in disgust, to the city.

It seemed to those who were acquainted with the Dervish movements that the break-up of the Kerreri camp was the end of the Khalifa's determination to move north. There would be a hot and uneventful summer, and with the Nile flood the expedition would begin its final advance. The news which was received on the 15th of February came as a great and pleasant surprise. Mahmud was crossing the Nile and proposed to advance on

Berber without reinforcements of any kind. The Sirdar, highly satisfied at this astounding piece of good fortune, immediately began
to mass his force nearer the confluence. The Seaforths began their
journey from Cairo, and the various battalions of the Egyptian
Army pressed forward towards Berber and Atbara fort. On the
25th, Mahmud being reported as having crossed to the right bank,
the general concentration was ordered.

Chapter 11

RECONNAISSANCE

The hazards which were courted by the daring occupation of Berber have been discussed in the last chapter. From October to December the situation was threatening. In December it suddenly became critical. Had the Emir Mahmud advanced with the Dervishes at Metemma even as late as the middle of January, he might possibly have recaptured Berber. If the great Omdurman army had taken the field, the possibility would have become a certainty. But it was not until the Khalifa had sent his own army back into the city that, being very badly informed of the numbers and disposition of the Egyptian force, he allowed the Metemma Dervishes to move.

Mahmud received permission to advance at the end of January. He eagerly obeyed the longed-for order. But the whole situation was now changed. The Egyptian Army was concentrated; the British brigade had arrived; the railway had reached Geneinetti; the miserable hamlet of Dakhila, at the confluence, had grown from a small depôt to an entrenched camp, against which neither Dervish science nor strength could by any possibility prevail. Perhaps Mahmud did not realise the amazing power of movement that the railway had given his foes; perhaps he still believed, with the Khalifa, that Berber was held only by 2,000 Egyptians; or else – and this is the most probable – he was reckless of danger and strong in his own conceit. At any rate, during the second week in February he began to transport himself across the Nile, with the plain design of an advance north. With all the procrastination of

157

an Arab he crawled leisurely forward towards the confluence of the rivers. At El Aliab some idea of the strength of the Atbara entrenchment seems to have dawned upon him. A council was held. Mahmud was for a continued advance and for making a direct attack on the enemy's position. Osman Digna urged a more prudent course. Many years of hard fighting against disciplined troops had taught the wily Hadendoa slaver the power of modern rifles, and much sound tactics besides. He pressed his case with jealous enthusiasm upon the commander he detested and despised. An insurmountable obstacle confronted them. Yet what could not be overcome might be avoided. The hardy Dervishes could endure privations which would destroy the soldiers of civilisation. Barren and inhospitable as was the desert, they might move round the army at the Atbara fort and once they were behind the Egyptians, these accursed ones were lost. The railway – that mysterious source of strength – could be cut. The host that drew its life along it must fight at a fearful disadvantage or perish miserably. Besides, he reminded Mahmud, they could count on help in Berber itself.

The agreement of the Emirs, called to the council, decided the Dervish leader. His confidence in himself was weakened, his hatred of Osman Digna increased. Nevertheless, following the older man's advice, he left Aliab on the 18th of March, and struck north-east into the desert towards the village and ford of Hudi on the Atbara River. Thence by a long desert march he might reach the Nile and Berber. But while his information of the Sirdar's force and movements was uncertain, the British General was better served. As soon, therefore, as Kitchener learned that the Dervishes had left the Nile and were making a detour around his left flank, he marched up the Atbara River to Hudi. This offered Mahmud the alternative of attacking him in a strong position or of making a still longer detour. He chose the latter, and, deflecting his march still more to the east, reached the Atbara at Nakheila. But from this point the distance to Berber was far too great for him to

158

cover. He could not carry enough water in his skins. The wells were few, and held against him. Further advance was impossible. So he waited and entrenched himself, uncertain what to do. Supplies were running short. His magazines at Shendi had been destroyed as soon as he had left the Nile. The Dervishes might exist, but they did not thrive, on the nuts of the *dôm* palms. Soldiers began to desert. Osman Digna, although his advice had been followed, was at open enmity.

And all this time his terrible antagonist watched him as a tiger gloats on a helpless and certain prey – silent, merciless, inexorable. The tiger crept forward two measured strides – from Ras-el-Hudi to Abadar, from Abadar to Umdabia – crouched for a moment, and then bounded with irresistible fury upon its prey and tore it to pieces. At daybreak on the morning of the 6th of April the whole army broke camp at Abadar and marched to the deserted village of Umdabia, where they bivouacked close by a convenient pool of the Atbara and seven miles nearer the Dervish camp. The camp at Umdabia lay in the scrub which grows by the banks of the Atbara, as by those of the Nile, and in order to profit by the open, level ground the four infantry brigades moved by parallel routes into the desert, and then formed facing south-east in column of brigade squares, the British brigade leading. The mounted forces, with four batteries of artillery, waited in camp until two o'clock the next morning, and did not break their march. The distance from the river-bank to the open plain was perhaps a mile and a half, and the whole infantry force had cleared the scrub by six o'clock. The sun was setting, and the red glow, brightening the sandy hillocks, made the western horizon indefinite, so that it was hard to tell where the desert ended and the sky began. On the great plain 12,000 infantry, conscious of their strength and eager to encounter the enemy, were beautifully arranged in four solid masses. Then the march began. The actual distance from the camp to the Dervish position was scarcely seven miles, but the circle necessary to avoid the bushes and the gradual bends of the river added perhaps another five to the length of the road. The pace of the advance was slow, and the troops had not gone far when the sun sank and, with hardly an interval of twilight, darkness enveloped everything.

No operation of a war is more critical than a night-march. Over and over again in every country frightful disaster has overtaken the force that has attempted it. In the gloom the shape and aspect of the ground are altered. Places well known by daylight appear strange and unrecognisable. The smallest obstacle impedes the column, which can only crawl sluggishly forward with continual checks and halts. The effect of the gloom upon the nerves of the soldiers is not less than on the features of the country. Each man tries to walk quietly, and hence all are listening for the slightest sound. Every eye seeks to pierce the darkness. In such hours doubts and fears come unbidden to the brain, and the marching men wonder whether they themselves will survive the event. And if suddenly out of the black silence there burst the jagged glare of rifles and the crash of a volley followed by the yell of an attacking foe, the steadiest troops may be thrown into confusion, and a panic, once afoot, stops only with the destruction or dispersal of the whole force.

For more than two hours the force advanced, moving across smooth swells of sand broken by rocks and with occasional small bushes. Several shallow *khors* traversed the road, and these rocky ditches, filled with a strange, sweet-scented grass, delayed the brigades until the pace was hardly two miles an hour.

At nine o'clock the army halted in a previously selected space, near the deserted village of Mutrus and about two miles from the river. Nearly half the distance to Mahmud's *zeriba* was accomplished, and barely four miles in the direct line divided the combatants; but since it was not desirable to arrive before the dawn, the soldiers, still formed in their squares, lay down upon the ground.

During the halt the moon had risen, and when at one o'clock

the advance was resumed, the white beams revealed a wider prospect and, glinting on the fixed bayonets, crowned the squares with a sinister glitter. For three hours the army toiled onwards at the same slow and interrupted crawl. Strict silence was now enforced, and all smoking was forbidden. The cavalry, the Camel Corps, and the five batteries had overtaken the infantry, so that the whole attacking force was concentrated. Meanwhile the Dervishes slept.

At three o'clock the glare of fires became visible to the south, and, thus arrived before the Dervish position, the squares, with the exception of the reserve brigade, were unlocked, and the whole force, assuming formation of attack, now advanced in one long line through the scattered bush and scrub, presently to emerge upon a large plateau which overlooked Mahmud's *zeriba* from a distance of about 900 yards.

It was still dark, and the haze that shrouded the Dervish camp was broken only by the glare of the watch-fires. The silence was profound. It seemed impossible to believe that more than 25,000 men were ready to join battle at scarcely the distance of half a mile. Yet the advance had not been unperceived, and the Arabs knew that their terrible antagonists crouched on the ridge waiting for the morning. At last, after what seemed an interminable period, the uniform blackness of the horizon was broken by the first glimmer of the dawn. Gradually the light grew stronger until, as a theatre curtain is pulled up, the darkness rolled away, the vague outlines in the haze became definite, and the whole scene was revealed.

The British and Egyptian Army lay along the low ridge in the form of a great bow – the British brigade on the left, MacDonald in the centre, Maxwell curving forward on the right. The whole crest of the swell of ground was crowned with a bristle of bayonets and the tiny figures of thousands of men sitting or lying down and gazing curiously before them. Behind them, in a solid square, was the transport, guarded by Lewis's brigade. The leading squadrons of the cavalry were forming leisurely towards the left flank. The four batteries and a rocket detachment, moving between the infantry, ranged themselves on two convenient positions about a hundred yards in front of the line of battalions. All was ready.

Half a mile away, at the foot of the ridge, a long irregular black line of thorn bushes enclosed the Dervish defences. Behind this *zeriba* low palisades and entrenchments bent back to the scrub by the river. Odd shapeless mounds indicated the positions of the gun-emplacements, and various casemates could be seen in the middle of the enclosure. Without, the bushes had been cleared away, and the smooth sand stretched in a gentle slope to where the army waited. Within were crowds of little straw huts and scattered bushes, growing thicker to the southward. Such was Mahmud's famous *zeriba*, which for more than a month had been the predominant thought in the minds of the troops. It was scarcely imposing, and at first the soldiers thought it deserted. Only a dozen stray horsemen sat silently on their horses outside the entrenchment, watching their enemies, and inside a few dirty-white figures appeared and disappeared behind the parapets. Yet, insignificant as the *zeriba* looked, the smoke of many fires cooking the morning meal showed that it was occupied by men; and gay banners of varied colour and device, flaunting along the entrenchments or within the enclosure, declared that some at least were prepared to die in its defence.

The hush of the hour and the suspense of the army were broken by the bang of a gun. Everyone on the ridge jumped up and looked towards the sound. A battery of Krupps a little to the right of the Cameron Highlanders had opened fire. Another gun further to the right was fired. Another shell burst over the straw huts among the palm-trees. The two Maxim-Nordenfeldt batteries had come into action. The officers looked at their watches. It was a quarter past six. The bombardment had begun.

Explosion followed explosion in quick succession until all four batteries were busily engaged. The cannonade grew loud and continuous. The rocket detachment began to fire, and the strange projectiles hissed and screamed as they left the troughs and jerked erratically towards the *zeriba*. At the very first shot all the dirty-white figures disappeared, bobbing down into their pits and shelters; but a few solitary horsemen remained motionless for a while in the middle of the enclosure, watching the effect of the fire, as if it had no concern with them.

After the bombardment had lasted about ten minutes a great cloud of dust sprang up in the *zeriba*, and hundreds of horsemen were seen scrambling into their saddles and galloping through a gap in the rear face out into the open sand to the right. To meet the possibility of an attempt to turn the left flank of the attack, the eight squadrons of cavalry and two Maxim guns jingled and clattered off in the direction of the danger. The dust, which the swift passage of so many horsemen raised, shut the scene from the eyes of the infantry, but continual dust-clouds above the scrub to the left and the noise of the Maxims seemed to indicate a cavalry fight. The Baggara horse, however, declined an unequal combat. Twice they showed some sort of front, and the squadrons thought they might find opportunity to charge; but a few rounds from the Maxims effectually checked the enemy. With the exception of one squadron detached on the right, the Egyptian cavalry force, however, remained on the left flank, and shielded the operations of the assaulting infantry.

Meanwhile the bombardment continued with accuracy and precision. The batteries searched the interior of the *zeriba*, threshing out one section after another, and working the whole ground regularly from front to rear. The *zeriba* and palisades were knocked about in many places, and at a quarter to seven a cluster of straw huts caught fire and began to burn briskly. At a quarter past seven the infantry were ordered to form in column for assault.

The plan of the attack for the army was simple. The long, deployed line were to advance steadily against the entrenchments, subduing by their continual fire that of the enemy. They were then to tear the *zeriba* to pieces. Covered by their musketry, the dense columns of assault which had followed the line were to enter the defences through the gaps, deploy to the right, and march through the enclosure, clearing it with the bayonet and by fire.

At twenty minutes to eight the Sirdar ordered his bugles to sound the general advance. The call was repeated by all the brigades, and the clear notes rang out above the noise of the artillery. The superior officers – with the exception of Hunter, Maxwell, and MacDonald – dismounted and placed themselves at the head of their commands. The whole mass of the infantry, numbering nearly eleven thousand men, immediately began to move forward upon the *zeriba*. The scene as this great force crested the ridge and advanced down the slope was magnificent and tremendous. Large solid columns of men, preceded by a long double line, with the sunlight flashing on their bayonets and displaying their ensigns, marched to the assault in regular and precise array. The pipes of the Highlanders, the bands of the Soudanese, and the drums and fifes of the English regiments added a wild and thrilling accompaniment. As soon as the advance masked the batteries, the guns were run forward with the firing line, in order effectually to support the attack. The deployed battalions opened a ceaseless and crushing fire on the entrenchment, and as the necessity of firing delayed the advance of the attacking columns, the pace did not exceed a slow march.

The Dervishes remained silent until the troops were within 300 yards. Then the smoke-puffs spurted out all along the stockades, and a sharp fusillade began, gradually and continually growing in intensity until the assaulting troops were exposed to a furious and effective fire. From 250 yards up to the position losses began to occur. The whole entrenchment was rimmed with flame and smoke, amid which the active figures of the Dervish riflemen were momentarily visible, and behind the filmy curtain solid masses of swordsmen and spearmen appeared. The fortunate interposition of a

THE BATTLE OF ATBARA

small knoll in some degree protected the advance of the Lincoln Regiment, but in both Highland battalions soldiers began to drop. The whole air was full of a strange chirping whistle. Numerous explosive bullets, fired by the Arabs, made queer startling reports. All the deployed battalions began to suffer. But they and the assaulting columns, regardless of the fire, bore down on the *zeriba* in all the majesty of war – an avalanche of men, stern, unflinching, utterly irresistible.

The loss during the passage of the *zeriba* and in the assault of the entrenchments was severe. Captain Findlay and Major Urquhart, of the Cameron Highlanders, were both mortally wounded in the fight at the stockades, and expired still cheering on their men. Major Napier, of the same regiment, and Captain Baillie, of the Seaforth Highlanders, received the wounds, of which they subsequently died, a few yards further on. At all points the troops broke into the enclosure. Behind the stockade there ran a treble trench. The whole interior was honeycombed with pits and holes. From these there now sprang thousands of Dervishes, desperately endeavouring to show a front to the attack. Many soldiers were killed and wounded in the narrow space. In the five minutes which were occupied in the passage of the obstruction about four hundred casualties occurred.

The British brigade had struck the extremity of the north front of the *zeriba*, and thus took the whole of the eastern face in *enfilade*, sweeping it with their terrible musketry from end to end, and strewing the ground with corpses. Although, owing to the lines of advance having converged, there was not room for more than half the force to deploy, the brigades pushed on. The conduct of the attack passed to the company commanders. All these officers kept their heads, and brought their companies up into the general lines as the front gradually widened and gaps appeared. So the whole force – companies, battalions, even brigades – mixed up together and formed in one dense, ragged, but triumphant line, marched on unchecked towards the river bed, driving their enemies in hopeless confusion before them. Yet, although the Dervishes were unable to make head against the attack, they disdained to run. Many hundreds held their ground, firing their rifles valiantly till the end. Others charged with spear and sword. The greater part retired in skirmishing order, jumping over the numerous pits, walking across the open spaces, and repeatedly turning round to shoot. The XIth Soudanese encountered the most severe resistance after the defences were penetrated. As their three deployed companies pressed on through the enclosure, they were confronted by a small inner *zeriba* stubbornly defended by the Emir Mahmud's personal bodyguard. These poured a sudden volley into the centre company at close range, and so deadly was the effect that nearly all the company were shot, falling to the ground still in their ranks. Notwithstanding this severe check the regiment, gallantly led by their colonel and supported by the Xth Soudanese, rushed this last defence and slew its last defenders. Mahmud was himself captured, and, on his being recognised, the intervention of a British officer alone saved him from the fury of the excited Soudanese.

At about twenty minutes past eight the whole force, with the Seaforth Highlanders well forward on the left, arrived at the bank of the Atbara, having marched completely through the position, and shot or bayoneted all in their path. Hundreds of Dervishes were still visible retiring across the dry bed of the river, and making for the scrub on the opposite bank. The leading companies of the Seaforth Highlanders and Lincolns, with such odd parties of Camerons as had been carried on with the attack, opened a murderous fire on these fugitives. Since they would not run their loss was heavy, and it was a strange sight – the last vivid impression of the day – to watch them struggling through the deep sand, with the dust knocked up into clouds by the bullets which struck all round them. Very few escaped, and the bodies of the killed lay thickly dotting the river-bed with heaps of dirty-white. Then at 8.25 the 'Cease fire' sounded, and the Battle of the

Atbara ended.

The losses had been severe. In the assault – a period not exceeding half an hour – eighteen British, sixteen native officers and 525 men had been killed or wounded, the greater part during the passage of the *zeriba*.

The actual pursuit was abortive. Colonel Lewis, with his two battalions, followed a line of advance which led south of the *zeriba*, and just before reaching the river bank found and fired upon a few Dervishes retreating through the scrub. All the cavalry and the Camel Corps crossed the Atbara and plunged into the bush on the further side. But so dense and tangled was the country that after three miles of peril and perplexity they abandoned the attempt, and the routed Arabs fled unmolested. The Baggara horse had ridden off during the action, headed by the prudent Osman Digna, and under that careful leadership suffered little loss. The rest of the army was, however, destroyed or dispersed. Of the powerful force of 12,000 fighting men which Mahmud had gathered at Metemma, scarcely 4,000 reached Gedaref in safety. These survivors were added to the army of Ahmed Fedil, and thus prevented from spreading their evil tidings among the populace at Omdurman. Osman Digna, Wad Bishara, and other important Emirs whose devotion and discretion were undoubted, alone returned to the capital.

As soon as the troops were re-formed, the *zeriba* was evacuated and the army drew up in line along the neighbouring ridge. It was then only nine o'clock, and the air was still cool and fresh. The soldiers lit fires, made some tea, and ate their rations of biscuits and meat. Gradually, as the hours passed, the sun became powerful. There was no shade, and only a few thin, leafless bushes rose from the sand. The hours of a day, peculiarly hot, even for the country and season, dragged wearily away. The water in the *fantasses* and bottles was hot and scarce. The pool of the Atbara was foul and tainted. In spite of the devoted efforts of the few medical officers who had been allowed to accompany the force, the wounded officers and soldiers endured the greatest miseries, and it is certain that several died of their wounds who might in happier circumstances have been saved.

Several hundred prisoners were taken. They were mostly negroes – for the Arabs refused to surrender, and fought to the last or tried to escape. The captive blacks, who fight with equal willingness on either side, were content to be enlisted in the Soudanese regiments; so that many of those who served the Khalifa on the Atbara helped to destroy him at Omdurman. The most notable prisoner was the Emir Mahmud – a tall, strong Arab, about thirty years old. Immediately after his capture he was dragged before the Sirdar. 'Why', inquired the General, 'have you come into my country to burn and kill?' 'I have to obey my orders, and so have you,' retorted the captive sullenly, yet not without a certain dignity. He was removed in custody – a fine specimen of proud brutality, worthy perhaps of some better fate than to linger indefinitely in the gaol at Rosetta.

As the Battle of the Atbara had been decisive, the whole Expeditionary Force went into summer quarters. The Egyptian Army was distributed into three principal garrisons – four battalions at Atbara camp, six battalions and the cavalry at Berber, three battalions at Abadia. The artillery and transport were proportionately divided. The British brigade encamped with two battalions at Darmali and two at the village of Selim, about a mile and a half distant.

For the final phase of the campaign three new gunboats had been ordered from England. These were now sent in sections over the Desert Railway. Sir H. Kitchener himself proceeded to Abadia to accelerate the construction of the vessels on which so much depended. Here during the heat of the summer he remained, maturing his plans, and waiting only for the rise of the river to complete the downfall of his foes.

CHAPTER 12

THE GRAND ADVANCE

All through the early months of the summer the preparations for the final advance were steadily proceeding. A second British brigade was ordered to the Soudan. A new battery of Howitzer artillery – the 37th – firing enormous shells charged with lyddite, was despatched from England. Two large 40-pounder guns were sent from Cairo. Another British Maxim battery of four guns was formed in Cairo from men of the Royal Irish Fusiliers. Three new screw gunboats of the largest size and most formidable pattern had been passed over the indefatigable railway in sections, and were now launched on the clear waterway south of the Atbara encampment; and last, but not least, the 21st Lancers[1] were ordered up the Nile. Events now began to move rapidly. There was no delay at the Atbara encampment. Even before the whole of the second brigade had arrived, some of its battalions were being despatched to Wad Hamed, the new point of concentration. This place was a few miles north of Shabluka, and only fifty-eight miles from Omdurman. It was evident, therefore, that the decisive moment of the three years' war approached. The Staff, the British infantry, one squadron, the guns, and the stores were carried south in steamers and barges. The Egyptian division marched to Wad Hamed by brigades. The horses of the batteries, the transport animals of the British division (about 1,400 in number), the chargers of the officers,

---

[1] *The author led a troop in this regiment during the final advance to Omdurman; and it is from this standpoint that the ensuing chapters are to some extent conceived.*

some cattle, and most of the war correspondents were sent along the left bank of the river escorted by two squadrons of the 21st Lancers and two Maxim guns.

All the thirteen squadrons of cavalry remained three days at Wad Hamed. After the fatigues of the march we were glad to have an opportunity of looking about, of visiting regiments known in other circumstances, and of writing a few letters. This last was the most important, for it was now known that after leaving Wad Hamed there would be no post or communication with Cairo and Europe until the action had been fought and all was over. The halt was welcome for another reason. The camp itself was well worth looking at. It lay lengthways along the river-bank, and was nearly two miles from end to end. The Nile secured it from attack towards the east. On the western and southern sides were strong lines of thorn bushes, staked down and forming a *zeriba*; and the north face was protected by a deep artificial watercourse which allowed the waters of the river to make a considerable inundation. Far away to the southward the white tents of the British division; a little nearer rows and rows of grass huts and blanket shelters, the bivouacs of the Egyptian and Soudanese brigades; the Sirdar's large white tent, with the red flag of Egypt flying from a high staff, on a small eminence; and to the right the grove of palm-trees in which the officers of the Egyptian cavalry had established themselves. The whole riverside was filled by a forest of masts; *gyassas*, barges, and steamers were moored closely together.

The road to the next camp was a long one; for though Royan island, opposite to which the site had been selected, was only seven miles in the direct line, it was necessary to march eight miles into the desert to avoid the Shabluka heights, and then to turn back to the Nile. The infantry were therefore provided with camel transport to carry sufficient water in small iron tanks for one night; and they were thus able to bivouac half-way, and to complete the journey on the next morning, thus making a two days' march. The mounted troops, who remained at Wad Hamed till all had gone south, were ordered to move on the 27th of August, and by a double march catch up the rest of the army.

Wad Hamed then ceased for the time being to exist except in name. All the stores and transport were moved by land or water to the south of Shabluka, and an advanced base was formed upon Royan island. Communications with the Atbara encampment and with Cairo were dropped, and the army carried with them in their boats sufficient supplies to last until after the capture of Omdurman. It was calculated that the scope of this operation would not be greater than three weeks, and on the 27th the army were equipped with twenty-one days' supplies, of which two were carried by the troops, five by the regimental barges, and fourteen in the army transport sailing-vessels. All surplus stores were deposited at Royan island, where a field hospital was also formed.

The total strength of the Expeditionary Force supplied for the culminating moment of the River War amounted to 8,200 British and 17,600 Egyptian soldiers, with 44 guns and 20 Maxims on land, with 36 guns and 24 Maxims on the river, and with 2,469 horses, 896 mules, 3,524 camels, and 229 donkeys, besides followers and private animals.

While the army were to move along the west bank of the river – the Omdurman side – a force of Arab irregulars, formed from the friendly tribes, would march along the east bank and clear it of any Dervishes. All the debris which the Egyptian advance had broken off the Dervish Empire was thus to be hurled against that falling State. Eager for plunder, anxious to be on the winning side, Sheikhs and Emirs from every tribe in the Military Soudan had hurried, with what following the years of war had left them, to Wad Hamed. On the 26th of August the force of irregulars numbered about 2,500 men, principally Jaalin survivors, but also comprising bands and individuals of Bisharin; of Hadendoa from Suakin; of Shukria, the camel-breeders; of Batahin, who had suffered a bloody diminution at the Khalifa's hands; of Shaiggia, Gordon's vexatious allies; and lastly some Gemilab Arabs under a reputed son of Zubehr Pasha. The command of the whole motley force was given to Major Stuart-Wortley, Lieutenant Wood accompanying him as Staff Officer; and the position of these officers among the cowed and untrustworthy Arabs was one of considerable peril.

While the infantry divisions were marching round the heights of Shabluka to the camp opposite Royan island, the steamers and gunboats ascended the stream and passed through the gorge, dragging up with them the whole fleet of barges and *gyassas*. The northern end of the narrow passage had been guarded by the five Dervish forts, which now stood deserted and dismantled. They were well built, and formed nearly a straight line – four on one bank and one on the other. Each fort had three embrasures, and might, when occupied, have been a formidable defence to the cataract.

The mounted forces marched from Wad Hamed at dawn on the 27th and, striking out into the desert, skirted the rocky hills. Besides the 21st Lancers and nine squadrons of Egyptian cavalry, the column included the Camel Corps, 800 strong, and a battery of Horse Artillery; and it was a fine sight to see all these horsemen and camel-men trotting swiftly across the sand by squadrons and companies, with a great cloud of dust rising from each and drifting away to the northward.

The *zeriba* of the camp at Royan had been already made and much of the ground cleared by the energy of the Soudanese division, which had been the first to arrive. An advanced depôt was established at Royan island, which was covered with white hospital tents, near which there was a forest of masts and sails. The barges and boats containing the stores and kits awaited the troops, and they had only to bivouac along the river-bank and shelter themselves as quickly as possible from the fierce heat of the sun. The eternal Nile flowed swiftly by the tents and shelters, and disappeared mysteriously in the gloom of the gorge; and on the further bank there rose a great mountain – Jebel Royan – from the top of which it was said that men might see Khartoum.

The whole army broke camp at Royan on the 28th of August at four o'clock in the afternoon, and marched to Wady el Abid, six miles further south. We now moved on a broad front, which could immediately be converted into a fighting formation. This was the first time that it had been possible to see the whole force – infantry, cavalry, and guns – on the march at once. In the clear air the amazing detail of the picture was striking. There were six brigades of infantry, composed of twenty-four battalions; yet every battalion showed that it was made up of tiny figures, all perfectly defined on the plain. A Soudanese brigade had been sent on to hold the ground with pickets until the troops had constructed a *zeriba*. But a single Dervish horseman managed to evade these and, just as the light faded, rode up to the Warwickshire Regiment and flung his broad-bladed spear in token of defiance. So great was the astonishment which this unexpected apparition created that the bold man actually made good his escape uninjured.

On the 29th the forces remained halted opposite Um Teref, and only the Egyptian cavalry went out to reconnoitre. They searched the country for eight or nine miles, and Colonel Broadwood returned in the afternoon, having found a convenient camping-ground, but nothing else. During the day the news of two river disasters arrived – the first to ourselves, the second to our foes. On the 28th the gunboat *Zafir* was steaming from the Atbara to Wad Hamed, intending thereafter to ascend the Shabluka Cataract. Suddenly – overtaken now, as on the eve of the advance on Dongola, by misfortune – she sprang a leak, and, in spite of every effort to run her ashore, foundered by the head in deep water near Metemma. The Sirdar received the news at Royan. His calculations were disturbed by the loss of a powerful vessel; but the days of struggling warfare were over, and the General knew that he had a safe margin of strength.

The other catastrophe afflicted the Khalifa, and its tale was brought to the advancing army by the Intelligence spies, who to the last – even when the forces were closing – tried to pass between them. Not content with building batteries along the banks, Abdullah, fearing the gunboats, had resolved to mine the river. An old officer of the old Egyptian Army, long a prisoner in Omdurman, was brought from his chains and ordered to construct mines. Two iron boilers were filled with gunpowder, and it was arranged that these should be sunk in the Nile at convenient spots. Buried in the powder of each was a loaded pistol with a string attached to the trigger. On pulling the string the pistol, and consequently the mine, would be exploded. So the Khalifa argued; nor was he wrong. It was resolved to lay one mine first. On the 17th of August the Dervish steamer *Ismailia* moved out into the middle of the Nile, carrying one of the boilers fully charged and equipped with pistol detonator. Arrived at the selected spot, the great cylinder of powder was dropped over the side. Its efficiency as a destructive engine was immediately demonstrated, for, on the string being pulled by accident, the pistol discharged itself, the powder exploded, and the *Ismailia* and all on board were blown to pieces.

Undeterred by the loss of life, and encouraged by the manifest power of the contrivance, the Khalifa immediately ordered the second of the two boilers to be sunk in the stream. As the old Egyptian officer had been killed by the explosion, the Emir in charge of the arsenal was entrusted with the perilous business. He rose, however, to the occasion, and, having first taken the precaution of letting the water into the boiler so as to damp the powder, he succeeded in laying the second mine in mid-stream, to the joy and delight of Abdullah, who, not understanding that it was now useless, overwhelmed him with praise and presents.

Beguiled with such stories and diversions, the day of rest at Wady el Abid passed swiftly. Night brought beetles, bugs, and ants, and several men were stung by scorpions – a most painful though not dangerous affair. Towards morning it began to rain, and everyone was drenched and chilled when the sun rose across the river from behind a great conical hill and dispersed the clouds into wisps of creamy flame. Then we mounted and set out.

When we had advanced a little further, there arose above the scrub the dark outlines of a rocky peak, the hill of Merreh. The whole of the 21st Lancers now concentrated, and, trotting quickly forward, occupied this position, whence a considerable tract of country was visible. We were hardly twenty-five miles from Khartoum, and of that distance at least ten miles were displayed. Yet there were no enemy. Had they all fled? Should we find Omdurman deserted or submissive? These were questions which occurred to everyone, and many answered them affirmatively. Colonel Martin had meanwhile heliographed back to the Sirdar that all the ground was up to this point clear, and that there were no Dervishes to be seen. After some delay orders were signalled back for one squadron to remain till sunset in observation on the hill and for the rest to return to camp.

With two troops thrown out a mile in front we waited watching on the hill. Time passed slowly, for the sun was hot. Suddenly it became evident that one of the advanced troops was signalling energetically. The message was spelt out. The officer with the troop perceived Dervishes in his front. We looked through our glasses. It was true. There, on a white patch of sand among the bushes of the plain, were a lot of little brown spots, moving slowly across the front of the cavalry outposts towards an Egyptian squadron, which was watching far out to the westward. There may have been seventy horsemen altogether. We could not take our eyes off those distant specks we had travelled so far, if possible, to destroy. Presently the Dervish patrol approached our right troop, and apparently came nearer than they imagined, for the officer who commanded opened fire on them with carbines, and we saw them turn and ride back, but without hurrying.

The camp to which we returned was a very different place from the one we had left in the morning. Instead of lying along the river-bank, it was pitched in the thinner scrub. The bushes had on all sides been cut down, the ground cleared, and an immense oblong *zeriba* was built, around which the six brigades were drawn up, and into which cavalry, guns, and transport were closely packed.

Very early next morning the advance was continued. The army paraded by starlight, and with the first streak of the dawn the cavalry were again flung far out in advance. Secure behind the screen of horsemen and Camel Corps, the infantry advanced in regular array. Up to the 27th of August the force marched by divisions; but on and after the 30th of August the whole force commenced to march in fighting formation. The British division was on the left, the Egyptian Army on the right. All the brigades marched in line, or in a slight echelon. The flank brigades kept their flank battalions in column or in fours. Other British battalions had six companies in the front line (in company column of fours) and two companies in support. The Egyptian brigades usually marched with three battalions in the front line and one in reserve, each of the three in the front line having four companies in front and two in support.

Day after day and hour after hour the advance was maintained. Arrived at the camping-ground, the *zeriba* had to be built; and this involved a long afternoon of fatigue. In the evening, when the dusty, tired-out squadrons returned, the troopers attended to their horses, and so went to sleep in peace. It was then that the dusty tired-out infantry provided sentries and pickets, who in a ceaseless succession paced the *zeriba* and guarded its occupants.

The position of the next camp was a strong one, on a high swell of open ground which afforded a clear field of fire in every direction. Everyone that night lay down to sleep with a feeling of keen expectancy. One way or the other all doubts would be settled the next day. The cavalry would ride over the Kerreri Hills if they were not occupied by the enemy, and right up to the walls of

Omdurman. If the Dervishes had any army – if there was to be any battle – we should know within a few hours. The telegrams which were despatched that evening were the last to reach England before the event. During the night heavy rain fell, and all the country was drenched. The telegraph-wire had been laid along the ground, as there had been no time to pole it. The sand when dry is a sufficient insulator, but when wet its non-conductivity is destroyed. Hence all communications ceased, and those at home who had husbands, sons, brothers, or friends in the Expeditionary Force were left in an uncertainty as great as that in which we slept – and far more painful.

CHAPTER 13

THE OPERATIONS OF THE FIRST OF SEPTEMBER

The British and Egyptian cavalry, supported by the Camel Corps and Horse Artillery, trotted out rapidly, and soon interposed a distance of eight miles between them and the army. As before, the 21st Lancers were on the left nearest the river, and the Khedivial squadrons curved backwards in a wide half-moon to protect the right flank. Meanwhile the gunboat flotilla was seen to be in motion. The white boats began to ascend the stream leisurely. The orders of the cavalry were to reconnoitre Omdurman; of the gunboats to bombard it.

As soon as the squadrons of the 21st Lancers had turned the shoulder of the steep Kerreri Hills, we saw in the distance a yellow-brown pointed dome rising above the blurred horizon. It was the Mahdi's Tomb, standing in the very heart of Omdurman. From the high ground the field-glass disclosed rows and rows of mud houses, making a dark patch on the brown of the plain. To the left the river, steel-grey in the morning light, forked into two channels, and on the tongue of land between them the gleam of a white building showed among the trees. Before us were the ruins of Khartoum and the confluence of the Blue and White Niles.

A black, solitary hill rose between the Kerreri position and Omdurman. A long, low ridge running from it concealed the ground beyond. For the rest there was a wide-rolling, sandy plain of great extent, surrounded on three sides by rocky hills and ridges, and patched with coarse, starveling grass or occasional bushes. By the banks of the river which framed the picture on the left stood a straggling mud village, and this, though we did not know it, was to be the field of Omdurman. It was deserted. Not a living creature could be seen. And now there were many who said once and for all that there would be no fight; for here we were arrived at the very walls of Omdurman, and never an enemy to bar our path.

It was about three miles to the last ridge which lay between us and the city. If there was a Dervish Army, if there was to be a battle, much must be visible from that ridge. We looked over. At first nothing was apparent except the walls and houses of Omdurman and the sandy plain sloping up from the river to distant hills. Then four miles away on our right front emerged a long black line with white spots. It was the enemy. It seemed to us, as we looked, that there might be 3,000 men behind a high, dense *zeriba* of thorn-bushes. That, said the officers, was better than nothing. It is scarcely necessary to describe our tortuous movements towards the Dervish position. Always edging nearer, the cavalry slowly approached, and halted in the plain about three miles away – three great serpents of men – the light-coloured one, the 21st Lancers; a much longer and a blacker one, the Egyptian squadrons; a mottled one, the Camel Corps and Horse Artillery.

It was now nearly eleven o'clock. Suddenly the whole black line which seemed to be *zeriba* began to move. It was made of men, not bushes. Behind it other immense masses and lines of men appeared over the crest; and while we watched, amazed by the wonder of the sight, the whole face of the slope became black with swarming savages. Four miles from end to end, and, as it seemed, in five great divisions, this mighty army advanced – swiftly. The whole side of the hill seemed to move. Between the masses horsemen galloped continually; before them many patrols dotted the plain; above them waved hundreds of banners, and the sun, glinting on many thousand hostile spear-points, spread a sparkling cloud.

It is now known that the Khalifa had succeeded in concentrating at Omdurman an army of more than 60,000 men. He remembered that all the former victories over the Egyptians had been won by the Dervishes attacking. He knew that in all the recent defeats they had stood on the defensive. He therefore determined not to oppose the advance at the Shabluka or on the march thence to Omdurman. All was to be staked on the issue of a great battle on the plains of Kerreri. The Mahdi's prophecy was propitious. When the 'Turks' arrived, they should be driven into the river. Accordingly the Khalifa had only watched the advance of the Expeditionary Force from Wad Hamed with a patrol of cavalry about 200 strong. On the 30th he was informed that the enemy drew near, and on the 31st he assembled his bodyguard and regular army, with the exception of the men needed for the river batteries, on the Omdurman parade ground. The next day all the male population of the city were compelled to join the army in the field, and only the gunners and garrisons on the river-face remained within. In spite, however, of his utmost vigilance, nearly 6,000 men deserted during the nights of the 31st of August and the 1st of September. This and the detachments in the forts reduced the force actually engaged in the battle to 52,000 men. The host that now advanced towards the British and Egyptian cavalry was perhaps 4,000 stronger.

Their array was regular and precise, and, facing north-east, stretched for more than four miles from flank to flank. A strong detachment of the *mulazemin* or guard was extended in front of the centre. Ali-Wad-Helu, with his bright green flag, prolonged the line to the left; and his 5,000 warriors, chiefly of the Degheim and Kenana tribes, soon began to reach out towards the Egyptian cavalry. The centre and main force of the army was composed of the regular troops, formed in squares under Osman Sheikh-ed-Din and Osman Azrak. This great body comprised 12,000 black riflemen and about 13,000 black and Arab spearmen. In their midst rose the large, dark green flag which the Sheikh-ed-Din had adopted to annoy Ali-Wad-Helu, of whose distinctive emblem he was inordinately jealous. The Khalifa with his own bodyguard, about 2,000 strong, followed the centre. In rear of all marched Yakub with the Black Flag and 13,000 men – nearly all swordsmen and spearmen, who with those extended in front of the army constituted the guard. The right wing was formed by the brigade of the Khalifa Sherif, consisting of 2,000 Danagla tribesmen, whose principal ensign was a broad red flag. Osman Digna, with about 1,700 Hadendoa, guarded the extreme right and the flank nearest Omdurman, and his fame needed no flag. Such was the great army which now moved swiftly towards the watching squadrons; and these, pausing on the sandy ridge, pushed out a fringe of tentative patrols, as if to assure themselves that what they saw was real.

The Egyptian cavalry had meanwhile a somewhat different view of the spectacle. Working on the right of the 21st Lancers, and keeping further from the river, the leading squadrons had reached the extreme western end of the Kerreri ridge at about seven o'clock. From here the Mahdi's Tomb was visible, and, since the rocks of Surgham did not obstruct the view from this point, the British officers, looking through their field-glasses, saw what appeared to be a long column of brown spots moving south-westwards across the wide plain which stretches away to the west of Omdurman. The telescope, an invaluable aid to reconnaissance, developed the picture. The brown objects proved to be troops of horses grazing; and beyond, to the southward, camels and white flapping tents could be distinguished. There were no signs that a retreat was in progress; but from such a distance – nearly four miles – no certain information could be obtained. Colonel Broadwood accordingly led his whole command south-westward towards a round-topped hill which rose about four miles from the end of the Kerreri ridge and was one of the more distant hill features bounding the plain on the western side. The Egyptian cavalry moved slowly across the desert to this new point of observation, and at half past eleven began to climb the lower slopes of the round-topped hill. Here the whole scene burst suddenly upon them. Scarcely three miles away the Dervish Army was advancing with the regularity of parade. The south wind carried the martial sound of horns and drums and – far more menacing – the deep murmur of a multitude to the astonished officers. Like the 21st Lancers – three miles away to their left, at the end of the long sandy ridge which runs westward from Surgham – the soldiers remained for a space spell-bound. But all eyes were soon drawn from the thrilling spectacle of the Dervish advance by the sound of guns on the river.

At about eleven o'clock the gunboats had ascended the Nile, and now engaged the enemy's batteries on both banks. Throughout the day the loud reports of their guns could be heard, and, looking from our position on the ridge, we could see the white vessels steaming slowly forward against the current, under clouds of black smoke from their furnaces and amid other clouds of white smoke from the artillery. The forts, which mounted nearly fifty guns, replied vigorously; but the British aim was accurate and their fire crushing. Despite the tenacity and courage of the Dervish gunners, they were driven from their defences and took refuge among the streets of the city. The great wall of Omdurman was breached in many places, and a large number of unfortunate non-combatants were killed and wounded.

Meanwhile the Arab irregulars, under Major Wortley, had been sharply engaged. That officer's orders were to co-operate with the flotilla by taking in rear the forts and fortified villages on the east bank of the river. As soon as the gunboats had silenced the lower forts, Major Wortley ordered the irregulars to advance on them and on the houses. He placed the Jaalin, who were prac- tically the only trustworthy men in his force, in reserve, and formed the tribes according to their capabilities and prejudices. On the order to attack being given, the whole force, some 3,000 strong, advanced on the buildings, from which the Dervishes at once opened fire. Arrived within 500 yards they halted, and began to discharge their rifles in the air; they also indulged in frantic dances expressive of their fury and valour, but declined to advance any further.

Major Wortley then ordered the Jaalin to attack. These – formed in a long column, animated by the desire for vengeance, and being besides brave men – moved upon the village at a slow pace, and, surrounding one house after another, captured it and slew all its defenders, including the Dervish Emir and 350 of his followers. The Jaalin themselves suffered a loss of about sixty killed and wounded.

The village being captured, and the enemy on the east bank killed or dispersed, the gunboats proceeded to engage the batteries higher up the river. The howitzer battery was now landed, and at 1.30 began to bombard the Mahdi's Tomb. This part of the proceedings was plainly visible to us, waiting and watching on the ridge, and its interest even distracted attention from the Dervish Army. The dome of the tomb rose tall and prominent above the mud houses of the city. A lyddite shell burst over it – a great flash, a white ball of smoke, and, after a pause, the dull thud of the distant explosion. Another followed. At the third shot, instead of the white smoke, there was a prodigious cloud of red dust, in which the whole tomb disappeared. When this cleared away we saw that, instead of being pointed, it was now flat-topped. Other shells continued to strike it with like effect, some breaking holes in the dome, others smashing off the cupolas, all enveloping it in dust.

All this time the Dervishes were coming nearer, and the steady and continuous advance of the great army compelled the Egyptian cavalry to mount their horses and trot off to some safer point of view. Colonel Broadwood conceived his direct line of retreat to camp threatened, and shortly after one o'clock he began a regular retirement. The Dervish horsemen contented themselves with firing occasional shots, and the boggy ground of the Khor Shambat was recrossed in safety.

THE BATTLE OF OMDURMAN—THE FIRST ATTACK

When the Arab horsemen saw all the cavalry retiring they became very bold, and numerous small groups of fives and sixes began to draw nearer at a trot. Accordingly, whenever the ground was favourable, the squadrons halted in turn for a few minutes to fire on them. In this way perhaps half a dozen were killed or wounded. The great army, however, still advanced majestically, pressing the cavalry back before it; and it was evident that if the Khalifa's movement continued, in spite of it being nearly one o'clock, there would be a collision between the main forces before the night.

The British and Egyptian Army had been ordered to stand to arms at two o'clock in formation to resist the attack which it seemed the Dervishes were about to deliver. But at a quarter to two the Dervish Army halted. Their drill was excellent, and they all stopped as by a single command. Then suddenly their riflemen discharged their rifles in the air with a great roar – a barbaric *feu de joie*. The smoke sprang up along the whole front of their array, running from one end to the other. After this they lay down on the ground, and it became certain that the matter would not be settled that day. We remained in our position among the sandhills of the ridge until the approach of darkness. As the light failed, we returned to the river to water and encamp, passing into the *zeriba* through the ranks of the British division, where officers and men, looking out steadfastly over the fading plain, asked us whether the enemy were coming – and, if so, when.

When the gunboats had completed their bombardment, had sunk a Dervish steamer, had silenced all the hostile batteries, and had sorely battered the Mahdi's Tomb, they returned leisurely to the camp, and lay moored close to the bank to lend the assistance of their guns in case of attack. As the darkness became complete they threw their powerful searchlights over the front of the *zeriba* and on to the distant hills. The wheeling beams of dazzling light swept across the desolate, yet not deserted, plain. The Dervish Army lay for the night along the eastern slope of the Shambat depression. All the 50,000 faithful warriors rested in their companies near the flags of their Emirs. The Khalifa slept in rear of the centre of his host, surrounded by his generals. Suddenly the whole scene was lit by a pale glare. Abdullah and the chiefs sprang up. Everything around them was bathed in an awful white illumination. Far away by the river there gleamed a brilliant circle of light – the cold, pitiless eye of a demon. The Khalifa put his hand on Osman Azrak's shoulder – Osman, who was to lead the frontal attack at dawn – and whispered, 'What is this strange thing?' 'Sire,' replied Osman, 'they are looking at us.' Thereat a great fear filled all their minds. The Khalifa had a small tent, which showed conspicuously in the searchlight. He had it hurriedly pulled down. Some of the Emirs covered their faces, lest the baleful rays should blind them. All feared that some terrible projectile would follow in the path of the light. And then suddenly it passed on – for the sapper who worked the lens could see nothing at that distance but the brown plain – and swept along the ranks of the sleeping army, rousing up the startled warriors, as a wind sweeps over a field of standing corn.

The moonlit camp, with its anxious generals, its weary soldiers, its fearful machinery of destruction, all strewn along the bank of the great river, remained plunged in silence, as if brooding over the chances of the morrow and the failures of the past. And hardly four miles away another army – twice as numerous, equally confident, equally brave – were waiting impatiently for the morning and the final settlement of the long quarrel.

CHAPTER 14

THE BATTLE OF OMDURMAN
2nd September 1898

The bugles all over the camp by the river began to sound at half-past four. Then it grew gradually lighter, and cavalry mounted their horses, the infantry stood to their arms, and the gunners went to their batteries; while the sun, rising over the Nile, revealed the wide plain, the dark rocky hills, and the waiting army.

Even before it became light several squadrons of British and Egyptian cavalry were pushed swiftly forward to gain contact with the enemy and learn his intentions. The first of these, under Captain Baring, occupied Surgham Hill, and waited in the gloom until the whereabouts of the Dervishes should be disclosed by the dawn. It was a perilous undertaking, for he might have found them unexpectedly near. As the sun rose, the 21st Lancers trotted out of the *zeriba* and threw out a spray of officers' patrols. As there had been no night attack, it was expected that the Dervish Army would have retired to their original position or entered the town. It was hardly conceivable that they would advance across the open ground to attack the *zeriba* by daylight. But these anticipations were immediately dispelled by the scene which was visible from the crest of the ridge.

It was a quarter to six. The light was dim, but growing stronger every minute. There in the plain lay the enemy, their numbers unaltered, their confidence and intentions apparently unshaken. Their front was now nearly five miles long, and composed of great masses of men joined together by thinner lines. Behind and near to the flanks were large reserves. From the ridge

191

they looked dark blurs and streaks, relieved and diversified with an odd-looking shimmer of light from the spear-points. At about ten minutes to six it was evident that the masses were in motion and advancing swiftly. Their Emirs galloped about and before their ranks. Scouts and patrols scattered themselves all over the front. Then they began to cheer. They were still a mile away from the hill, and were concealed from the Sirdar's army by the folds of the ground. The noise of the shouting was heard, albeit faintly, by the troops down by the river. But to those watching on the hill a tremendous roar came up in waves of intense sound, like the tumult of the rising wind and sea before a storm.

The British and Egyptian forces were arranged in line, with their back to the river. The flanks were secured by the gunboats lying moored in the stream. Before them was the rolling sandy plain, looking from the slight elevation of the ridge smooth and flat as a table. To the right rose the rocky hills of the Kerreri position, near which the Egyptian cavalry were drawn up – a dark solid mass of men and horses. On the left the 21st Lancers, with a single squadron thrown out in advance, were halted watching their patrols, who climbed about Surgham Hill, stretched forward beyond it, or perched, as we did, on the ridge.

Although the Dervishes were steadily advancing, a belief that their musketry was inferior encouraged a nearer view, and we trotted round the south-west slopes of Surgham Hill until we reached the sandhills on the enemy's side, among which the regiment had waited the day before. Thence the whole array was visible in minute detail. It seemed that every single man of all the thousands could be examined separately. The pace of their march was fast and steady, and it was evident that it would not be safe to wait long among the sandhills. Yet the wonder of the scene exercised a dangerous fascination, and for a while we tarried.

The emblems of the more famous Emirs were easily distinguishable. On the extreme left the chiefs and soldiers of the bright green flag gathered under Ali-Wad-Helu; between this and the centre the large dark green flag of Osman Sheikh-ed-Din rose above a dense mass of spearmen, preceded by long lines of warriors armed presumably with rifles; over the centre, commanded by Yakub, the sacred black banner of the Khalifa floated high and remarkable; while on the right a great square of Dervishes was arrayed under an extraordinary number of white flags, amid which the red ensign of Sherif was almost hidden. All the pride and might of the Dervish Empire were massed on this last great day of its existence. Riflemen who had helped to destroy Hicks, spearmen who had charged at Abu Klea, Emirs who saw the sack of Gondar, Baggara fresh from raiding the Shillooks, warriors who had besieged Khartoum – all marched, inspired by the memories of former triumphs and embittered by the knowledge of late defeats, to chastise the impudent and accursed invaders.

The advance continued. The Dervish left began to stretch out across the plain towards Kerreri – as I thought, to turn our right flank. Their centre, under the Black Flag, moved directly towards Surgham. The right pursued a line of advance south of that hill. This mass of men were the most striking of all. They could not have mustered fewer than 6,000. Their array was perfect. They displayed a great number of flags – perhaps 500 – which looked at the distance white, though they were really covered with texts from the Koran, and which by their admirable alignment made this division of the Khalifa's army look like the old representations of the Crusaders in the Bayeux tapestry.

If there was one arm in which the Arabs were beyond all comparison inferior to their adversaries, it was in guns. Yet it was with this arm that they opened their attack. In the middle of the Dervish line now marching in frontal assault were two puffs of smoke. About fifty yards short of the thorn fence two red clouds of sand and dust sprang up, where the projectiles had struck. It looked like a challenge. It was immediately answered. Great clouds of smoke appeared all along the front of the British and Soudanese brigades. One after another four batteries opened on the enemy at a range of about 3,000 yards. The sound of the cannonade rolled up to us on the ridge, and was re-echoed by the hills. Above the heads of the moving masses shells began to burst, dotting the air with smoke-balls and the ground with bodies. But a nearer tragedy impended. The 'White Flags' were nearly over the crest. In another minute they would become visible to the batteries. Did they realise what would come to meet them? They were in a dense mass, 2,800 yards from the 32nd Field Battery and the gun-boats. The ranges were known. It was a matter of machinery. The more distant slaughter passed unnoticed, as the mind was fasci-nated by the approaching horror. In a few seconds swift destruction would rush on these brave men. They topped the crest and drew out into full view of the whole army. Their white ban-ners made them conspicuous above all. As they saw the camp of their enemies, they discharged their rifles with a great roar of musketry and quickened their pace. For a moment the white flags advanced in regular order, and the whole division crossed the crest and were exposed. Forthwith the gunboats, the 32nd British Field Battery, and other guns from the *zeriba* opened on them. About twenty shells struck them in the first minute. Some burst high in the air, others exactly in their faces. Others, again, plunged into the sand and, exploding, dashed clouds of red dust, splinters, and bullets amid their ranks. The white banners toppled over in all directions. Yet they rose again immediately, as other men pressed forward to die for the Mahdi's sacred cause and in the defence of the successor of the True Prophet. It was a terrible sight, for as yet they had not hurt us at all, and it seemed an unfair advantage to strike thus cruelly when they could not reply. Under the influence of the shells the mass of the 'White Flags' dissolved into thin lines of spearmen and skirmishers, and came on in altered formation and diminished numbers, but with unabated enthusiasm. And now, the whole attack being thoroughly exposed, it became the duty of the cavalry to clear the front as quickly as possible, and leave the further conduct of the debate to the infantry and the

Maxim guns. All the patrols trotted or cantered back to their squadrons, and the regiment retired swiftly into the *zeriba*, while the shells from the gunboats screamed overhead and the whole length of the position began to burst into flame and smoke.

The tumult grew louder and more intense, until even the flickering stutter of the Maxims could scarcely be heard above the continuous din. Eighty yards away, and perhaps twenty feet above us, the 32nd Field Battery was in action. The officers, some standing on biscuit-boxes, peered through their glasses and studied the effect. Of this I had one glimpse. Eight hundred yards away a ragged line of men were coming on desperately, struggling forward in the face of the pitiless fire – white banners tossing and collapsing; white figures subsiding in dozens to the ground; little white puffs from their rifles, larger white puffs spreading in a row all along their front from the bursting shrapnel.

The infantry fired steadily and stolidly, without hurry or excitement, for the enemy were far away and the officers careful. Besides, the soldiers were interested in the work and took great pains. But presently the mere physical act became tedious. The tiny figures seen over the slide of the back-sight seemed a little larger, but also fewer at each successive volley. The rifles grew hot – so hot that they had to be changed for those of the reserve companies. And all the time out on the plain on the other side bullets were shearing through flesh, smashing and splintering bone; valiant men were struggling on through a hell of whistling metal, exploding shells, and spurting dust – suffering, despairing, dying. Such was the first phase of the Battle of Omdurman.

The Khalifa's plan of attack appears to have been complex and ingenious. It was, however, based on an extraordinary miscalculation of the power of modern weapons. He first ordered about 15,000 men, drawn chiefly from the army of Osman Sheikh-ed-Din and placed under the command of Osman Azrak, to deliver a frontal attack. He himself waited with an equal force near Surgham Hill to watch the result. If it succeeded, he would move forward with his bodyguard, the flower of the Arab Army, and complete the victory. If it failed, there was yet another chance. The Dervishes who were first launched against the *zeriba* were not by any means his best or most reliable troops. Their destruction might be a heavy loss, but it would not end the struggle. While the attack was proceeding, the valiant left, consisting of the rest of the army of Osman Sheikh-ed-Din, might move unnoticed to the northern flank and curve round on to the front of the *zeriba* held by the Egyptian brigade. Ali-Wad-Helu was meanwhile to march to the Kerreri Hills, and remain out of range and, if possible, out of sight among them. Should the frontal and flank attacks be unhappily repulsed, the 'enemies of God', exulting in their easy victory, would leave their strong place and march to the capture of the city. Then, while they were yet dispersed on the plain, with no *zeriba* to protect them, the chosen warriors of the True Religion would abandon all concealment, and hasten in their thousands to the utter destruction of the accursed – the Khalifa with 15,000 falling upon them from behind Surgham; Ali-Wad-Helu and all that remained of Osman's army assailing them from Kerreri. Attacked at once from the north and south, and encompassed on every side, the infidels would abandon hope and order, and Kitchener might share the fate of Hicks and Gordon. Two circumstances prevented the accomplishment of this plan. The second attack was not executed simultaneously by the two divisions of the Dervish Army; and even had it been, the power of the musketry would have triumphed, and though the Expeditionary Force might have sustained heavier losses the main result could not have been affected. The last hopes of barbarism had passed with the shades of night.

Colonel Broadwood, with nine squadrons of cavalry, the Camel Corps, and the Horse Artillery, had been ordered to check the Dervish left, and prevent it enveloping the down-stream flank of the *zeriba*, as this was held by the Egyptian brigade, which it was not thought desirable to expose to the full weight of an attack.

With this object he had occupied the Kerreri ridge with the Horse battery and the Camel Corps, holding his cavalry in reserve in rear of the centre.

The Kerreri ridge, to which reference has so frequently been made, consists of two main features, which rise to the height of about 300 feet above the plain, are each above a mile long, and run nearly east and west, with a dip or trough about 1,000 yards wide between them. The eastern ends of these main ridges are perhaps 1,000 yards from the river, and in this intervening space there are several rocky under-features and knolls. The Kerreri Hills, the spaces between them, and the smaller features are covered with rough boulders and angular stones of volcanic origin, which render the movements of horses and camels difficult and painful.

The cavalry horses and camels were in the dip between the two ridges; and the dismounted men of the Camel Corps were deployed along the crest of the most southerly of the ridges, with their right at the desert end. Next in order to the Camel Corps, the centre of the ridge was occupied by the dismounted cavalry. The Horse Artillery were on the left. The remainder of the cavalry waited in the hollow behind the guns.

The tempestuous advance of Osman soon brought him into contact with the mounted force. His real intentions are still a matter of conjecture. Whether he had been ordered to attack the Egyptian brigade, or to drive back the cavalry, or to disappear behind the Kerreri Hills in conformity with Ali-Wad-Helu, is impossible to pronounce. His action was, however, clear. He could not safely assail the Egyptians with a powerful cavalry force threatening his left rear. He therefore continued his move across the front of the *zeriba*. Keeping out of the range of infantry fire, bringing up his right, and marching along due north, he fell upon Broadwood. This officer, who had expected to have to deal with small bodies on the Dervish flank, found himself suddenly exposed to the attack of nearly 15,000 men, many of whom were riflemen. The

Sirdar, seeing the situation from the *zeriba*, sent him an order to withdraw within the lines of infantry. Colonel Broadwood, however, preferred to retire through the Kerreri Hills to the northward, drawing Osman after him. He replied to that effect.

The Dervishes, advancing in a north-easterly direction, attacked the Kerreri Hills obliquely. They immediately enveloped the right flank of the mounted troops holding them. As soon as the Dervish riflemen gained a point west and in prolongation of the trough between the two ridges, they not only turned the right flank, but also threatened the retreat of the defenders of the southerly ridge; for they were able to sweep the trough from end to end with their fire. As soon as it became certain that the southerly ridge could not be held any longer, Colonel Broadwood retired the battery to the east end of the second or northern ridge. This was scarcely accomplished when the dip was enfiladed, and the cavalry and Camel Corps who followed lost about fifty men and many horses and camels killed and wounded. It was now painfully evident that in rocky ground the Dervishes could go faster on their feet than the soldiers on their camels. Pressing on impetuously at a pace of nearly seven miles an hour, and unchecked by artillery fire from the *zeriba* and from the Horse battery, the Arabs rapidly diminished the distance between themselves and their enemies. In these circumstances Colonel Broadwood decided to send the Camel Corps back to the *zeriba* under cover of a gunboat, which, observing the progress of the fight, was coming down stream to assist. The distance which divided the combatants was scarcely 400 yards and decreasing every minute. The cavalry were drawn up across the eastern or river end of the trough. The guns of the Horse battery fired steadily from their new position on the northern ridge. But the Camel Corps were still struggling in the broken ground, and it was clear that their position was one of great peril. The Dervishes already carpeted the rocks of the southern ridge with dull yellow swarms, and, heedless of the shells which still assailed them in reverse from the *zeriba*, continued to push their attack home. On the very instant that they saw the Camel Corps make for the river they realised that those they had deemed their prey were trying, like a hunted animal, to run to ground within the lines of infantry. With that instinctive knowledge of war which is the heritage of savage peoples, the whole attack swung to the right, changed direction from north to east and rushed down the trough and along the southern ridge towards the Nile, with the plain intention of cutting off the Camel Corps and driving them into the river.

The moment was critical. It appeared to the cavalry commander that the Dervishes would actually succeed, and their success must involve the total destruction of the Camel Corps. The whole nine squadrons of cavalry assumed a preparatory formation. The British officers believed that a terrible charge impended. They would meet in direct collision the swarms of men who were hurrying down the trough. The diversion might enable the Camel Corps to escape. But the ground was bad; the enemy's force was overwhelming; the Egyptian troopers were prepared to obey – but that was all. There was no exalted enthusiasm such as at these moments carries sterner breeds to victory. Nevertheless, the operation appeared inevitable. The Camel Corps were already close to the river. But thousands of Dervishes were running swiftly towards them at right angles to their line of retreat, and their only hope lay in maintaining themselves by their fire near the river-bank until help could reach them, and, in order to delay and weaken the Dervish attack the cavalry would have to make a desperate charge.

But at the critical moment the gunboat arrived on the scene and began suddenly to blaze and flame from Maxim guns, quick-firing guns and rifles. The range was short; the effect tremendous. The terrible machine floating gracefully on the waters – a beautiful white devil – wreathed itself in smoke. The river slopes of the Kerreri Hills, crowded with the advancing thousands, sprang up into clouds of dust and splinters of rock. The charging Dervishes sank down in tangled heaps. The masses in rear paused, irresolute. The approach of another gunboat completed their discomfiture. The Camel Corps, hurrying along the shore, slipped past the fatal point of interception, and saw safety and the *zeriba* before them.

Exasperated by their disappointment, the soldiers of Osman Sheik-ed-Din turned again upon the cavalry, and, forgetting in their anger the mobile nature of their foe, pursued the elusive squadrons three long miles to the north. The cavalry, intensely relieved by the escape of the Camel Corps, played with their powerful antagonist, as the banderillo teases the bull. Colonel Broadwood thus succeeded in luring this division of the Dervish Army far away from the field of battle where they were sorely needed.

Both gunboats, having watched the Camel Corps safely into the *zeriba,* now returned with the current and renewed their attack upon the Arabs. Opening a heavy and accurate fire upon the river flank, they drove them westward and away from the Nile. Through the gap thus opened Broadwood and his squadrons trotted to rejoin the main body.

While these things were passing on the northern flank, the frontal attack was in progress. The debris of the 'White Flags' joined the centre and the whole 14,000 pressed forward against the *zeriba*, spreading out by degrees and abandoning their dense formations, and gradually slowing down. At about 800 yards from the British division the advance ceased and they could make no headway. Opposite the Soudanese who were armed only with the Martini-Henry rifle, the assailants came within 300 yards and one brave old man, carrying a flag, fell at 150 paces from the shelter trench. But the attack was shattered. The leader, clad in his new *jibba* of many colours rode on steadfastly towards the inexorable firing line, until, pierced by several bullets, he fell lifeless. Such was the end of that stubborn warrior of many fights – wicked Osman Azrak, faithful unto death. The surviving Dervishes lay down on the ground. Unable to advance, they were unwilling to retire; and

British Commanders | 1 Lewis 2 MacDonald 3 Maxwell 4 Wauchope 5 Lyttelton 6 Collinson & Transport 7 21ST Lancers
▷ SIRDAR

A & B (Green Flags) (later)

A (Light Green Flag)

Um Matragan

Kerreri Hills

B (Dark Green Flag)

Kerreri

Broadwood Returning

Gunboats

Broadwood

N

The Khalifa's Attack: 9.40 a.m.

E (Black Flag)

D

The Frontal Attack 6.45 a.m.

C

2

1

British Counter-Attack

2
3
4
5 7
6

Gunboats

NILE

D & E (Black Flag)

J. Surgham

White Flags

Ibraham Khalil retreating

To Omdurman

A Ali Wad Helu B Osman Sheikh C Osman Azrak
D Khalifa E Yakub

0   Mile   1

THE BATTLE OF OMDURMAN – THE KHALIFA'S ATTACK

their riflemen, taking advantage of the folds of the plain, opened and maintained an unequal combat. By eight o'clock it was evident that the whole attack had failed.

The Sirdar and his generals were all agreed on one point. They must occupy Omdurman before the Dervish Army could get back there. They could fight as many Dervishes as cared to come in the plain; among the houses it was different. The Arabs were out in the desert. A great part of their army was even as far away as Kerreri. The troops could move on interior lines. They were bound to reach Omdurman first. The order was therefore given to march on the city at once. But first the Surgham ridge must be reconnoitred, and the ground between the *zeriba* and Omdurman cleared of the Dervishes – with infantry if necessary, but with cavalry if possible, because that would be quicker. The 21st Lancers were again called upon to act.

As the fusillade slackened, the Lancers stood to their horses. Then General Gatacre, with Captain Brooke and the rest of his Staff, came galloping along the rear of the line of infantry and guns, and shouted for Colonel Martin. There was a brief conversation, an order, and we were all scrambling into our saddles and straightening the ranks in high expectation. We started at a trot, two or three patrols galloping out in front, towards the high ground, while the regiment followed in mass – a great square block of ungainly brown figures and little horses, hung all over with water-bottles, saddle-bags, picketing-gear; the polish of peace gone; but still a regiment of light cavalry in active operation against the enemy.

The crest of the ridge was only half a mile away. It was found unoccupied. The rocky mass of Surgham obstructed the view and concealed the great reserve collected around the Black Flag. But southward, between us and Omdurman, the whole plain was exposed. It was infested with small parties of Dervishes, moving about, mounted and on foot, in tens and twenties. Three miles away a broad stream of fugitives, of wounded, and of deserters flowed from the Khalifa's army to the city. The sight was sufficient to excite the fiercest instincts of cavalry. Only the scattered parties in the plain appeared to prevent a glorious pursuit. The signalling officer was set to heliograph back to the Sirdar that the ridge was unoccupied and that several thousand Dervishes could be seen flying into Omdurman. Pending the answer, we waited; and looking back northwards, across the front of the *zeriba*, where the first attack had been stopped, perceived a greyish-white smudge, perhaps a mile long. The glass disclosed details – hundreds of tiny white figures heaped or scattered; dozens hopping, crawling, staggering away; a few horses standing stolidly among the corpses; a few unwounded men dragging off their comrades. Then the heliograph in the *zeriba* began to talk in flashes of light that opened and shut capriciously. The actual order is important. 'Advance', said the helio, 'and clear the left flank, and use every effort to prevent the enemy re-entering Omdurman.' That was all, but it was sufficient. In the distance the enemy could be seen re-entering Omdurman in hundreds. They must be stopped, and incidentally these small parties in the plain might be brushed away. We remounted; the ground looked smooth and unbroken; yet it was desirable to reconnoitre. Two patrols were sent out. The first struck out towards Omdurman, and began to push in between the scattered Dervishes, who fired their rifles and showed great excitement. The other patrol, under Lieutenant Grenfell, were sent to see what the ground looked like from further along the ridge and on the lower slopes of Surgham. They, too, had had good fortune in their adventurous ride. They reported that in a shallow and apparently practicable *khor* about three-quarters of a mile to the south-west, and between the regiment and the fugitives, there was drawn up a formed body of Dervishes about 1,000 strong. Colonel Martin decided on this information to advance and attack this force, which alone interposed between him and the Arab line of retreat. Then we started.

But all this time the enemy had been busy. At the beginning

of the battle the Khalifa had posted a small force of 700 men on his extreme right, to prevent his line of retreat to Omdurman being harassed. This detachment was composed entirely of the Hadendoa tribesmen of Osman Digna's flag, and was commanded by one of his subordinate Emirs, who selected a suitable position in the shallow *khor*. As soon as the 21st Lancers left the *zeriba* the Dervish scouts on the top of Surgham carried the news to the Khalifa. It was said that the English cavalry were coming to cut him off from Omdurman. Abdullah thereupon determined to strengthen his extreme right; and he immediately ordered four regiments, each 500 strong, drawn from the force around the Black Flag and under the Emir Ibrahim Khalil, to reinforce the Hadendoa in the *khor*. While we were waiting for orders on the ridge these men were hurrying southwards along the depression, and concealed by a spur of Surgham Hill. The Lancer patrol reconnoitred the *khor*, at the imminent risk of their lives, while it was only occupied by the original 700 Hadendoa. Galloping back, they reported that it was held by about 1,000 men. Before they reached the regiment this number was increased to 2,700. This, however, we had no means of knowing. The Khalifa, having despatched his reinforcement, rode on his donkey with a scanty escort nearly half a mile from the Black Flag towards the *khor*, in order to watch the event, and in consequence he was within 500 yards of the scene.

We advanced at a walk in mass for about 300 yards. The scattered parties of Dervishes fell back and melted away, and only one straggling line of men in dark blue waited motionless a quarter of a mile to the left front. They were scarcely a hundred strong. The regiment formed into line of squadron columns, and continued at a walk until within 300 yards of this small body of Dervishes. There was complete silence, intensified by the recent tumult. Far beyond the thin blue row of Dervishes the fugitives were visible streaming into Omdurman. And should these few devoted men impede a regiment? Yet it were wiser to examine their position from the other flank before slipping a squadron at them. The heads of the squadrons wheeled slowly to the left, and the Lancers, breaking into a trot, began to cross the Dervish front in column of troops. Thereupon and with one accord the blue-clad men dropped on their knees, and there burst out a loud crackling fire of musketry. It was hardly possible to miss such a target at such a range. Horses and men fell at once. The only course was plain and welcome to all. The Colonel, nearer than his regiment, already saw what lay behind the skirmishers. He ordered 'Right wheel into line' to be sounded. The trumpet jerked out a shrill note, heard faintly above the trampling of the horses and the noise of the rifles. On the instant all the sixteen troops swung round and locked up into a long galloping line, and the 21st Lancers were committed to their first charge in war.

Two hundred and fifty yards away the dark-blue men were firing madly in a thin film of light-blue smoke. Their bullets struck the hard gravel into the air, and the troopers, to shield their faces from the stinging dust, bowed their helmets forward, like the Cuirassiers at Waterloo. The pace was fast and the distance short. Yet, before it was half covered, the whole aspect of the affair changed. A deep crease in the ground – a dry watercourse, a *khor* – appeared where all had seemed smooth, level plain; and from it there sprang, with the suddenness of a pantomime effect and a high-pitched yell, a dense white mass of men nearly as long as our front and about twelve deep. A score of horsemen and a dozen bright flags rose as if by magic from the earth. Eager warriors sprang forward to anticipate the shock. The rest stood firm to meet it. The Lancers acknowledged the apparition only by an increase of pace. Each man wanted sufficient momentum to drive through such a solid line. The flank troops, seeing that they over-lapped, curved inwards like the horns of a moon. But the whole event was a matter of seconds. The riflemen, firing bravely to the last, were swept head over heels into the *khor*, and jumping down with them, at full gallop and in the closest order, the British squadrons struck the fierce brigade with one loud furious shout.

The collision was prodigious. Nearly thirty Lancers, men and horses, and at least two hundred Arabs were overthrown. The shock was stunning to both sides, and for perhaps ten wonderful seconds no man heeded his enemy. Terrified horses wedged in the crowd, bruised and shaken men, sprawling in heaps, struggled, dazed and stupid, to their feet, panted, and looked about them. Several fallen Lancers had even time to remount. Meanwhile the impetus of the cavalry carried them on.

Stubborn and unshaken infantry hardly ever meet stubborn and unshaken cavalry. Either the infantry run away and are cut down in flight, or they keep their heads and destroy nearly all the horsemen by their musketry. On this occasion two living walls had actually crashed together. The Dervishes fought manfully. They tried to hamstring the horses. They fired their rifles, pressing the muzzles into the very bodies of their opponents. They cut reins and stirrup-leathers. They flung their throwing-spears with great dexterity. They tried every device of cool, determined men prac-tised in war and familiar with cavalry; and, besides, they swung sharp, heavy swords which bit deep. The hand-to-hand fighting on the further side of the *khor* lasted for perhaps one minute. Then the horses got into their stride again, the pace increased, and the Lancers drew out from among their antagonists. Within two minutes of the collision every living man was clear of the Dervish mass. All who had fallen were cut at with swords till they stopped quivering.

Two hundred yards away the regiment halted, rallied, faced about, and in less than five minutes were re-formed and ready for a second charge. The men were anxious to cut their way back through their enemies. We were alone together – the cavalry regiment and the Dervish brigade. The ridge hung like a curtain between us and the army. The general battle was forgotten, as it was unseen. This was a private quarrel. The other might have been a massacre; but here the fight was fair, for we too fought with sword and spear. Indeed the advantage of ground and numbers lay with them. All prepared to settle the debate at once and for ever. But some realisation of the cost of our wild ride began to come to those who were responsible. Riderless horses galloped across the plain. Men, clinging to their saddles, lurched helplessly about, covered with blood from perhaps a dozen wounds. Horses, streaming from tremendous gashes, limped and staggered with their riders. In 120 seconds five officers, 65 men, and 119 horses out of fewer than 400 had been killed or wounded.

The Dervish line, broken by the charge, began to re-form at once. They closed up, shook themselves together, and prepared with constancy and courage for another shock. But on military considerations it was desirable to turn them out of the *khor* first and thus deprive them of their vantage-ground. The regiment again drawn up, three squadrons in line and the fourth in column, now wheeled to the right, and, galloping round the Dervish flank, dismounted and opened a heavy fire with their magazine carbines. Under the pressure of this fire the enemy changed front to meet the new attack, so that both sides were formed at right angles to their original lines. When the Dervish change of front was completed, they began to advance against the dismounted men. But the fire was accurate, and there can be little doubt that the moral effect of the charge had been very great, and that these brave enemies were no longer unshaken. Be this as it may, the fact remains that they retreated swiftly, though in good order, towards the ridge of Surgham Hill, where the Khalifa's Black Flag still waved, and the 21st Lancers remained in possession of the ground – and of their dead.

Such is the true and literal account of the charge. An officer was despatched with the news to the Sirdar, and on the instant both cannonade and fusillade broke out again behind the ridge, and grew in a crashing crescendo until the whole landscape seemed to vibrate with the sound of explosions. The second phase of the battle had begun.

Even before the 21st Lancers had reconnoitred Surgham

ridge, the Sirdar had set his brigades in motion towards Omdurman. He was determined, even at a very great risk, to occupy the city before the army in the plain could return to defend it. The advantage might be tremendous. Nevertheless the movement was premature. The Khalifa still remained undefeated west of Surgham Hill; Ali-Wad-Helu lurked behind Kerreri; Osman was rapidly re-forming. There were still at least 35,000 men on the field. Nor, as the event proved, was it possible to enter Omdurman until they had been beaten.

As soon as the infantry had replenished their ammunition, they wheeled to the left in echelon of brigades, and began to march towards Surgham ridge. The movements of a great force are slow. It was not desirable that the British division, which led the echelon, should remain in the low ground north of Surgham – where they were commanded, had no field of fire, and could see nothing – and accordingly both these brigades moved forward almost together to occupy the crest of the ridge. Thus two steps of the ladder were run into one, and Maxwell's brigade, which followed Wauchope's, was 600 yards further south than it would have been had the regular echelon been observed. In the *zeriba* MacDonald had been next to Maxwell. But a very significant change in the order was now made. General Hunter evidently conceived the rear of the echelon threatened from the direction of Kerreri. Had the earth swallowed all the thousands who had moved across the plain towards the hills? At any rate, he would have his best brigade and his most experienced general in the post of possible danger. He therefore ordered Lewis's brigade to follow Maxwell, and left MacDonald last of all, strengthening him with three batteries of artillery and eight Maxim guns. Collinson marched with the transport. MacDonald moved out westward into the desert to take his place in the echelon, and also to allow Lewis to pass him as ordered. Lewis hurried on after Maxwell, and, taking his distance from him, was thus also 600 yards further south than the regular echelon admitted. The step which had been absorbed when both British brigades moved off – advisedly – together, caused a double gap between MacDonald and the rest of the army. And this distance was further increased by the fact that while he was moving west, to assume his place in correct echelon, the other five brigades were drawing off to the southward. Hence MacDonald's isolation.

At 9.15 the whole army was marching south in echelon, with the rear brigade at rather more than double distance. Collinson had already started with the transport, but the field hospitals still remained in the deserted *zeriba*, busily packing up. The medical staff had about 150 wounded on their hands. The Sirdar's orders had been that these were to be placed on the hospital barges, and that the field hospitals were to follow the transport. But the moving of wounded men is a painful and delicate affair, and by a stupid and grievous mistake the three regular hospital barges, duly prepared for the reception of the wounded, had been towed across to the right bank. It was necessary to use three ammunition barges, which, although in no way arranged for the reception of wounded, were luckily at hand. Meanwhile time was passing, and the doctors, who worked with devoted energy, became suddenly aware that, with the exception of a few detachments from the British division and three Egyptian companies, there were no troops within half a mile, and none between them and the dark Kerreri Hills. The two gunboats which could have guarded them from the river were down stream, helping the cavalry; MacDonald with the rear brigade was out in the plain; Collinson was hurrying along the bank with his transport. They were alone and unprotected. The army and the river together formed a huge V pointing south. The northern extremity – the gorge of the redan, as it were – gaped open towards Kerreri; and from Kerreri there now began to come, like the first warning drops before a storm of rain, small straggling parties of Dervish cavalry. The interior of the V was soon actually invaded by these predatory patrols, and one troop of perhaps a score of Baggara horse watered their ponies within 300 yards of the unprotected hospitals. Behind, in the distance, the banners of an army began to reappear. The situation was alarming. The wounded were bundled on to the barges, although, since there was no steamer to tow them, they were scarcely any safer when embarked. While some of the medical officers were thus busied, Colonel Sloggett galloped off, and, running the gauntlet of the Baggara horsemen, hurried to claim protection for the hospitals and their helpless occupants. In the midst of this excitement and confusion the wounded from the cavalry charge began to trickle in.

When the British division had moved out of the *zeriba*, a few skirmishers among the crags of Surgham Hill alone suggested the presence of an enemy. Each brigade, formed in four parallel columns of route, which closed in until they were scarcely forty paces apart, and both at deploying interval – the second brigade nearer the river, the first almost in line with it and on its right – hurried on, eager to see what lay beyond the ridge. All was quiet, except for a few 'sniping' shots from the top of Surgham. But gradually as Maxwell's brigade – the third in the echelon – approached the hill, these shots became more numerous, until the summit of the peak was spotted with smokepuffs. The British division moved on steadily, and, leaving these bold skirmishers to the Soudanese, soon reached the crest of the ridge. At once and for the first time the whole panorama of Omdurman – the brown and battered dome of the Mahdi's Tomb, the multitude of mud houses, the glittering fork of water which marked the confluence of the rivers – burst on their vision. For a moment they stared entranced. Then their attention was distracted; for trotting, galloping, or halting and gazing stupidly about them, terrified and bewildered, a dozen riderless troop-horses appeared over the further crest – for the ridge was flat-topped – coming from the plain, as yet invisible, below. It was the first news of the Lancers' charge. Details soon followed in the shape of the wounded, who in twos and threes began to make their way between the battalions, all

covered with blood and many displaying most terrible injuries –
faces cut to rags, bowels protruding, fishhook spears still stuck in
their bodies – realistic pictures from the darker side of war. Thus
absorbed, the soldiers hardly noticed the growing musketry fire
from the peak. But suddenly the bang of a field-gun set all eyes
looking backward. A battery had unlimbered in the plain between
the *zeriba* and the ridge, and was beginning to shell the summit of
the hill. The report of the guns seemed to be the signal for the
whole battle to reopen. From far away to the right rear there came
the sound of loud and continuous infantry firing, and immediately
Gatacre halted his division.

Almost before the British had topped the crest of the ridge,
before the battery had opened from the plain, while Colonel
Sloggett was still spurring across the dangerous ground between
the river and the army, the Sirdar knew that his enemy was again
upon him. Looking back from the slopes of Surgham, he saw that
MacDonald, instead of continuing his march in echelon, had halted
and deployed. The veteran brigadier had seen the Dervish formations on the ridge to the west of Surgham, realised that he was
about to be attacked, and, resolving to anticipate the enemy,
immediately brought his three batteries into action at 1,200 yards.
Five minutes later the whole of the Khalifa's reserve, 15,000
strong, led by Yakub with the Black Flag, the bodyguard and 'all
the glories' of the Dervish Empire, surged into view from behind
the hill and advanced on the solitary brigade with the vigour of
the first attack and thrice its chances of success. Thereupon Sir
Herbert Kitchener ordered Maxwell to change front to the right
and storm Surgham Hill. He sent Major Sandbach to tell Lewis to
conform and come into line on Maxwell's right. He galloped
himself to the British division – conveniently halted by General
Gatacre on the northern crest of the ridge – and ordered Lyttelton
with the 2nd Brigade to form facing west on Maxwell's left south
of Surgham, and Wauchope with the 1st Brigade to hurry back to
fill the wide gap between Lewis and MacDonald. Last of all he

sent an officer to Collinson and the Camel Corps with orders that they should swing round to their right rear and close the open part of the V. By these movements the army, instead of facing south in echelon, with its left on the river and its right in the desert, was made to face west in line, with its left in the desert and its right reaching back to the river. It had turned nearly a complete somersault.

In obedience to these orders Lyttelton's brigade brought up their left shoulders, deployed into line, and advanced west; Maxwell's Soudanese scrambled up the Surgham rocks, and, in spite of a sharp fire, cleared the peak with the bayonet and pressed on down the further side; Lewis began to come into action on Maxwell's right; MacDonald, against whom the Khalifa's attack was at first entirely directed, remained facing south-west, and was soon shrouded in the smoke of his own musketry and artillery fire. The three brigades which were now moving west and away from the Nile attacked the right flank of the Dervishes assailing MacDonald, and, compelling them to form front towards the river, undoubtedly took much of the weight of the attack off the isolated brigade. There remained the gap between Lewis and MacDonald. But Wauchope's brigade – still in four parallel columns of route – had shouldered completely round to the north, and was now doubling swiftly across the plain to fill the unguarded space. With the exception of Wauchope's brigade and of Collinson's Egyptians, the whole infantry and artillery force were at once furiously engaged.

The firing became again tremendous, and as each fresh battalion was brought into line the tumult steadily increased. The three leading brigades continued to advance westward in one long line looped up over Surgham Hill, and with the right battalion held back in column. As the forces gradually drew nearer, the possibility of the Dervishes penetrating the gap between Lewis and MacDonald presented itself and the flank battalion was wheeled into line so as to protect the right flank. The aspect of the

Dervish attack was at this moment most formidable. Enormous masses of men were hurrying towards the smoke-clouds that almost hid MacDonald. Other masses turned to meet the attack which was developing on their right. Within the angle formed by the three brigades facing west and MacDonald facing nearly south a great army of not fewer than 15,000 men was enclosed, like a flock of sheep in a fold, by the thin brown lines of the British and Egyptian brigades. As the 7th Egyptians, the right battalion of Lewis's brigade and nearest the gap between that unit and MacDonald, deployed to protect the flank, they became unsteady, began to bunch and waver, and actually made several retrograde movements. There was a moment of danger; but General Hunter, who was on the spot, himself ordered the two reserve companies of the 15th Egyptians under Major Hickman to march up behind them with fixed bayonets. Their morale was thus restored and the peril averted. The advance of the three brigades continued.

Yakub found himself utterly unable to withstand the attack from the river. His own attack on MacDonald languished. The musketry was producing terrible losses in his crowded ranks. The valiant Wad Bishara and many other less famous Emirs fell dead. Gradually he began to give ground. It was evident that the civilised troops were the stronger. But even before the attack was repulsed, the Khalifa, who watched from a close position, must have known that the day was lost.

The three brigades advancing drove the Khalifa's Dervishes back into the desert. Along a mile of front an intense and destructive fire flared and crackled. The Maxim guns pulsated feverishly. Two were even dragged by the enterprise of a subaltern to the very summit of Surgham, and from this elevated position intervened with bloody effect. Thus the long line moved forward in irresistible strength. In the centre, under the red Egyptian flag, careless of the bullets which that conspicuous emblem drew, and which inflicted some loss among those around him, rode the Sirdar, stern and sullen, equally unmoved by fear or enthusiasm.

Before that terrible line the Khalifa's division began to break up. The whole ground was strewn with dead and wounded, among whose bodies the soldiers picked their steps with the customary Soudan precautions. Surviving thousands struggled away towards Omdurman and swelled the broad stream of fugitives upon whose flank the 21st Lancers already hung vengefully. Yakub and the defenders of the Black Flag disdained to fly, and perished where they stood, beneath the holy ensign, so that when their conquerors reached the spot the dark folds of the banner waved only over the dead.

While all this was taking place – for events were moving at speed – the 1st British Brigade were still doubling across the rear of Maxwell and Lewis to fill the gap between the latter and MacDonald. As they had wheeled round, the regiments gained on each other according to their proximity to the pivot flank. The brigade assumed a formation which may be described as an echelon of columns of route, with the Lincolns, who were actually the pivot regiment, leading. By the time that the right of Lewis's brigade was reached and the British had begun to deploy, it was evident that the Khalifa's attack was broken and that his force was in full retreat. In the near foreground the Arab dead lay thick. Crowds of fugitives were trooping off in the distance. The Black Flag alone waved defiantly over the corpses of its defenders. In the front of the brigade the fight was over. But those who looked away to the right saw a different spectacle. What appeared to be an entirely new army was coming down from the Kerreri Hills. While the soldiers looked and wondered, fresh orders arrived. A mounted officer galloped up. There was a report that terrible events were happening in the dust and smoke to the northward. The spearmen had closed with MacDonald's brigade; were crumpling his line from the flank; had already broken it. Such were the rumours. The orders were more precise. The nearest regiment – the Lincolnshire – was to hurry to MacDonald's threatened flank to meet the attack. The rest of the brigade was to change front half right, and remain in support. The Lincolnshires, breathless but elated, forthwith started off again at the double. They began to traverse the rear of MacDonald's brigade, dimly conscious of rapid movements by its battalions, and to the sound of tremendous independent firing, which did not, however, prevent them from hearing the venomous hiss of bullets.

Had the Khalifa's attack been simultaneous with that which was now developed, the position of MacDonald's brigade must have been almost hopeless. In the actual event it was one of extreme peril. The attack in his front was weakening every minute, but the far more formidable attack on his right rear grew stronger and nearer in inverse ratio. Both attacks must be met. The moment was critical; the danger near. All depended on MacDonald, and that officer, who by valour and conduct in war had won his way from the rank of a private soldier to the command of a brigade, was equal to the emergency.

To meet the Khalifa's attack he had arranged his force facing south-west, with three battalions in line and the fourth held back in column of companies in rear of the right flank – an inverted L-shaped formation. As the attack from the south-west gradually weakened and the attack from the north-west continually increased, he broke off his battalions and batteries from the longer side of the L and transferred them to the shorter. He timed these movements so accurately that each face of his brigade was able to exactly sustain the attacks of the enemy. As soon as the Khalifa's force began to waver he ordered the XIth Soudanese and a battery on his left to move across the angle in which the brigade was formed, and deploy along the shorter face to meet the impending onslaught of Ali-Wad-Helu. Perceiving this, the IXth Soudanese, who were the regiment in column on the right of the original front, wheeled to the right from column into line without waiting for orders, so that two battalions faced towards the Khalifa and two towards the fresh attack. By this time it was clear that the

Khalifa was practically repulsed, and MacDonald ordered the Xth Soudanese and another battery to change front and prolong the line of the IXth and XIth. He then moved the 2nd Egyptians diagonally to their right front, so as to close the gap at the angle between their line and that of the three other battalions. These difficult manoeuvres were carried out under a heavy fire, which in twenty minutes caused over 120 casualties in the four battalions – exclusive of the losses in the artillery batteries – and in the face of the determined attacks of an enemy who outnumbered the troops by seven to one and had only to close with them to be victorious. Amid the roar of the firing and the dust, smoke, and confusion of the change of front, the general found time to summon the officers of the IXth Soudanese around him, rebuked them for having wheeled into line in anticipation of his order, and requested them to drill more steadily in brigade.

The three Soudanese battalions were now confronted with the whole fury of the Dervish attack from Kerreri. The bravery of the blacks was no less conspicuous than the wildness of their musketry. They evinced an extraordinary excitement – firing their rifles without any attempt to sight or aim, and only anxious to pull the trigger, re-load, and pull it again. In vain the British officers strove to calm their impulsive soldiers. In vain they called upon them by name, or, taking their rifles from them, adjusted the sights themselves. The independent firing was utterly beyond control. Soon the ammunition began to be exhausted, and the soldiers turned round clamouring for more cartridges, which their officers doled out to them by twos and threes in the hopes of steadying them. It was useless. They fired them all off and clamoured for more. Meanwhile, although suffering fearfully from the close and accurate fire of the three artillery batteries and eight Maxim guns, and to a less extent from the random firing of the Soudanese, the Dervishes drew nearer in thousands, and it seemed certain that there would be an actual collision. The valiant blacks prepared themselves with delight to meet the shock, notwithstanding the overwhelming numbers of the enemy. Scarcely three rounds per man remained throughout the brigade. The batteries opened a rapid fire of case-shot. Still the Dervishes advanced, and the survivors of their first wave of assault were scarcely 100 yards away. Behind them both green flags pressed forward over enormous masses of armed humanity, rolling on as they now believed to victory.

At this moment the Lincoln Regiment began to come up. As soon as the leading company cleared the right of MacDonald's brigade, they formed line, and opened an independent fire obliquely across the front of the Soudanese. Groups of Dervishes in twos and threes were then within 100 yards. The great masses were within 300 yards. The independent firing lasted two minutes, during which the whole regiment deployed. Its effect was to clear away the leading groups of Arabs. The deployment having been accomplished with the loss of a dozen men, including Colonel Sloggett, who fell shot through the breast while attending to the wounded, section volleys were ordered. With excellent discipline the independent firing was instantly stopped, and the battalion began with machine-like regularity to carry out the principles of modern musketry, for which their training had efficiently prepared them and their rifles were admirably suited. They fired on an average sixty rounds per man, and finally repulsed the attack.

The Dervishes were weak in cavalry, and had scarcely 2,000 horsemen on the field. About 400 of these, mostly the personal retainers of the various Emirs, were formed into an irregular regiment and attached to the flag of Ali-Wad-Helu. Now when these horsemen perceived that there was no more hope of victory, they arranged themselves in a solid mass and charged the left of MacDonald's brigade. The distance was about 500 yards, and, wild as was the firing of the Soudanese, it was evident that they could not possibly succeed. Nevertheless, many carrying no weapon in their hands, and all urging their horses to their utmost speed, they rode unflinchingly to certain death. All were killed and fell as they entered the zone of fire – three, twenty, fifty, two hundred, sixty, thirty, five and one out beyond them all – a brown smear across the sandy plain. A few riderless horses alone broke through the ranks of the infantry.

After the failure of the attack from Kerreri the whole Anglo-Egyptian army advanced westward, in a line of bayonets and artillery nearly two miles long, and drove the Dervishes before them into the desert, so that they could by no means rally or reform. At half past eleven Sir H. Kitchener shut up his glasses, and, remarking that he thought the enemy had been given 'a good dusting', gave the order for the brigades to resume their interrupted march on Omdurman.

Meanwhile the great Dervish Army, who had advanced at sunrise in hope and courage, fled in utter rout, pursued by the Egyptian cavalry, harried by the 21st Lancers, and leaving more than 9,000 warriors dead and even greater numbers wounded behind them.

Thus ended the Battle of Omdurman – the most signal triumph ever gained by the arms of science over barbarians.

CHAPTER 15

THE FALL OF THE CITY

Now, when the Khalifa Abdullah saw that the last army that remained to him was broken, that all his attacks had failed, and that thousands of his bravest warriors were slain, he rode from the field of battle in haste, and, regaining the city, proceeded like a brave and stubborn soldier to make preparations for its defence, and, like a prudent man, to arrange for his own flight should further resistance be impossible. He ordered his great war-drum to be beaten and the *ombya* to be blown, and for the last time those dismal notes boomed through the streets of Omdurman. They were not heeded. The Arabs recognised that all was lost. Besides, to return to the city was difficult and dangerous.

As soon as it was apparent that the surrender of individuals was accepted, the Dervishes began to come in and lay down their arms — at first by twos and threes, then by dozens, and finally by scores. Meanwhile those who were still intent on flight made a wide detour to avoid the cavalry, and streamed past our front at a mile's distance in uninterrupted succession. The disarming and escorting of the prisoners delayed our advance, and many thousands of Dervishes escaped from the field. But the position of the cavalry and the pressure they exerted shouldered the routed army out into the desert, so that retiring they missed the city of Omdurman altogether, and, disregarding the Khalifa's summons to defend it and the orders of their Emirs, continued their flight to the south. To harry and annoy the fugitives a few troops were dismounted with carbines, and a constant fire was made on such as did not attempt to come in and surrender. Yet the crowds continued to run the gauntlet, and at least 20,000 men made good their escape. Many of these were still vicious, and replied to our fire with bullets, fortunately at very long range. It would have been madness for 300 Lancers to gallop in among such masses, and we had to be content with the results of the carbine fire.

While all this had been going on, the advance of the army on Omdurman was continuing. Nor was it long before we saw the imposing array of infantry topping the sandhills near Surgham and flooding out into the plain which lay between them and the city. High over the centre brigade flew the Black Flag of the Khalifa, and underneath a smaller flash of red marked the position of the Headquarters Staff. The black masses of men continued to move slowly across the open ground while we fired at the flying Arabs, and at twelve o'clock we saw them halt near the river about three miles from the city. Orders now reached us to join them, and as the sun was hot, the day dragged, all were tired and hungry, and the horses needed water, we were not long in complying, and the remnants of the Dervish Army made good their retreat unmolested.

It was not until four o'clock that the cavalry received orders to ride round the outside of the city and harry such as should seek to escape. The Egyptian squadrons and the 21st Lancers started forthwith, and, keeping about a mile from the houses of the suburbs, proceeded to make the circle of the town. The infantry had already entered it, as was evident from a continual patter of shots and an occasional rattle of the Maxim guns. The leading Soudanese brigade – Maxwell's – had moved from Khor Shambat at 2.30, formed in line of company columns and in the following order:

↑ *Direction of Advance* ↑

XIVth Soudanese	XIIth Soudanese	Maxims	8th Egyptians	32nd Field Battery	XIIIth Soudanese

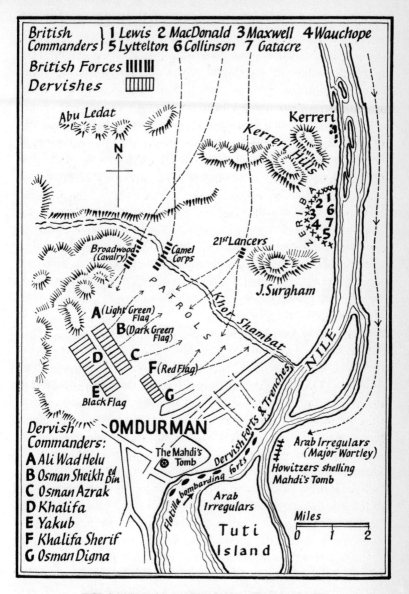

British Commanders: 1 Lewis 2 MacDonald 3 Maxwell 4 Wauchope 5 Lyttelton 6 Collinson 7 Gatacre

British Forces ▮▮▮▮▮▮

Dervishes ▯▯▯▯▯

Abu Ledat

Kerreri

Kerreri Hills

N

ZERIBA ✕✕✕✕✕ 1 6 2 3 4 7 5

Broadwood (Cavalry)

Camel Corps

21st Lancers

J. Surgham

PATROLS

Khor Shambat

NILE

A (Light Green) Flag

B (Dark Green Flag)

D   C

F (Red Flag)

E   G

Black Flag

Dervish Forts & Trenches

OMDURMAN

The Mahdi's Tomb

Dervish Forts

Flotilla bombarding forts

Arab Irregulars (Major Wortley)

Howitzers shelling Mahdi's Tomb

Dervish Commanders:
A Ali Wad Helu
B Osman Sheikh ed Din
C Osman Azrak
D Khalifa
E Yakub
F Khalifa Sherif
G Osman Digna

Arab Irregulars

Tuti Island

Miles
0   1   2

THE BATTLE OF OMDURMAN - FINAL STAGE

221

The Sirdar, attended by his whole Staff, with the Black Flag of the Khalifa carried behind him and accompanied by the band of the XIth Soudanese, rode in front of the XIVth battalion. The regiments were soon enveloped by the numberless houses of the suburbs and divided by the twisting streets; but the whole brigade pressed forward on a broad front. Behind followed the rest of the army – battalion after battalion, brigade after brigade – until all, swallowed up by the maze of mud houses, were filling the open spaces and blocking and choking the streets and alleys with solid masses of armed men, who marched or pushed their way up to the great wall.

For two miles the progress through the suburbs continued, and the General, hurrying on with his Staff, soon found himself, with the band, the Maxims, and the artillery, at the foot of the great wall. Several hundred Dervishes had gathered for its defence; but the fact that no *banquette* had been made on which they could stand to fire prevented their resistance from being effective. A few ill-aimed shots were, however, fired, to which the Maxim guns replied with vigour. In a quarter of an hour the wall was cleared. The Sirdar then posted two guns of the 32nd Field Battery at its northern angle, and then, accompanied by the remaining four guns and the XIVth Soudanese, turned eastwards and rode along the foot of the wall towards the river, seeking some means of entry into the inner city. The breach made by the gunboats was found temporarily blocked by wooden doors, but the main gate was open, and through this the General passed into the heart of Omdurman. Within the wall the scenes were more terrible than in the suburbs. The effects of the bombardment were evident on every side. Women and children lay frightfully mangled in the roadway. Dead Dervishes, already in the fierce heat beginning to decompose, dotted the ground. The houses were crammed with wounded. Hundreds of decaying carcasses of animals filled the air with a sickening smell. Here, as without the wall, the anxious inhabitants renewed their protestations of loyalty and welcome;

and interpreters, riding down the narrow alleys, proclaimed the merciful conditions of the conquerors and called on the people to lay down their arms. Great piles of surrendered weapons rose in the streets, guarded by Soudanese soldiers. All Dervishes who did not immediately surrender were shot or bayoneted, and bullets whistled at random along or across the streets. But while women crowded round his horse, while sullen men fired carefully from houses, while beaten warriors cast their spears on the ground and others, still resisting, were despatched in corners, the Sirdar rode steadily onward through the confusion, the stench, and the danger, until he reached the Mahdi's Tomb.

At the mosque two fanatics charged the Soudanese escort, and each killed or badly wounded a soldier before he was shot. The day was now far spent, and it was dusk when the prison was reached. The General was the first to enter that foul and gloomy den. Charles Neufeld and some thirty heavily shackled prisoners were released. Neufeld, who was placed on a pony, seemed nearly mad with delight, and talked and gesticulated with queer animation. 'Thirteen years', he said to his rescuer, 'have I waited for this day.' From the prison, as it was now dark, the Sirdar rode to the great square in front of the mosque, in which his headquarters were established, and where both British brigades were already bivouacking. The rest of the army settled down along the road-ways through the suburbs, and only Maxwell's brigade remained in the city to complete the establishment of law and order – a business which was fortunately hidden by the shades of night.

While the Sirdar with the infantry of the army was taking possession of Omdurman, the British and Egyptian cavalry had moved round to the west of the city. There for nearly two hours we waited, listening to the dropping fusillade which could be heard within the great wall and wondering what was happening. Large numbers of Dervishes and Arabs, who, laying aside their *jibbas*, had ceased to be Dervishes, appeared among the houses at the edge of the suburbs. Several hundreds of these, with two or three Emirs, came out to make their submission; and we were presently so loaded with spears and swords that it was impossible to carry them, and many interesting trophies had to be destroyed. It was just getting dark when suddenly Colonel Slatin galloped up. The Khalifa had fled! The Egyptian cavalry were at once to pursue him. The 21st Lancers must await further orders. Slatin appeared very much in earnest. He talked with animated manner to Colonel Broadwood, questioned two of the surrendered Emirs closely, and hurried off into the dusk, while the Egyptian squadrons, mounting, also rode away at a trot.

It was not for some hours after he had left the field of battle that Abdullah realised that his army had not obeyed his summons, but were continuing their retreat, and that only a few hundred Dervishes remained for the defence of the city. He seems, if we judge from the accounts of his personal servant, an Abyssinian boy, to have faced the disasters that had overtaken him with singular composure. He rested until two o'clock, when he ate some food. Thereafter he repaired to the Tomb, and in that ruined shrine, amid the wreckage of the shell-fire, the defeated sovereign appealed to the spirit of Mohammed Ahmed to help him in his sore distress. It was the last prayer ever offered over the Mahdi's grave. The celestial counsels seem to have been in accord with the dictates of common-sense, and at four o'clock the Khalifa, hearing that the Sirdar was already entering the city, and that the English cavalry were on the parade ground to the west, mounted a small donkey, and, accompanied by his principal wife, a Greek nun, as a hostage, and a few attendants, rode leisurely off towards the south. Eight miles from Omdurman a score of swift camels awaited him, and on these he soon reached the main body of his routed army. Here he found many disheartened friends; but the fact that, in this evil plight, he found any friends at all must be recorded in his favour and in that of his subjects. When he arrived he had no escort – was, indeed, unarmed. The fugitives had good reason to be savage. Their leaders had led them only to their ruin. To cut the throat of this one man who was the cause of all their sufferings was as easy as they would have thought it innocent. Yet none assailed him. The tyrant, the oppressor, the scourge of the Soudan, the hypocrite, the abominated Khalifa; the embodiment, as he has been depicted to European eyes, of all the vices; the object, as he was believed in England, of his people's bitter hatred, found safety and welcome among his flying soldiers. The surviving Emirs hurried to his side. Many had gone down on the fatal plain. Osman Azrak, the valiant Bishara, Yakub, and scores whose strange names have not obscured these pages, but who were, nevertheless, great men of war, lay staring up at the stars. Yet those who remained never wavered in their allegiance. Ali-Wad-Helu, whose leg had been shattered by a shell splinter, was senseless with pain; but the Sheikh-ed-Din, the astute Osman Digna, Ibrahim Khalil, who withstood the charge of the 21st Lancers, and others of less note rallied to the side of the appointed successor of Mohammed Ahmed, and did not, even in this extremity, abandon his cause. And so all hurried on through the gathering darkness, a confused and miserable multitude – dejected warriors still preserving their trashy rifles, and wounded men hobbling pitifully along; camels and donkeys laden with household goods; women crying, panting, dragging little children; all in thousands – nearly 30,000 altogether; with little food and less water to sustain them; the desert before them, the gunboats on the Nile, and behind the rumours of pursuit and a broad trail of dead and dying to mark the path of flight.

In the battle and capture of Omdurman the losses of the Expeditionary Force were as follows: 20 officers, 462 men.

The Dervish losses were, from computations made on the field and corrected at a later date, ascertained to be 9,700 killed, and wounded variously estimated at from 10,000 to 16,000. There were, besides, 5,000 prisoners.

CHAPTER 16

'THE FASHODA INCIDENT'

The long succession of events, of which I have attempted to give
some account, has not hitherto affected to any great extent other
countries than those which are drained by the Nile. But this
chapter demands a wider view, since it must describe an incident which might easily have convulsed Europe, and from which
far-reaching consequences have arisen.

The undisputed facts are few. Towards the end of 1896 a
French expedition was despatched from the Atlantic into the heart
of Africa under the command of Major Marchand. The re-
occupation of Dongola was then practically complete, and the
British Government were earnestly considering the desirability of
a further advance. In the beginning of 1897 a British expedition,
under Colonel Macdonald, and comprising a dozen carefully
selected officers, set out from England to Uganda, landed at
Mombasa, and struck inland. The misfortunes which fell upon this
enterprise are beyond the scope of this account, and I shall not
dwell upon the local jealousies and disputes which marred it. It is
sufficient to observe that Colonel Macdonald was provided with
Soudanese troops who were practically in a state of mutiny and
actually mutinied two days after he assumed command. The
officers were compelled to fight for their lives. Several were
killed. A year was consumed in suppressing the mutiny and the
revolt which arose out of it. If the object of the expedition was
to reach the Upper Nile, it was soon obviously unattainable, and
the Government were glad to employ the officers in making

geographical surveys.

At the beginning of 1898 it was clear to those who, with the fullest information, directed the foreign policy of Great Britain that no results affecting the situation in the Soudan could be expected from the Macdonald Expedition. The advance to Khartoum and the reconquest of the lost provinces had been irrevocably undertaken. An Anglo-Egyptian force was already concentrating at Berber. Lastly, the Marchand Mission was known to be moving towards the Upper Nile, and it was a probable contingency that it would arrive at its destination within a few months. It was therefore evident that the line of advance of the powerful army moving south from the Mediterranean and of the tiny expedition moving east from the Atlantic must intersect before the end of the year, and that intersection would involve a collision between the Powers of Great Britain and France.

With these introductory reflections we may return to the theatre of war.

On the 7th of September, five days after the battle and capture of Omdurman, the *Tewfikia*, a small Dervish steamer – one of those formerly used by General Gordon – came drifting and paddling down the river. Her Arab crew soon perceived by the Egyptian flags which were hoisted on the principal buildings, and by the battered condition of the Mahdi's Tomb, that all was not well in the city; and then, drifting a little further, they found themselves surrounded by the white gunboats of the 'Turks', and so incontinently surrendered. The story they told their captors was a strange one. They had left Omdurman a month earlier, in company with the steamer *Safia*, carrying a force of 500 men, with the Khalifa's orders to go up the White Nile and collect grain. For some time all had been well; but on approaching the old Government station of Fashoda they had been fired on by black troops commanded by white officers under a strange flag – and fired on with such effect that they had lost some forty men killed and wounded. Doubting who these formidable enemies might be, the foraging expedition had turned back, and the Emir in command, having disembarked and formed a camp at a place on the east bank called Reng, had sent the *Tewfikia* back to ask the Khalifa for instructions and reinforcements. The story was carried to the Sirdar and ran like wildfire through the camp. Many officers made their way to the river, where the steamer lay, to test for themselves the truth of the report. The woodwork of the hull was marked with many newly made holes, and cutting into these with their penknives the officers extracted bullets – not the roughly cast leaden balls, the bits of telegraph wire, or old iron which savages use, but the conical nickel-covered bullets of small-bore rifles such as are fired by civilised forces alone. Here was positive proof. A European Power was on the Upper Nile: which? Some said it was the Belgians from the Congo; some that an Italian expedition had arrived; others thought that the strangers were French; others, again, believed in the Foreign Office – it was a British expedition, after all. The Arab crew were cross-examined as to the flag they had seen. Their replies were inconclusive. It had bright colours, they declared; but what those colours were and what their arrangement might be they could not tell.

The camp for the most part received the news with a shrug. After their easy victory the soldiers walked delicately. They knew that they belonged to the most powerful force that had ever penetrated the heart of Africa. If there was to be more war, the Government had but to give the word, and the Grand Army of the Nile would do by these newcomers as they had done by the Dervishes.

On the 8th the Sirdar started up the White Nile for Fashoda with five steamers, the XIth and XIIIth Battalions of Soudanese, two companies of the Cameron Highlanders, Peake's battery of artillery, and four Maxim guns. Three days later he arrived at Reng, and there found, as the crew of the *Tewfikia* had declared, some 500 Dervishes encamped on the bank, and the *Safia* steamer moored to it. These stupid fellows had the temerity to open fire on the vessels. Whereat the *Sultan*, steaming towards their *dêm*, replied with a fierce shellfire which soon put them to flight. The *Safia*, being under steam, made some attempt to escape – whither, it is impossible to say – and Commander Keppel by a well-directed shell in her boilers blew her up, much to the disgust of the Sirdar, who wanted to add her to his flotilla.

After this incident the expedition continued its progress up the White Nile. The *sudd* which was met with two days' journey south of Khartoum did not in this part of the Nile offer any obstacle to navigation, as the strong current of the river clears the waterway; but on either side of the channel a belt of the tangled weed, varying from twelve to twelve hundred yards in breadth, very often prevented the steamers from approaching the bank to tie up. The banks themselves depressed the explorers by their melancholy inhospitality. At times the river flowed past miles of long grey grass and swampland, inhabited only by hippopotami. At times a vast expanse of dreary mud-flats stretched as far as the eye could see. At others the forest, dense with an impenetrable undergrowth of thorn-bushes, approached the water, and the active forms of monkeys and even of leopards darted among the trees. Whether forest, mud-flat, or prairie it was a wet land steaming under a burning sun and humming with mosquitoes and all kinds of insect life.

Onward and southward toiled the flotilla, splashing the brown water into foam and startling the strange creatures on the banks, until on the 18th of September they approached Fashoda. The gunboats waited, moored to the bank for some hours of the afternoon, to allow a message which had been sent by the Sirdar to the mysterious Europeans, to precede his arrival, and early in the morning of the 19th a small steel rowing-boat was observed coming down stream to meet the expedition. It contained a Senegalese sergeant and two men, with a letter from Major Marchand announcing the arrival of the French troops and their formal occupation of the Soudan. It, moreover, congratulated the

Sirdar on his victory, and welcomed him to Fashoda in the name of France.

A few miles' further progress brought the gunboats to their destination, and they made fast to the bank near the old Government buildings of the town. Major Marchand's party consisted of eight French officers or non-commissioned officers, and 120 black soldiers drawn from the Niger district. They possessed three steel boats fitted for sail or oars, and a small steam launch, the *Faidherbe*, which latter had, however, been sent south for reinforcements. They had six months' supplies of provisions for the French officers, and about three months' rations for the men; but they had no artillery, and were in great want of small-arm ammunition. Their position was indeed precarious. The little force was stranded, without communications of any sort, and with no means of either withstanding an attack or of making a retreat. They had fired away most of their cartridges at the Dervish foraging party, and were daily expecting a renewed attack. Indeed, it was with consternation that they had heard of the approach of the flotilla. The natives had carried the news swiftly up the river that the Dervishes were coming back with five steamers, and for three nights the French had been sleeplessly awaiting the assault of a powerful enemy.

Their joy and relief at the arrival of a European force were undisguised. The Sirdar and his officers on their part were thrilled with admiration at the wonderful achievements of this small band of heroic men. Two years had passed since they left the Atlantic coast. For four months they had been absolutely lost from human ken. They had fought with savages; they had struggled with fever; they had climbed mountains and pierced the most gloomy forests. Five days and five nights they had stood up to their necks in swamp and water. A fifth of their number had perished; yet at last they had carried out their mission and, arriving at Fashoda on the 10th of July, had planted the tricolour upon the Upper Nile.

Moved by such reflections the British officers disembarked.

231

Major Marchand, with a guard of honour, came to meet the General. They shook hands warmly. 'I congratulate you', said the Sirdar, 'on all you have accomplished.' 'No', replied the Frenchman, pointing to his troops; 'it is not I, but these soldiers who have done it.' And Kitchener, telling the story afterwards, remarked, 'Then I knew he was a gentleman.'

Into the diplomatic discussions that followed, it is not necessary to plunge. The Sirdar politely ignored the French flag, and, without interfering with the Marchand Expedition and the fort it occupied, hoisted the British and Egyptian colours with all due ceremony, amid musical honours and the salutes of the gunboats. A garrison was established at Fashoda, consisting of the XIth Soudanese, four guns of Peake's battery, and two Maxims, the whole under the command of Colonel Jackson, who was appointed military and civil commandant of the Fashoda district.

At three o'clock on the same afternoon the Sirdar and the gunboats resumed their journey to the south, and the next day reached the mouth of the Sobat, sixty-two miles from Fashoda. Here other flags were hoisted and another post formed with a garrison of half the XIIIth Soudanese battalion and the remaining two guns of Peake's battery. The expedition then turned northwards, leaving two gunboats – the *Sultan* and the *Abu Klea* – at the disposal of Colonel Jackson.

I do not attempt to describe the international negotiations and discussions that followed the receipt of the news in Europe, but it is pleasing to remember that a great crisis found England united. The determination of the Government was approved by the loyalty of the Opposition, supported by the calm resolve of the people, and armed with the efficiency of the fleet. At first indeed, while the Sirdar was still steaming southward, wonder and suspense filled all minds; but when suspense ended in the certainty that eight French adventurers were in occupation of Fashoda and claimed a territory twice as large as France, it gave place to a deep and bitter anger. They should go. They should evacuate Fashoda, or else all the might, majesty, dominion, and power of everything that could by any stretch of the imagination be called 'British' should be employed to make them go.

Those who find it difficult to account for the hot, almost petulant, flush of resolve that stirred the nation must look back over the long history of the Soudan drama. It had always been a duty to reconquer the abandoned territory. When it was found that this might be safely done, the duty became a pleasure. The operations were watched, with extravagant attention, and while they progressed the earnestness of the nation increased. As the tides of barbarism were gradually driven back, the old sea-marks came one after another into view. Names of towns that were half forgotten – or remembered only with sadness – reappeared on the posters, in the gazettes, and in the newspapers. We were going back. 'Dongola', 'Berber', 'Metemma' – who had not heard of them before? Now they were associated with victory.

When the final triumph, long expected, came in all its completeness it was hailed with a shout of exultation, and the people of Great Britain, moved far beyond their wont, sat themselves down to give thanks to their God, their Government, and their General. Suddenly, on the chorus of their rejoicing there broke a discordant note. They were confronted with the fact that a 'friendly Power' had, unprovoked, endeavoured to rob them of the fruits of their victories. They now realised that while they had been devoting themselves to great military operations, in broad daylight and the eye of the world, and prosecuting an enterprise on which they had set their hearts, other operations – covert and deceitful – had been in progress in the heart of the Dark Continent, designed solely for the mischievous and spiteful object of depriving them of the produce of their labours.

Great Britain was determined to have Fashoda or fight; and as soon as this was made clear, the French were willing to give way. Fashoda was a miserable swamp, of no particular value to them. Marchand, Lord Salisbury's 'explorer in difficulties upon the

Upper Nile', was admitted by the French Minister to be merely an 'emissary of civilisation'. It was not worth their while to embark on the hazards and convulsions of a mighty war for either swamp or emissary. Besides, the plot had failed. The negro tribes gazed with wonder on the strangers, but had no intention of fighting for them. The pride and barbarism of the Khalifa rejected all overtures and disdained to discriminate between the various breeds of the accursed 'Turks'. Finally, the victory of Omdurman and its forerunner – the Desert Railway – had revolutionised the whole situation in the Nile valley. After some weeks of tension, the French Government consented to withdraw their expedition from the region of the Upper Nile.

Meanwhile events were passing at Fashoda. The town, the site of which had been carefully selected by the old Egyptian Government, is situated on the left bank of the river, on a gentle slope of ground which rises about four feet above the level of the Nile at full flood. During the rainy season, which lasts from the end of June until the end of October, the surrounding country is one vast swamp, and Fashoda itself becomes an island. It is not, however, without its importance; for it is the only spot on the west shore for very many miles where landing from the river is possible. All the roads – mere camel-tracks – from Lower Kordofan meet at the Government post, but are only passable in the dry season. The soil is fertile, and, since there is a superabundance of sun and water, almost any crop or plant can be grown. The French officers, with the adaptive thrift of their nation, had already, in spite of the ravages of the water-rats, created a good vegetable garden, from which they were able to supplement their monotonous fare. The natives, however – aboriginal negroes of the Dinka and Shillook tribes – are unwilling to work, except to provide themselves with the necessaries of life; and since these are easily obtained, there is very little cultivation, and the fertility of the soil may be said to increase the poverty of the country. At all seasons of the year the climate of Fashoda is pestilential, and the malarial fever attacks

every European or Egyptian, breaking down the strongest consti-
tutions, and in many cases causing death.[1]

On this dismal island, far from civilisation, health, or comfort,
the Marchand Mission and the Egyptian garrison lived in polite
antagonism for nearly three months. The French fort stood at the
northern end. The Egyptian camp lay outside the ruins of the
town. Civilities were constantly exchanged between the forces,
and the British officers repaid the welcome gifts of fresh vegetables
by newspapers and other conveniences. The Senegalese riflemen
were smart and well-conducted soldiers, and the blacks of the
Soudanese battalion soon imitated their officers in reciprocating
courtesies. A feeling of mutual respect sprang up between Colonel
Jackson and Major Marchand. The dashing commandant of the
XIth Soudanese, whose Egyptian medals bear no fewer than fourteen clasps, was filled with a generous admiration for the French
explorer. Realising the difficulties, he appreciated the magnificence
of the achievement; and as he spoke excellent French a good and
almost cordial understanding was established, and no serious disagreement occurred. But, notwithstanding the polite relations, the
greatest vigilance was exercised by both sides, and whatever civilities were exchanged were of a formal nature.

The Dinkas and Shillooks had on the first arrival of the
French made submission, and had supplied them with provisions.
They knew that white men were said to be coming, and they did
not realise that there were different races among the whites.
Marchand was regarded as the advance guard of the Sirdar's army.
But when the negroes gradually perceived that these bands of
white men were at enmity with each other – were, in fact, of rival
tribes – they immediately transferred their allegiance to the
stronger force, and, although their dread of the Egyptian flag was
at first very marked, boycotted the French entirely.

---

[1] *The place is most unhealthy, and in March 1899 (the driest season of the year) out of
a garrison of 317 men only 37 were fit for duty.* – Sir William Garstin's Report:
Egypt, No. 5, 1899.

In the middle of October despatches from France arrived for Marchand by steamer; and that officer, after reading them, determined to proceed to Cairo. Jackson, who was most anxious that no disagreement should arise, begged him to give positive orders to his subordinate to maintain the *status quo*, as had been agreed. Marchand gladly consented, and departed for Omdurman, where he visited the battlefield, and found in the heaps of slain a grim witness of the destruction from which he had been saved, and so on to Cairo, where he was moved to tears and speeches. But in his absence Captain Germain, who succeeded to the command, diverged from his orders. No sooner had Marchand left than Germain, anxious to win distinction, embarked upon a most aggressive policy. He occupied the Dinka country on the right bank of the river, pushed reconnoitring parties into the interior, prevented the Dinka Sheikhs from coming to make their submission at Fashoda, and sent his boats and the *Faidherbe* steam launch, which had returned from the south, beyond the northern limits which the Sirdar had prescribed and Marchand had agreed to recognise.

Colonel Jackson protested again and again. Germain sent haughty replies, and persisted in his provoking policy. At last the British officer was compelled to declare that if any more patrols were sent into the Dinka country, he would not allow them to return to the French post. Whereat Germain rejoined that he would meet force with force. All tempers were worn by fever, heat, discomfort, and monotony. The situation became very difficult, and the tact and patience of Colonel Jackson alone averted a conflict which would have resounded in all parts of the world. He confined his troops strictly to their lines, and moved as far from the French camp as was possible. But there was one dark day when the French officers worked in their shirts with their faithful Senegalese to strengthen the entrenchments, and busily prepared for a desperate struggle. On the other side little activity was noticeable. The Egyptian garrison, although under arms, kept out of sight, but

236

a wisp of steam above the funnels of the redoubtable gunboats showed that all was ready.

At length in a fortunate hour Marchand returned, reproved his subordinate, and expressed his regrets to Colonel Jackson. Then it became known that the French Government had ordered the evacuation of Fashoda. Some weeks were spent in making preparations for the journey, but at length the day of departure arrived. At 8.20 on the morning of the 11th of December the French lowered their flag with salute and flourish of bugle. The British officers, who remained in their own camp and did not obtrude themselves, were distant but interested spectators. On the flag ceasing to fly, a *sous-officier* rushed up to the flagstaff and hurled it to the ground, shaking his fists and tearing his hair in a bitterness and vexation from which it is impossible to withhold sympathy, in view of what these men had suffered uselessly and what they had done. The French then embarked, and at 9.30 steamed southward, the *Faidherbe* towing one oblong steel barge and one old steel boat, the other three boats sailing, all full of men. As the little flotilla passed the Egyptian camp a guard of honour of the XIth Soudanese saluted them and the band struck up their national anthem. The French acknowledged the compliment by dipping their flag, and in return the British and Egyptian flags were also lowered. The boats then continued their journey until they had rounded the bend of the river, when they came to land, and, honour being duly satisfied, Marchand and his officers returned to breakfast with Colonel Jackson. The meeting was very friendly. Jackson and Germain exchanged most elaborate compliments, and the commandant, in the name of the XIth Soudanese, presented the expedition with the banner of the Emir who had attacked them, which had been captured at Reng. Marchand shook hands all round, and the British officers bade their gallant opponents a final farewell.

Once again the eight Frenchmen, who had come so far and accomplished so much, set out upon their travels, to make a safe though tedious journey through Abyssinia to the coast, and thence home to the country they had served faithfully and well, and which was not unmindful of their services.

It only remains to discuss the settlement made between the conquerors of the Soudan. Great Britain and Egypt had moved hand in hand up the great river, sharing, though unequally, the cost of the war in men and money. The prize belonged to both. The direct annexation of the Soudan by Great Britain would have been an injustice to Egypt. Moreover, the claim of the conquerors to Fashoda and other territories rested solely on the former rights of Egypt. On the other hand, if the Soudan became Egyptian again, it must wear the fetters of that imprisoned country. Mixed Tribunals, Ottoman Suzerainty, and other vexatious burdens would be added to the difficulties of Soudan administration. To free the new country from the curse of internationalism was a paramount object. The Soudan Agreement by Great Britain and Egypt, published on the 7th of March 1899, achieves this. Like most of the best work done in Egypt by the British Agency, the Agreement was slipped through without attracting much notice. Under its authority a State has been created in the Nile Valley which is neither British nor Ottoman, nor anything else so far known to the law of Europe. International jurists are confronted with an entirely new political status. A diplomatic 'Fourth Dimension' has been discovered. Great Britain and Egypt rule the country together. The allied conquerors have become the joint-possessors. 'What does this Soudan Agreement mean?' the Austrian Consul-General asked Lord Cromer; and the British Agent, whom twenty-two years' acquaintance with Egyptian affairs had accustomed to anomalies, replied, 'It means simply this'; and handed him the inexplicable document, under which the conquered country may some day march to Peace and Plenty.

CHAPTER 17

ON THE BLUE NILE

The authority of the Khalifa and the strength of his army were for ever broken on the 2nd of September, and the Battle of Omdurman is the natural climax of this tale of war. After the victory the public interest was no longer centred in the Soudan. The last British battalion had been carried north of Assuan; the last Press correspondent had hurried back to Cairo or London. But the military operations were by no means over.

The enemy had been defeated. It remained to reconquer the territory. The Dervishes of the provincial garrisons still preserved their allegiance to the Khalifa. Several strong Arab forces kept the field. Distant Kordofan and even more distant Darfur were as yet quite unaffected by the great battle at the confluence of the Niles. There were rumours of Europeans in the Far South.

The unquestioned command of the waterways which the Sirdar enjoyed enabled the greater part of the Egyptian Soudan to be at once formally re-occupied. All towns or stations on the main rivers and their tributaries were at the mercy of the gunboats. It was only necessary to send troops to occupy them and to hoist the British and Egyptian flags. Two expeditions were forthwith sent up the White and Blue Niles to establish garrisons, and as far as possible to subdue the country. The first, under the personal command of the Sirdar, left Omdurman on the 8th of September, and steamed up the White Nile towards Fashoda. The events which followed that momentous journey have already been related. The second expedition consisted of the gunboats *Sheikh* and *Hafir*, together with two companies and the brass band of the Xth Soudanese and a Maxim battery, all under the command of General Hunter. Leaving Omdurman on the 19th of September, they started up the Blue Nile to Abu Haraz.

On the 22nd of September a considerable part of the army of Osman Digna, which had not been present at the Battle of Omdurman, was found encamped on the Ghezira, a few miles north of Rufaa. The Sheikhs and Emirs, on being summoned by General Hunter, surrendered, and a force of about 2,000 men laid down their arms.

But there was one Dervish force which had no intention of surrendering to the invaders. Ahmed Fedil, a zealous and devoted adherent of the Khalifa, had been sent, after the defeat on the Atbara, to collect all the Dervishes and bring them to join the growing army at Omdurman. The Emir was hurrying to his master's assistance with a strong and well disciplined force of no fewer than 8,000 men when, while yet sixty miles from the city, he received the news of 'the stricken field'. He immediately halted, and sought to hide the disaster from his soldiers by announcing that the Khalifa had been victorious and no longer needed their assistance. The truth was not, however, long concealed; for a few days later two emissaries despatched by Slatin arrived at the Dervish camp and announced the destruction of the Omdurman army, the flight of the Khalifa, and the fall of the city. The messengers were authorised to offer Ahmed terms; but that implacable Dervish flew into a rage, and, having shot one, sent the other, covered with insults and stripes, to tell the 'Turks' that he would fight to the bitter end. His Dervishes, whose families and women had been left with large stores of grain and ammunition in Gedaref, under a strong garrison of 3,000 men, urged their commander to return and collect these possessions.

On the 7th of September Colonel Parsons, in command of the forces at Kassala, in conformity with previous instructions, set out for Gedaref. It was known that Ahmed Fedil had marched towards Omdurman. It was believed that Gedaref was only weakly held, and the opportunity of cutting the most powerful remaining Dervish army from its base was too precious to be neglected. But the whole available strength of the Kassala garrison was 1,350 motley soldiers, untried, little disciplined, worn with waiting and wasted by disease, without cavalry, artillery, or machine guns, and with only seven British officers.

During the night of the 21st, when the column was within twelve miles of Gedaref, startling news arrived. A deserter from the Dervishes made his way into the camp and informed Colonel Parsons that the Emir Saadalla awaited him with 3,500 men two miles before the town. The situation was grave. A retreat through the broken country in the face of a powerful enemy seemed impossible. There was no alternative but to attack.

Very early on the morning of the 22nd – the same day on which General Hunter on the Blue Nile was compelling Musa Digna and his followers to surrender – Colonel Parsons and the Kassala column set forth to march into Gedaref and to fight whatever force it might contain. At half past seven, and about three miles from Gedaref, the enemy's scouts were encountered. At eight o'clock the column halted, and Colonel Parsons and his officers ascended a small knoll to reconnoitre.

A most menacing spectacle confronted them. Four lines of white figures rising out of the grass showed by their length the number, and by their regularity, the discipline of the enemy. Subsequent investigation has shown that the Emir Saadalla marched out of Gedaref with 1,700 riflemen, 1,600 spearmen, and 300 horse.

The valley was rocky, and overgrown; but to the right of the track there rose a high saddleback hill, the surface of which looked more open, and which appeared to command the approaches from Gedaref. The troops knew nothing of the country; the Dervishes understood it thoroughly. The high ground gave at least advantage of view. Colonel Parsons resolved to occupy it.

241

The order was given, and the column began to double across the valley towards the saddleback. The Dervishes, perceiving the nature of the movement, hurried their advance in the hope of catching the troops on the move, but they were too late. Colonel Parsons and his force reached the saddleback safely, and advanced along it in column in the direction of Gedaref.

The Dervishes, seeing that the troops had already reached the hill, swung to their left and advanced to the attack. Thereupon at half past eight the column wheeled into line to meet them, and standing in the long grass, which even on the summit of the hill was nearly breast-high, opened a heavy and destructive fire. The enemy, although suffering severe loss, continued to struggle bravely onward, replying vigorously to the musketry of the soldiers. At nine o'clock, while the frontal attack was still undecided, Colonel Parsons became aware that a strong force of Dervishes had moved round the left rear and were about to attack the hospital and transport. He at once sent to warn Captain Fleming, R.A.M.C., who combined the duties of medical officer and commander of the baggage column, of the impending assault. The Arab Sheikhs, who in the absence of officers were acting as orderlies, had scarcely brought the news to Fleming, when the enemy, some 300 strong, rushed with great determination upon the baggage, and the escort of 120 Arab irregulars at once broke and fled. The situation became desperate; but Ruthven with thirty-four Slavery Department camel-men hastened to meet the exultant enemy and protect the baggage column. In spite of all their efforts the rear of the baggage column was broken and cut up. The survivors fell back towards their main body, hotly pressed by the enemy.

At this moment Captain Ruthven observed one of his native officers, lying wounded on the ground, about to fall into the hands of the Dervishes and perish miserably. He immediately went back and, being a man of great physical strength, carried the body off in his arms. The enemy were, however, so close that he was three times compelled to set his burden down and defend himself with his revolver. Meanwhile the retirement towards the main body continued and accelerated.

Colonel Parsons and his force were now between two fires. The frontal attack was within 200 yards. The rear attack, flushed with success, were hurrying impetuously forward. The defeat and consequent total destruction of the Kassala column appeared certain. But in the nick of time the Dervish frontal attack, which had been suffering heavily from the fire of the troops, wavered; and when the Arab battalion and the 16th Egyptians advanced upon them, they broke and fled. Colonel Parsons at once endeavoured to meet the rear attack. The 16th Egyptians, on being called upon by their commanding officer, Captain McKerrell, faced steadily about to encounter the fresh attack.

The heavy fire of the regular battalion checked the Dervish advance, and Captain Fleming, the rest of the dismounted camelmen, and Ruthven, still carrying his native officer,[1] found safety in their ranks. A short fierce musketry combat followed at a range of less than a hundred yards, at the end of which the assailants of the baggage convoy were completely repulsed. The action was now practically over and success was won.

The town of Gedaref surrendered at noon. The Dervish Emir, Nur Angara, who with 200 black riflemen and two brass guns had been left in command of the garrison, made haste to submit. The remainder of the Dervishes, continuing their flight under the Emir Saadalla, hurried to tell the tale of defeat to Ahmed Fedil.

The victory had been won, the enemy were routed, and the town was taken: it had now to be defended. The position was good and adaptable. It consisted of three large enclosures, capable of holding the entire force, situated in echelon, so as to protect each other by their fire, and with strong brick walls six feet high. All were at once set to work to clear the approaches, to level the mud houses without, and to build ramparts or *banquettes* within the walls. While the infantry were thus engaged, Ruthven and his

---

[1] *For his gallantry on this occasion Captain Ruthven received the Victoria Cross.*

camel-men made daily reconnaissances of the surrounding country.

By great good fortune a convoy of ammunition from Mugatta reached Gedaref on the afternoon of the 27th. At dawn the next day Ruthven reported that the advance guard of Ahmed Fedil was approaching the town. The attack began at half past eight. The Dervishes, who fought with their customary gallantry, simultane-ously assaulted the north, south, and west faces of the defences. Creeping forward through the high *doura*, they were able to get within 300 yards of the enclosures. But the intervening space had been carefully cleared of cover, and was swept by the musketry of the defenders. All attempts to cross this ground – even the most determined rushes – proved vain. After an hour's heavy fusillade the attack weakened, and presently ceased altogether.

The Dervishes remained for two days in the palm grove two miles to the west of the town, but on the 1st of October Ahmed Fedil was forced to retire to a more convenient camp eight miles to the southward. Here for the next three weeks he remained, savage and sulky; until the arrival of a relief expedition to the Kassala column forced him to realise that he had no chance of recapturing the town.

After his defeat before Gedaref, Ahmed Fedil reverted to his intention of joining the Khalifa in Kordofan, and he withdrew southwards towards the Dinder river with a following that still numbered more than 5,000. To pass the Nile in the face of the gunboats appeared impossible. He did not, however, believe that steamers could navigate the higher reaches of the rivers, and in the hopes of finding a safe crossing-place he directed his march so as to strike the Blue Nile south of Karkoj. Moving leisurely, and with frequent delays to pillage the inhabitants, he arrived on the Dinder, twenty-five miles to the east of Karkoj, on the 7th of November. Here he found two powerful vessels already patrolling it. Again frustrated, he turned southwards, meaning to cross above the Rosaires Cataract, which was without doubt impassable to steamers.

During the end of November the Sheikh Bakr, who had deserted the Dervishes after their retreat from Gedaref, arrived at Karkoj where Colonel Lewis, who had been marching through the centre of the Ghezira to re-establish the Egyptian authority, had halted, with 350 irregulars. He claimed to have defeated his former chief many times, and produced a sack of heads as evidence of his success. His loyalty being thus placed beyond doubt, he was sent to keep contact with the Dervishes and encouraged by the permission to appropriate whatever spoils of war he could capture.

Meanwhile Ahmed Fedil was working his way slowly southward along a deep *khor* which runs almost parallel to the Blue Nile and is perhaps twenty miles from it. As soon as the position of the Dervish Emir was definitely known, Colonel Lewis moved his force from Karkoj to Rosaires. On the 20th of December, information was received that on the 18th Ahmed Fedil had reached the village of Dakhila, about twenty miles south of the Rosaires post; that he himself had immediately crossed with his advanced guard, and was busily passing the women and children across the river on rafts.

On the 22nd, therefore, Colonel Lewis hurried the Sheikh Bakr up the west bank to cut off their flocks and harass the Dervishes who had already crossed the river. The irregulars accordingly departed; and the next day news was brought that the Dervish force was almost equally divided by the Blue Nile, half being on one bank and half on the other.

Colonel Lewis determined to attack what part of Ahmed Fedil's force still remained on the east bank of the river, and on Christmas Day, at five o'clock in the afternoon, he marched with every man he could muster in the direction of Dakhila.

Moving in single file along a track which led through a dense forest of thorny trees, the column reached Abu Zogholi, a village thought to be half, but really not one-third, of the way to Dakhila, at eleven o'clock on Christmas night. Here they bivouacked until

245

THE CAMPAIGN ON THE BLUE NILE

3 a.m. on the 26th, when the march was resumed in the same
straggling order through the same tangled scrub. Daylight found
them still several miles from the Dervish position, and it was not
until eight o'clock that the enemy's outposts were discovered.
After a few shots the Arab picquet fell back, and the advance
guard, hurrying after them, emerged from the forest upon the
open ground of the river-bank. Into this space the whole column
gradually debouched.

246

THE ACTION NEAR ROSAIRES

The Dervish position was well chosen and of great defensive strength. A little to the north of Dakhila the Blue Nile bifurcates – one rapid but shallow stream flowing fairly straight under the east bank; another very deep stream running in a wide curve under the west bank, cutting into it so that it is precipitous. These two branches of the river enclose an island a mile and a quarter long by 1,400 yards wide, and on this island, surrounded by a natural moat of swiftly flowing water, was the Dervish *dêm*. The western side of the island rose into a line of low sandhills covered with scrub and grass, with a steep reverse slope towards the foreshore of the river-bank; and here, in this excellent cover, what eventually proved to be three-quarters of the force of Ahmed Fedil were drawn up. Backed against the deep arm of the river they had no choice, nor indeed any other wish, but to fight. Before them stretched a bare slope of heavy shingle, 1,000 yards wide, over which their enemies must advance to the attack. Behind them the high precipitous west bank of the river, which rose in some places to a height of fifty feet, was lined with the 300 riflemen who had already crossed; and from this secure position Ahmed Fedil and four of his Emirs were able to watch, assist, and direct the defence of the island. The force on the island was under the sole command of the Emir Saadalla, of Gedaref repute.

The prospect was uninviting. Colonel Lewis discovered that he had absurdly under-rated the strength and discipline of the Dervish force. It had been continually reported that the defeats at Gedaref had demoralised them, and that their numbers did not exceed 2,000 men. Moreover, he had marched to the attack in the belief that they were equally divided on both sides of the river. Retreat was, however, impossible. Strong as was the position of the enemy, the direct assault was actually safer than a retirement through the nineteen miles of gloomy forest which lay between the adventurous column and Rosaires. At nine o'clock the two Maxims, which represented the artillery of the little force, came into action in good positions, while the Xth Soudanese and most of the irregulars lined the east bank. Musketry and Maxim fire was now opened at long range. The Dervishes replied, and it soon became evident that no long-range fire could dislodge them; and Colonel Lewis resolved, in spite of the great disparity of force and disadvantage of ground, to attack them with the bayonet. Some time was spent in finding fords across the interposing arm of the river, and it was not until past ten o'clock that Bakr's men crossed on to the island, and, supported by a company of the Xth Soudanese, advanced towards the enemy's right and took up a position at about 800 yards from their line, to cover the rest of the passage.

Colonel Lewis now determined to turn the enemy's left from the north, attack them in flank, and roll them into the deep part of the river. With the Xth Soudanese, under Colonel Nason and Major Fergusson, he marched northwards along the river's edge, sheltering as far as possible under the curve of the bank from the fire. Having reached the position from which it was determined to deliver the attack, the battalion deployed into line, and, changing front half left, advanced obliquely by alternate companies across the bare shingle towards the sandhills. As they advanced, a galling fire was opened upon the left flank by two hundred Dervishes admirably placed on a knoll.

The Dervish musketry now became intense. The Soudanese began to drop on all sides, and the ground was soon dotted with the bodies of the killed and wounded. But undaunted by fire and cross-fire, the heroic black soldiers pressed forward without the slightest check or hesitation, and, increasing their pace to a swift run, reached the first sandhills and found cover beneath them.

The rapidity of their advance had exhausted the Soudanese, and Lewis ordered Nason to halt under cover of the sandhills for a few minutes, so that the soldiers might get their breath before the final effort. Thereupon the Dervishes, seeing that the troops were no longer advancing, and believing that the attack was repulsed, resolved to clinch the matter. Ahmed Fedil from the west

249

bank sounded the charge on drum and bugle, and with loud shouts of triumph and enthusiasm the whole force on the island rose from among the upper sandhills, and, waving their banners, advanced impetuously in counter-attack. But the Xth Soudanese, panting yet unconquerable, responded to the call of their two white officers, and, crowning the little dunes behind which they had sheltered, met the exultant enemy with a withering fire and a responding shout.

The range was short and the fire effective. The astonished Arabs wavered and broke; and then the soldiers, nobly led, swept forward in a long scattered line and drove the enemy from one sandy ridge to another, until all who were not killed or wounded were penned at the extreme southern end of the island, with the deep unfordable arm of the river behind them and the fierce black soldiers, roused to fury by their losses, in front.

The Sheikh Bakr, with his men and the rest of the irregulars, joined the victorious Soudanese, and from the cover of the sand-hills, now in the hands of the troops, a terrible fire was opened upon the Dervishes crowded together on the bare and narrow promontory and on the foreshore. Some tried to swim across the rushing river to their friends on the west bank. Many were drowned – among them Saadalla, who sank horse and man beneath the flood. Others took refuge from the fire by standing up to their necks in the stream. The greater part, however, escaped to a smaller island a little further up the river. But the cover was bad, and, after being exposed for an hour and a half to the musketry of two companies, the survivors – 300 strong – surrendered.

By 11.30 the whole island was in the possession of the troops.

Ahmed Fedil escaped with scarcely a dozen followers to join the Khalifa.

CHAPTER 18

THE END OF THE KHALIFA

The Khalifa still remained in Kordofan. After he had made good his escape from the battlefield of Omdurman, Abdullah had hurried in the direction of El Obeid. In the beginning of November he moved westward to Aigailla. Here he was joined by the Emir El Khatem with the El Obeid garrison. This chief and his followers had never been engaged with the 'Turks', and were consequently fresh and valiant. Their arrival greatly encouraged the force which the Khalifa had rallied. A large *dêm* was formed at Aigailla, and here, since the water was plentiful during December, Abdullah abode quietly, sending his raiding parties to collect grain and other supplies.

As soon as the Sirdar, who had returned from England, received the news he determined to make an attempt to capture the Khalifa; and on the 29th of December sent for Colonel Kitchener, to whom he had decided to entrust this honourable enterprise. The colonel was directed to take a small mixed force into Kordofan and to reconnoitre the enemy's position. If possible, he was to attack and capture Abdullah, whose followers were believed not to exceed 1,000 ill-armed men.

The prime difficulty of the operation was the want of water. The Khalifa's position was nearly 125 miles from the river. The intervening country is, in the wet season, dotted with shallow lakes, but by January these are reduced to mud puddles and only occasional pools remain. All the water needed by the men, horses, and mules of the column must therefore be carried. The camels must

251

go thirsty until one of the rare pools might be found. Now, the capacity of a camel for endurance without drinking is famous; but it has its limits. It was thought that, partly by the water carried in skins, partly by the drying-up pools, and partly by the camel's power of endurance, it might be just possible for a force of about 1,200 men to strike out 125 miles into the desert, to have three days to do their business in, and to come back to the Nile. The force were supplied with food up till the 9th of February, and their radius of action, except as restricted by water, was nineteen days. This was further extended five days by the arrangement of a convoy which was to set out on the 30th of January to meet them as they returned.

The column – numbering 1,604 officers and men and 1,624 camels and other beasts of burden – started from Kohi at 3 p.m. on the 23rd of January. The country through which their route lay was of barren and miserable aspect. Ten miles from the river all vestiges of animal life disappeared. The land was a vast unprofitable thicket, whose interlacing thorn bushes, unable to yield the slightest nourishment to living creatures, could yet obstruct their path.

Through this the straggling column, headed in the daylight by the red Egyptian flag and at night by a lantern on a pole, wound its weary way, the advanced guard cutting a path with axes and marking the track with strips of calico. Three long marches brought them on the 25th to Gedid.

The march was resumed on the 26th. The trees were now larger; the scrub became a forest; the sandy soil changed to a dark red colour; but otherwise the character of the country was unaltered. The column rested at Abu Rokba. A few starving inhabitants who occupied the huts pointed out the grave of the Khalifa's father and the little straw house in which Abdullah was wont to pray during his visits.

At the end of the next march, which was made by day, the guides discovered a large pool of good water, and all drank deeply in thankful joy. A small but strong *zeriba* was built near

THE SHIRKELA RECONNAISSANCE

this precious pool, and the reserve food and a few sick men were left with a small garrison under an Egyptian officer. The column resumed their journey. On the 29th they reached Aigailla, and here, with feelings of astonishment scarcely less than Robinson Crusoe experienced at seeing the footprint in the sand, they came upon the Khalifa's abandoned camp. A wide space had been cleared of bush, and beyond stood the encampment – a great multitude of yellow spear-grass dwellings, perfectly clean, neatly arranged in streets and squares, and stretching for miles. The aspect of this strange deserted town, rising, silent as a cemetery, out of the awful scrub, chilled everyone who saw it. Its size might indeed concern their leader. At the very lowest computation it had contained 20,000 people. How many of these were fighting men? Certainly not fewer than 8,000 or 9,000. Yet the expedition had

253

been sent on the assumption that there were scarcely 1,000 warriors with the Khalifa!

Observing every precaution of war, the column crawled forward, and the cavalry and Camel Corps, who covered the advance, soon came in contact with the enemy's scouts. Shots were exchanged and the Arabs retreated. The column halted three miles to the east of this position, and, forming a strong *zeriba*, passed the night in expectation of an attack. Nothing, however, happened, and at dawn Mitford was sent out with some mounted 'friendlies' to reconnoitre. At ten o'clock he returned, and his report was startling. He estimated not fewer than 2,000 Arab riflemen in the front line.

The small force were 125 miles from their base; behind them lay an almost waterless country, and in front was a powerful enemy. An informal council of war was held. The Sirdar had distinctly ordered that there was to be no waiting; the troops were either to attack or retire. Colonel Kitchener decided to retire. The homeward march was not less long and trying than the advance, and neither hopes of distinction nor glamour of excitement cheered the weary soldiers.

Towards the end of the journey the camels, terribly strained by their privation of water, began to die, and it was evident that the force would have no time to spare. On the 5th of February the column reached Kohi, and the Kordofan Field Force, having overcome many difficulties and suffered many hardships, was broken up.

For nearly a year no further operations were undertaken against the Khalifa, and he remained all through the spring and summer of 1899 supreme in Kordofan, reorganising his adherents and plundering the country – a most serious element of unrest. The barren and almost waterless regions into which he had withdrawn presented very difficult obstacles to any military expedition, and although powerful forces were still concentrated at Khartoum, the dry season and the uncertain whereabouts of the

enemy prevented action. But towards the end of August trustworthy information was received by the Intelligence
Department, that the Khalifa, with all his army, was encamped at
Jebel Gedir – that same mountain in Southern Kordofan to which
nearly twenty years before he and the Mahdi had retreated after
the flight from Abba island. Here among old memories which his
presence revived he became at once a centre of fanaticism. Night
after night he slept upon the Mahdi's stone; and day after day tales
of his dreams were carried by secret emissaries not only
throughout the Western Soudan, but into the Ghezira and even
to Khartoum. And now, his position being definite and his action
highly dangerous, it was decided to move against him.

It was at first universally believed that the Khalifa's intention
was to retire to an almost inaccessible distance – to El Obeid or
Southern Darfur. But soon strange rumours began to run about
the bazaars of Omdurman of buried weapons and whispers of
revolt. For a few days a vague feeling of unrest pervaded the native
city, and then suddenly on the 12th of November came precise
and surprising news. The Khalifa was not retreating to the south
or to the west, but advancing northward with Omdurman, not El
Obeid, as his object. He had resolved to stake all that yet remained
to him in one last desperate attempt to recapture his former
capital; and so, upon the 12th of November, his advanced guard,
under the Emir Ahmed Fedil, struck the Nile opposite Abba
island.

The name of Abba island may perhaps carry the reader back
to the very beginning of this story. Here, eighteen years before, the
Mahdi had lived and prayed after his quarrel with the haughty
Sheikh; here Abdullah had joined him; here the flag of the revolt
had been set up, and the first defeat had been inflicted upon the
Egyptian troops. It is a curious instance of the occasional sym-
metry of history that final destruction should have befallen the
last remains of the Mahdist movement so close to the scene of its
origin!

The news which had reached Khartoum set all wheels in motion. Kitchener hurried south from Cairo, and arrived in Khartoum on the 18th. A field force of some 2,300 troops – one troop of cavalry, the 2nd Field Battery, the 1st Maxim Battery, the Camel Corps, IXth Soudanese, XIIIth Soudanese, and one company 2nd Egyptians – was immediately formed, and the command entrusted to Sir Reginald Wingate. There were besides some 900 Arab riflemen and a few irregular mounted scouts. On the 20th these troops were concentrated at Fashi Shoya, whence Colonel Lewis had obliged Ahmed Fedil to withdraw, and at 3.30 on the afternoon of the 21st the expedition started in a south-westerly direction upon the track of the enemy.

The troops bivouacked some ten miles south-west of Fashi Shoya, and then marched in bright moonlight to Nefisa, encountering only a Dervish patrol of about ten men. At Nefisa was found the evacuated camp of Ahmed Fedil, containing a quantity of grain which he had collected from the riverain district, and, what was of more value, a sick but intelligent Dervish who stated that the Emir had just moved to Abu Aadel, five miles further on.

Accordingly cavalry, Camel Corps, Maxims, and irregulars set off at their best pace: and after them at 9.15 hurried the infantry, refreshed by a drink at the water tanks and a hasty meal. As they advanced the scrub became denser, and all were in broken and obstructed ground when, at about ten o'clock, the sound of Maxim firing and the patter of musketry proclaimed that the cavalry under Colonel Mahon had come into contact. The firing soon became more rapid, and as the infantry approached it was evident that the mounted troops were briskly engaged. The position which they occupied was a low ridge comparatively bare of scrub; from this it was possible at a distance of 800 yards to overlook the Dervish encampment huddled around the water pools. It was immediately evident that the infantry and the battery were arriving none too soon. The Dervishes, who had hitherto contented themselves with maintaining a ragged and desultory fire from the scrub, now sallied forth into the open and delivered a most bold and determined charge upon the guns. The intervening space was little more than 200 yards, and for a moment the attack looked as if it might succeed. But upon the instant the IXth and XIIIth Soudanese, who had been doubled steadily for upwards of two miles, came into line, filling the gap between Mahon's guns and dismounted Camel Corps and the irregular riflemen; and so the converging fire of the whole force was brought to bear upon the enemy – now completely beaten and demoralised. Three hundred and twenty corpses were counted, and at least an equal number must have been wounded. Ahmed Fedil and one or two of his principal Emirs escaped to the southward and to the Khalifa.

It was learned from the prisoners that the Khalifa, with about 5,000 fighting men, was moving northwards towards the wells of Gedid, of which we have already heard in the Shirkela reconnaissance, and which were some twenty-five miles from the scene of the fight. The troops were already fatigued by their severe exertions. The water pool was so foul that even the thirsty camels refused to drink of it, and moreover scarcely any water remained in the tanks. It was therefore of vital importance to reach the wells of Gedid. But supposing exhausted troops famishing for water reached them only to be confronted by a powerful Dervish force already in possession! Sir Reginald Wingate decided, however, to face the risk, and at a few minutes before midnight the column set out again on its road. The ground was broken; the night was sultry: and as the hours passed by the sufferings of the infantry began to be most acute. Many men fell exhausted to the ground; and it was with a feeling of immense relief that at nine o'clock on the morning of the 24th news was received from the cavalry that the wells had been occupied by them without opposition. All the water in the tanks was at once distributed, and thus refreshed the infantry struggled on and settled down at midday around a fine pool of comparatively pure water.

At Gedid, as at Nefisa, a single Dervish was captured, and from him it was learned that the Khalifa's army was encamped seven miles to the south-east. It was now clear that his position was strategically most unfavourable. His route to the north lay barred; his retreat to the south lay through waterless and densely wooded districts; and as the seizure of the grain supplies which had resulted from Fedil's foraging excursions rendered his advance or retirement a matter of difficulty, it seemed probable he would stand. Wingate, therefore, decided to attack him at dawn.

Leaving the transport under guard by the water with instructions to follow at four o'clock, the troops moved off at midnight. At three o'clock, when about three miles from the enemy's position, the force was deployed into fighting formation. The irregular riflemen covered the front; behind them the XIIIth and IXth Soudanese; and behind these, again, the Maxims and the artillery were disposed. Cautiously and silently the advance was resumed, and now in the distance the beating of war drums and the long booming note of the Khalifa's horn broke on the stillness, proclaiming that the enemy were not unprepared. At a few minutes before four o'clock another low ridge, also comparatively bare of scrub, was reached and occupied as a position. The cavalry were now withdrawn from the front, a few infantry picquets were thrown out, and the rest of the force lay down in the long grass of the little ridge and waited for daylight.

After about an hour the sky to the eastward began to grow paler with the promise of the morning and in the indistinct light the picquets could be seen creeping gradually in; while behind them along the line of the trees faint white figures, barely distinguishable, began to accumulate. Sir Reginald Wingate, fearing lest a sudden rush should be made upon him, now ordered the whole force to stand up and open fire; and forthwith a loud crackling fusillade began. It was immediately answered. The enemy's fire flickered along a wide half-circle and developed continually with greater vigour opposite the Egyptian left, which was consequently

258

reinforced. As the light improved, large bodies of shouting Dervishes were seen advancing; but the fire was too hot, and their Emirs were unable to lead them far beyond the edge of the wood. So soon as this was perceived Wingate ordered a general advance; and the whole force, moving at a rapid pace down the gentle slope, drove the enemy through the trees into the camp about a mile and a half away. Here, huddled together under their straw shelters, 6,000 women and children were collected, all of whom, with many unwounded combatants, made signals of surrender and appeals for mercy. The 'cease fire' was sounded at half past six. Then, and not till then, was it discovered how severe the loss of the Dervishes had been. In one space not much more than a score of yards square lay all the most famous Emirs of the once far-reaching Dervish domination. The Khalifa Abdullah, pierced by several balls, was stretched dead on his sheepskin; on his right lay Ali-Wad-Helu, on his left Ahmed Fedil. Before them was a line of lifeless bodyguards; behind them a score of less important chiefs; and behind these, again, a litter of killed and wounded horses. Such was the grim spectacle which in the first light of the morning met the eyes of the British officers, to some of whom it meant the conclusion of a perilous task prolonged over many years. And while they looked in astonishment not unmingled with awe, there scrambled unhurt from under a heap of bodies the little Emir Yunes, of Dongola, who added the few links necessary to complete the chain.

At Omdurman Abdullah had remained mounted behind the hill of Surgham, but in this his last fight he had set himself in the forefront of the battle. Almost at the first discharge, his son Osman, the Sheikh-ed-Din, was wounded, and as he was carried away he urged the Khalifa to save himself by flight; but the latter, with a dramatic dignity sometimes denied to more civilised warriors, refused. Dismounting from his horse, and ordering his Emirs to imitate him, he seated himself on his sheepskin and there determined to await the worst of fortune. And so it came to pass that in this last scene in the struggle with Mahdism the stage was cleared of all its striking characters, and Osman Digna alone purchased by flight a brief ignoble liberty, soon to be followed by a long ignoble servitude.

Twenty-nine Emirs, 3,000 fighting men, 6,000 women and children surrendered themselves prisoners. The Egyptian losses were three killed and twenty-three wounded.

The long story now approaches its conclusion. The River War is over. In its varied course, which extended over fourteen years and involved the untimely destruction of perhaps 300,000 lives, many extremes and contrasts have been displayed. But the result is at length achieved, and the flags of England and Egypt wave unchallenged over the valley of the Nile.

INDEX

A CATALOG OF SELECTED
DOVER BOOKS
IN ALL FIELDS OF INTEREST

A CATALOG OF SELECTED DOVER

BOOKS IN ALL FIELDS OF INTEREST

CONCERNING THE SPIRITUAL IN ART, Wassily Kandinsky. Pioneering work by father of abstract art. Thoughts on color theory, nature of art. Analysis of earlier masters. 12 illustrations. 80pp. of text. 5⅜ x 8¼. 23411-8

ANIMALS: 1,419 Copyright-Free Illustrations of Mammals, Birds, Fish, Insects, etc., Jim Harter (ed.). Clear wood engravings present, in extremely lifelike poses, over 1,000 species of animals. One of the most extensive pictorial sourcebooks of its kind. Captions. Index. 284pp. 9 x 12. 23766-4

CELTIC ART: The Methods of Construction, George Bain. Simple geometric techniques for making Celtic interlacements, spirals, Kells-type initials, animals, humans, etc. Over 500 illustrations. 160pp. 9 x 12. (Available in U.S. only.) 22923-8

AN ATLAS OF ANATOMY FOR ARTISTS, Fritz Schider. Most thorough reference work on art anatomy in the world. Hundreds of illustrations, including selections from works by Vesalius, Leonardo, Goya, Ingres, Michelangelo, others. 593 illustrations. 192pp. 7⅞ x 10¼. 20241-0

CELTIC HAND STROKE-BY-STROKE (Irish Half-Uncial from "The Book of Kells"): An Arthur Baker Calligraphy Manual, Arthur Baker. Complete guide to creating each letter of the alphabet in distinctive Celtic manner. Covers hand position, strokes, pens, inks, paper, more. Illustrated. 48pp. 8¼ x 11. 24336-2

EASY ORIGAMI, John Montroll. Charming collection of 32 projects (hat, cup, pelican, piano, swan, many more) specially designed for the novice origami hobbyist. Clearly illustrated easy-to-follow instructions insure that even beginning paper-crafters will achieve successful results. 48pp. 8¼ x 11. 27298-2

THE COMPLETE BOOK OF BIRDHOUSE CONSTRUCTION FOR WOOD-WORKERS, Scott D. Campbell. Detailed instructions, illustrations, tables. Also data on bird habitat and instinct patterns. Bibliography. 3 tables. 63 illustrations in 15 figures. 48pp. 5¼ x 8½. 24407-5

BLOOMINGDALE'S ILLUSTRATED 1886 CATALOG: Fashions, Dry Goods and Housewares, Bloomingdale Brothers. Famed merchants' extremely rare catalog depicting about 1,700 products: clothing, housewares, firearms, dry goods, jewelry, more. Invaluable for dating, identifying vintage items. Also, copyright-free graphics for artists, designers. Co-published with Henry Ford Museum & Greenfield Village. 160pp. 8¼ x 11. 25780-0

HISTORIC COSTUME IN PICTURES, Braun & Schneider. Over 1,450 costumed figures in clearly detailed engravings—from dawn of civilization to end of 19th century. Captions. Many folk costumes. 256pp. 8⅜ x 11¾. 23150-X

THE STORY OF THE TITANIC AS TOLD BY ITS SURVIVORS, Jack Winocour (ed.). What it was really like: Panic, despair, shocking inefficiency, and a little heroism. More thrilling than any fictional account. 26 illustrations. 320pp. 5⅜ x 8½. 20610-6

FAIRY AND FOLK TALES OF THE IRISH PEASANTRY, William Butler Yeats (ed.). Treasury of 64 tales from the twilight world of Celtic myth and legend: "The Soul Cages," "The Kildare Pooka," "King O'Toole and his Goose," many more. Introduction and Notes by W. B. Yeats. 352pp. 5⅜ x 8½. 26941-8

BUDDHIST MAHAYANA TEXTS, E. B. Cowell and others (eds.). Superb, accurate translations of basic documents in Mahayana Buddhism, highly important in history of religions. The Buddha-karita of Asvaghosha, Larger Sukhavativyuha, more. 448pp. 5⅜ x 8½. 25552-2

ONE TWO THREE . . . INFINITY: Facts and Speculations of Science, George Gamow. Great physicist's fascinating, readable overview of contemporary science: number theory, relativity, fourth dimension, entropy, genes, atomic structure, much more. 128 illustrations. Index. 352pp. 5⅜ x 8½. 25664-2

EXPERIMENTATION AND MEASUREMENT, W. J. Youden. Introductory manual explains laws of measurement in simple terms and offers tips for achieving accuracy and minimizing errors. Mathematics of measurement, use of instruments, experimenting with machines. 1994 edition. Foreword. Preface. Introduction. Epilogue. Selected Readings. Glossary. Index. Tables and figures. 128pp. 5⅜ x 8½. 40451-X

DALI ON MODERN ART: The Cuckolds of Antiquated Modern Art, Salvador Dali. Influential painter skewers modern art and its practitioners. Outrageous evaluations of Picasso, Cézanne, Turner, more. 15 renderings of paintings discussed. 44 calligraphic decorations by Dali. 96pp. 5⅜ x 8½. (Available in U.S. only.) 29220-7

ANTIQUE PLAYING CARDS: A Pictorial History, Henry René D'Allemagne. Over 900 elaborate, decorative images from rare playing cards (14th–20th centuries): Bacchus, death, dancing dogs, hunting scenes, royal coats of arms, players cheating, much more. 96pp. 9¼ x 12¼. 29265-7

MAKING FURNITURE MASTERPIECES: 30 Projects with Measured Drawings, Franklin H. Gottshall. Step-by-step instructions, illustrations for constructing handsome, useful pieces, among them a Sheraton desk, Chippendale chair, Spanish desk, Queen Anne table and a William and Mary dressing mirror. 224pp. 8⅛ x 11¼. 29338-6

THE FOSSIL BOOK: A Record of Prehistoric Life, Patricia V. Rich et al. Profusely illustrated definitive guide covers everything from single-celled organisms and dinosaurs to birds and mammals and the interplay between climate and man. Over 1,500 illustrations. 760pp. 7½ x 10⅛. 29371-8

Paperbound unless otherwise indicated. Available at your book dealer, online at **www.doverpublications.com**, or by writing to Dept. GI, Dover Publications, Inc., 31 East 2nd Street, Mineola, NY 11501. For current price information or for free catalogues (please indicate field of interest), write to Dover Publications or log on to **www.doverpublications.com** and see every Dover book in print. Dover publishes more than 500 books each year on science, elementary and advanced mathematics, biology, music, art, literary history, social sciences, and other areas.